W9-CEH-007

THEATRE: A WAY OF SEEING

THEATRE

A Way of Seeing

❧

M. S. Barranger

Tulane University

Wadsworth Publishing Company
Belmont, California
A Division of Wadsworth, Inc.

Senior Editor: Rebecca Hayden
Production Editor: Carolyn Tanner
Designer: Detta Penna
Copy Editors: John Taylor, Gary McDonald
Technical Illustrator: Paul Gilman

© 1980 by Wadsworth, Inc. All rights reserved. No part of this book may be reproduced, stored in a retrieval system, or transcribed, in any form or by any means, electronic, mechanical, photocopying, recording, or otherwise, without the prior written permission of the publisher, Wadsworth Publishing Company, Belmont, California 94002, a division of Wadsworth, Inc.

Printed in the United States of America
1 2 3 4 5 6 7 8 9 10–84 83 82 81 80

Cover photo by Martha Swope shows the 1973–74 Broadway production of Candide.

Acknowledgments begin on page 300.

Library of Congress Cataloging in Publication Data

Barranger, M. S.
    Theatre, a way of seeing.

    Bibliography: p. 292
    Includes index.
    1. Theater.   I.   Title.
PN2037.B32   792   79-20829
ISBN 0-534-00763-5

Preface

Theatre as a way of seeing is the subject of this book. We will talk about the nature of the theatre experience—who sees, what is seen, where, and how it is seen—from our own viewpoint, that of an audience engaged in the direct experience of a complex art.

I have organized the book to discuss theatre as an experience of art and life: places, people, language, stories, movements, designs, sounds, and forms. The book is divided into eleven chapters. Eight deal with theatrical spaces, theatre artists, and dramatic forms; two discuss play reading and theatrical language; and the last chapter examines theatre criticism and the theatre review—its form and influence on our daily experience of theatre. In addition, there are photo essays (photographs and captions) illustrating theatre's variety, color, styles, and shapes. If instructors want to change the order of the chapters, they will find that they can do so.

Written for use in the basic course, this book introduces the student to theatre as a way of seeing men and women in action—what they do and why they do it. Since the students are probably discovering theatre for the first time, I have limited to *fourteen* the number of plays used as examples of trends, styles, and forms: *Agamemnon, Othello, Hamlet, Tartuffe, Ghosts, The Cherry Orchard, A Streetcar Named Desire, The Caucasian Chalk Circle, The Bald Soprano, Waiting for Godot, Who's Afraid of Virginia Woolf?, Marat/ Sade, America Hurrah!,* and *The River Niger.*

I have also provided some tools to help the student with problems of history, biography, definition, and example: play synopses; short biographies of playwrights, actors, directors, and designers; study questions; and a glossary of theatre terms. All terms that appear in boldface in the text are defined in the glossary. Where possible, terms are briefly defined within the text itself.

Finally, this book is in no way a definitive treatment of theatre practice, history, or literature, but an attempt to put students in touch with theatre as a fine art and humanistic event. Most important, it introduces students to theatre as an immediate experience, engaging actors and audience for a brief time in a special place. The Greeks called that special place a *theatron,* or "seeing place." Let us make *theatre as a way of seeing* our guide to understanding and enjoying the theatre experience.

My thanks are due to colleagues and students for their encouragement and assistance in the preparation of this book. Those who advised on the manuscript at various stages of its development were: Dianne Breitwieser (St. Louis Community College), Paul Cravath (Tulane University), Bill J. Harbin (Louisiana State University), Charles Harbour (University of Montevallo), E. James Hooks (University of Florida–Gainesville), Violet B. Ketels (Temple University), Judith F. Lyons (Temple University), Dorothy L. Marshall (Webster College), Richard A. Weaver (Texas Tech University), Robert Yowell (University of Arkansas at Little Rock). My colleagues in the Theatre and Speech Department at Tulane University were also most encouraging and helpful. Ronald A. Gural made available to me his director's promptbook on *Who's Afraid of Virginia Woolf?,* and Kenneth F. Peters advised me in the area of theatre design. Paul D. Reinhardt (University of Texas–Austin) was also of great assistance in developing the photo essay on theatre design. Finally, Rebecca Hayden of Wadsworth Publishing Company deserves special mention for her efforts as editor.

M. S. Barranger
New Orleans

Contents

Chapter 6   The Image Makers: The Designers   121

Chapter 7   Structures of Seeing   149

To Heather

THEATRE: A WAY OF SEEING

1

Discovering Theatre

*While we are watching, men and women make theatre happen
before us. In the theatre we see men and women in action—
what they do and why they do it—and we discover our
world's special qualities by seeing them through others' eyes.*

I can take any empty space and call it a bare
stage. A man walks across this empty space
whilst someone else is watching him, and this is
all that is needed for an act of theatre to be
engaged.

Peter Brook, *The Empty Space*

Theatre—like dance, music, opera, or film—places human experiences before a group of people—an audience. In this first chapter, we want to ask what makes theatre different from other arts. What makes theatre unique and special? What is theatre as a way of seeing?

THE IMMEDIATE ART

Unlike a painting or a novel prepared long before we see it, theatre takes place as we watch. For theatre to happen, two groups of people, actors and audience, must come together at a certain time and in a certain place. There the actors go onstage and present themselves to the audience in a story usually about human beings. The audience shares in the story and the occasion.

There is a living quality about theatre because it centers on these two groups of people. Painting and sculpture, which are not performed before an audience, do not share this quality. Dance, music, and opera share with theatre the human being as performer, but they do not share theatre's unique way of imitating reality. Unlike other arts, theatre presents actual human beings playing fictional characters who move, speak, and "live" before us in recognizable places and events; for a short time we share in an experience with them that is entertaining, provocative, imitative, and magical.

THE SPECIAL PLACE

At the heart of the theatre experience is the act of seeing and being seen. We are told that the word *theatre* comes from the Greek word *theatron,* seeing place. At one time or another during the history of Western culture, this place for seeing has been a primitive dancing circle, a Greek amphitheatre, a church, an Elizabethan stage, an arena, a garage, a street, and a **proscenium theatre.** Today, it may be a Broadway theatre, a university playhouse, or a renovated warehouse. But neither the stage's shape nor the building's architecture makes it a theatre. The use of space to imitate human experience for an audience to see makes that space special—a seeing place.

THE GRAND ILLUSION

Theatre creates the *illusion* that we are sharing an experience with others for the first time. As members of the audience we tacitly agree with the actors that for the time of the performance the play is a living reality; we know that theatre is not life, but we suspend this knowledge for the few hours we watch the play. We share with the actors the illusion that life is being lived on stage. We are watching and sharing the experiences of others. The actors contribute to the illusion, for they are both actors and characters. We are simultaneously aware that Oedipus, the central character in Sophocles' *Oedipus the King,* is a character and that he is played by an actor. Theatre's grand illusion is that life is taking shape before us for the first time, and that the actors are other than who they are. In the theatre we *suspend our disbelief* and give way to theatre's magic and illusion.

Sophocles, one of several Greek playwrights whose work survives today, wrote the greatest of Greek tragedies, *Oedipus the King,* in 427 B.C. He wrote three plays about the Oedipus story: *Antigone* and *Oedipus at Colonus* are the other two.

Oedipus the King is the story of a man who flees from Corinth to avoid fulfilling a prophecy that he will kill his father and marry his mother. On his journey he kills an old man (an apparent stranger but actually his real father, the king of Thebes) and his servants at a place where three roads meet. He then proceeds to Thebes and solves the riddle of the Sphinx. As a reward he is made king and married to the widowed queen, who is actually his mother, Jocasta. He rules well and has four children.

The play opens with Thebes stricken by a plague. Oedipus has sent his brother-in-law Creon to consult the Delphic oracle about the cause of the plague, declaring that he will rid the city of the infection. As Oedipus pursues the plague's source, he learns more and more about himself. Finally Oedipus comes face to face with himself as his father's killer, as his mother's son and husband, and as his children's father and brother. He puts out his eyes when he learns the truth and Jocasta kills herself. By his own decree he is exiled from Thebes and wanders blind into the countryside.

Oedipus the King is one of the world's greatest tragedies; it is about human guilt and innocence, knowledge and ignorance, power and helplessness. Its fundamental idea is that wisdom comes to us through suffering.

Thespis (c. 534 B.C.) is the Greek actor credited with the invention of drama. Virtually nothing is known about him, but legend has it that Thespis, a chorus leader, added to the choral narrative a prologue and lines to be spoken by an actor impersonating a character. One theory maintains that tragedy as we know it evolved from this dialogue between actor and chorus. Interestingly enough, the Greek word for actor is *hypokrites,* meaning "answerer."

AUDIENCE AND ACTOR

The two basic components of theatre are the actor and the audience. The history of the theatre has been, in one sense, the record of the changing physical relationships of actor and audience. The audience has moved from the hillside of the Greek amphitheatre to a place before the Christian altar, to standing room around the Elizabethan theatre's platform stage, to seats in a darkened hall before a curtained proscenium stage, to the floor and scaffolding of a modern environmental production.

In the same historical sequence, the actor has moved from the dancing circle of the Greek theatre to the church, to the open stage of the Elizabethan theatre, to the recessed stage of the proscenium theatre, to the environmental space of some contemporary productions. The historical trends and social institutions of the theatre are important but not crucial to this discussion of theatre as a way of seeing. What is crucial is an understanding of the common denominators, unchanged since the legendary Thespis stepped apart from the Greek chorus and created dialogue for the listener. These common factors are *actor, space,* and *audience.*

Whether the physical space becomes more elaborate or less so, whether the performance occurs indoors or out, the actor-audience relationship is theatre's vital ingredient. In one sense the formula for theatre is simple: *A man or woman stands in front of an audience, imitates someone else, and interacts with another performer.*

THE LIVING EXPERIENCE

The actor-audience relationship distinguishes theatre from that extraordinarily popular medium of our culture: *film.* When we go to a movie we sit in a darkened room looking at a screen filled with light images. We respond to the large *image* of the actor and not to the actor's *physical presence.* For this reason, *film is a nonimmediate art.*

Although films are often made from plays, and many stage plays from *Hamlet* to *The Sound of Music* to *Equus* have been made into highly popular films, theatre and film are different. Films use actors as characters in action who express themselves in dialogue, but the actors' images and activities are revealed to us on celluloid. Unlike theatre-goers, film audiences are in the presence of images from the past, not of living human beings in the present. Film is not the living, *immediate* experience that theatre is. And just as the film audience does not experience the actors' flesh-and-blood presence, the film actor does not experience the audience's instant response.

Although film makes use of actors, they are subordinate to the photographic images that the film editor has arranged. Both film and theatre use people as subjects, but film as a medium is a twentieth-century technological invention, a means of recording and preserving the image of reality. Theatre is "alive"—in immediate communion with its audience. Film captures that "aliveness" on celluloid for all time.

For example, the great performances of Marlon Brando and Vivien Leigh as Stanley Kowalski and Blanche DuBois in *A Streetcar Named Desire* are captured in the

Figure 1-1.   The film image. The still from the 1951 movie version of Tennessee Williams's play A Streetcar Named Desire *captures for all time this moment between Vivien Leigh as Blanche DuBois and Marlon Brando as Stanley Kowalski. Each time we see the movie (and it may be ten times), we can experience again this moment between these two particular actors. A similar moment in the theatre is lost to us even as it takes place before us on the stage. (Photo from The Museum of Modern Art Film Stills Archives.)*

1951 film. But the wonderful theatrical performances of Laurette Taylor, Jessica Tandy, and Elizabeth Ashley in plays by Tennessee Williams are lost to us as the performance ends. Theatre is a frustrating, evanescent art, lasting only those two or three hours it takes to see the play. The experience can be repeated night after night as long as the show is running, but once the play is closed and the cast dispersed, the performance is lost and the theatre dark.

Although admittedly frustrating, this intriguing qual-

Figure 1-2. A Streetcar Named Desire. *A tender moment between actors Jessica Tandy as Blanche DuBois and Karl Malden as Mitch in the original New York production (1947) directed by Elia Kazan with Marlon Brando as Stanley Kowalski and Kim Hunter as Stella. (Photo from the Vandamm Collection, The New York Public Library at Lincoln Center.)*

A *Streetcar Named Desire* was written by Tennessee Williams and first produced at the Barrymore Theatre, New York, in 1947. Her family's Mississippi estate sold, Blanche DuBois arrives at the New Orleans tenement home of Stella and Stanley Kowalski, her pregnant sister and brother-in-law. Blanche's faded gentility clashes with Stanley's male ego. As she seeks protection from the world, she competes with Stanley for Stella's affections but finds herself no match for his sexual hold over her sister. She tries to charm Mitch, Stanley's poker-playing friend, into marrying her. However, Stanley destroys Blanche's hopes for marriage by telling Mitch about her past drunkenness and promiscuity. As Stella reproaches Stanley for his cruelty, her labor pains begin and Stanley rushes her to the hospital.

Blanche is visited by a drunken Mitch, who accuses her of lying to him and makes an effort to seduce her. Stanley returns to find Blanche dressed for a party, fantasizing about an invitation to go on a cruise with a wealthy friend. Angered by her pretensions, Stanley starts a fight with her that ends in rape. In a final scene some weeks later, Blanche, her mind gone, is taken from the Kowalski home to a mental hospital.

Williams' tragedy is about human duplicity and desperation in which fragile people are overcome by the violence and vulgarity of Williams' South.

ity of theatre, which American critic Brooks Atkinson calls the "bright enigma," is the source of its vitality and liveliness.

ENTERTAINMENT

There are many kinds of entertainment. Watching a basketball game, for example, is entertaining. What is it about the theatre that makes its entertainment value different from that of an athletic event?

In both theatre and basketball activities we take pleasure in observing the skill of the performers. But part of the pleasure in watching a basketball game is finding out who's going to win, and it is this unpredictable or random quality of the sporting event that distinguishes it from the ritual quality of theatre. Each time a team plays another team the outcome is different, but once the theatrical performance is set, it varies little from night to night.

In addition, the players in a basketball game do not know how the game will turn out. In the theatre, the actors, director, and designers have planned their event with great care from beginning to end. We say that the performance is "set" in rehearsals. Each night actors recreate the same characters and reenact the same story; at predetermined times, actors do certain things, move, handle props, make gestures; the stage lights change and the scenery shifts upon cue. And although we take pleasure in observing the skill, talent, and intelligence of the performers in both basketball and theatre, there is a special pleasure that attaches to our participation with actors in an activity that for them is a ritualized performance.

If any random quality exists in theatrical performance, it comes from the particular *feedback* the performers obtain from each separate audience, which may vary from attentive rapport to an impatient shifting about in seats. Certain kinds of feedback, like laughter and applause, are almost second nature to us. But there is another, less tangible kind of communication between actor and audience. Like the Zen archer who becomes one with the arrow in flight, a great actor can establish an emotional kinship with the audience. The audience's attention, breathing, energy, and tensions send out signals to the actor and vice versa. For a brief spell, an emotional oneness is achieved between them. At the end of such a performance, the audience's applause is like the breaking of a spell, releasing energy and tension. These are the moments we remember in the theatre, when the actor's emotional life melds with the audience's living humanity.

THE COLLABORATIVE ART

Theatre is a team effort. It is made to happen, not by one individual, but by many artists, workers, and spectators. Unlike sculpture, painting, or writing, theatre is a collaborative art. Directors, designers, and actors collaborate as artists to create a special world. Working together they transform an empty stage into an environment where actors live out special moments of their make-believe lives in their make-believe worlds. And the audience, as we have seen, becomes part of this collaboration, responding from night to night to the success or failure of their collective efforts.

LIFE'S DOUBLE

Theatre is a way of seeing men and women in action—what they do and why they do it. Because human beings are both theatre's subject and its means of expression, theatre is one of the most immediate ways of experiencing another's concept of life—of what it means to be human.

It has been said by Shakespeare and others that there is a doubleness about the theatrical experience that provides a sense of life reflected before us in a special mirror—the stage. For instance, the audience experiences the actor both as actor—the living presence of another human being—and as fictional character. Likewise the performing space is both a stage and at the same time an imaginary world created by the playwright, designer, director, and actor. Sometimes this world is familiar to us—the stage might resemble a modern living room or a hotel room. Sometimes it is unfamiliar, like Othello's island of

Othello (1604) is Shakespeare's play about the noble Moor of Venice who marries a Venetian lady, Desdemona, and falls prey to Iago's villainy on the island of Cyprus. Iago has been denied a promotion by Othello, who has chosen Cassio for his lieutenant. Iago resents his treatment and begins to improvise plans to revenge himself on Othello. He and his friend Roderigo alert Desdemona's father, Brabantio, to his daughter's elopement with Othello. They are brought to the duke's house, where Othello defends himself against Brabantio's charge that he practiced witchcraft on Desdemona to get her to marry him. Othello and Desdemona assure the duke of their love, and the duke sends Othello to defend Cyprus against a Turkish invasion. On Cyprus, Iago plants doubts in Othello's mind about Desdemona's faithfulness (Cassio is the supposed lover), and provides Othello with proof of her affair —a handkerchief belonging to Desdemona, which Iago gets from his wife, Emilia, a lady-in-waiting to Desdemona. With this "proof," Othello kills Desdemona in bed. When he finds out too late that she is innocent and that Iago has plotted his downfall, Othello kills himself as punishment. Iago is condemned by the duke.

Othello is Shakespeare's tragedy about the power of evil disguised as good. As Othello comes to see the world through Iago's eyes, he is transformed from a noble soldier into a jealous murderer. Too late, he discovers that he has killed an innocent wife and been destroyed by Iago's malevolence.

Cyprus, Oedipus' plague-ridden Thebes, or Vladimir's deserted landscape in *Waiting for Godot*.

The Elizabethans thought the theatre mirrored life. Shakespeare had Hamlet describe the purpose of acting, or "playing," in this way:

. . . the purpose of playing, whose end, both at the first and now, was and is, to hold, as 'twere, the mirror up to nature, to show virtue her own feature, scorn her own image, and the very age and body of the time his form and pressure. (III, ii)

The Elizabethan idea of the stage as a mirror, related as it is to the act of seeing, can help us understand the dynamics of theatre. Looking into a mirror is, in a sense, like going to the theatre. When we look into a mirror we see our double—an image of ourselves—and possibly a background. The image can be made to move; we make certain judgments about it; it communicates to us certain attitudes and concerns about our humanness. Our human-

11

Figure 1-3.   Othello's world. Paul Robeson as Othello and Jose Ferrer as Iago in Margaret Webster's 1944 production of Othello *in New York City. Othello's doubts have begun to take hold, and the actors' postures betray the tension between them. (Photo from the Vandamm Collection, The New York Public Library at Lincoln Center.)*

ity as reflected in the mirror has shape, color, texture, form, attitude, and emotion; it is even capable of limited movement within the mirror's frame. Onstage the actor's living presence as a fictional character—as Othello or Desdemona, Vladimir or Estragon—creates that doubleness which is theatre's special quality. It is both a stage world and an illusion of a real world.

Theatre is life's double, but it is also something more than a reflection of life. It is a form of art—a *selected reflection*. It is life's reflection *organized meaningfully*.

Waiting for Godot, by the Irish playwright Samuel Beckett, was first produced at the Théâtre de Babylone, Paris, in 1953. On a country road in a deserted landscape marked by a single leafless tree, Estragon and Vladimir are waiting for someone named Godot. To pass the time, they play games, quarrel, make up, fall asleep. In comes Pozzo, a tyrannical person, leading Lucky by a rope tied around his neck. Pozzo demonstrates that Lucky is his obedient servant, and Lucky entertains them with a monologue that is a jumble of politics and theology. They disappear into the darkness, and Godot's messenger (a boy) announces that Mr. Godot will not come today. In Act II, a leaf has sprouted on the tree, suggesting that time has passed, but the two tramps are occupied in the same way. They play master-and-slave games, trade hats, argue about everything. Pozzo and Lucky return; one is blind and the other dumb. Godot again sends word that he will not come today, but perhaps tomorrow. As the play ends, Vladimir and Estragon, alone, continue waiting. In this play Beckett shows us how each of us waits for a Godot—for whatever it is that we hope for—and how, so occupied, we wait out a lifetime.

DISCOVERY

Theatre people often call the performance "magic time" because performances start with a magical effect. The houselights dim, the front curtain goes up (if there is one), and the audience *discovers* a hidden world.

In one sense, then, theatre is *discovery.* Let us compare two plays briefly to see how this discovery process works. Starting with two actors on a bare platform, the complex world of *Hamlet* gradually reveals itself. As the ghost appears to Hamlet demanding that he avenge his father's murder by his uncle Claudius, Shakespeare reveals a fallen and disordered world. Appearances are deceptive: The innocent appear to be guilty, and the devious seem honest. We find out about Claudius' villainy, Hamlet's "madness," and the murderous plots that end in the fatal duel. Hamlet's delayed revenge results in the destruction of two families and a kingdom. Witnessing that destruction, we discover that Shakespeare's revenge play is, in truth, a complex tragedy about the power of human evil and political sickness to paralyze the human will and corrupt the imagination. All this begins with two castle guards complaining about the cold weather as they go about their duties—literally two actors on a bare stage.

Figure 1-4. Four actors on a bare stage. American actor Sam Waterston as Hamlet kneels before Claudius, Gertrude, and Polonius in the 1975 New York Shakespeare Festival production at the Delacorte Theatre in Central Park. (Photo by George E. Joseph.)

Hamlet (c. 1600) is Shakespeare's greatest tragedy. Although the Danish court is celebrating King Claudius' wedding to Queen Gertrude (Hamlet's mother), Prince Hamlet still mourns the death of his father.

The ghost of his father appears and tells Hamlet that he has been secretly murdered by Claudius. Hamlet swears to take vengeance, but he must first prove to himself that Claudius is guilty. He has a group of strolling players put on a play in which a similar murder is depicted. Claudius' reaction to the play betrays him and Hamlet plots revenge. By accident he kills Polonius, the Lord Chamberlain and father to Ophelia, who loves Hamlet. Hamlet is exiled for killing Polonius, and Ophelia is driven mad. Laertes, Polonius' son, vows revenge and challenges Hamlet to a duel. To ensure that Hamlet is killed, Claudius poisons Laertes' sword and prepares a cup of poison for Hamlet to drink during the duel. In the closing scene, Gertrude accidentally drinks from the poisoned cup and dies, Hamlet kills Claudius, Laertes kills Hamlet and is killed in turn by his own poisoned sword, which Hamlet picked up in the confusion. Hamlet's cousin, Fortinbras, is made king of Denmark.

The *trope,* made up of chanted dialogue, was the beginning of medieval church drama and the first step toward creating plays after the dark ages. The tenth-century *Quem Quaeritis,* from a Benedictine abbey in Switzerland, consisted of questions and answers sung by the two halves of the choir during an Easter Mass. The Angels and the Marys were not actually impersonated, but the seeds of character and dialogue were there. Ultimately, the trope expanded into a little play or opera. It is interesting that a question and answer, so familiar to us in theatrical dialogue today, was used so long ago to introduce the Easter Mass.

Question (by the ANGELS): Whom do ye seek in the sepulcher, O followers of Christ?
Answer (by the MARYS): Jesus of Nazareth, who was crucified, just as he foretold. ANGELS: He is not here: He is risen, just as he foretold. Go, announce that he is risen from the sepulcher.

Let us consider a more recent play. A curtain rises in a proscenium theatre to reveal two tramps waiting under a wasted tree for someone named Godot. During the next two hours we discover that their situation is in many ways like our own. Samuel Beckett's tramps in *Waiting for Godot* eat, sleep, joke, suffer, quarrel, despair, and hope while waiting out their lives. As we watch the play, we discover that, like Vladimir and Estragon, we are also waiting for things to happen and time to pass.

When we go to the theatre we discover a writer's perception of humanity in a particular time and place. It is not unreasonable, then, that many plays begin and end with questions. When theatre emerged from the dark ages after the decline of the Greek and Roman cultures, one of the earliest recorded pieces was the *Quem Quaeritis* trope, which begins with the question "Whom seek ye?" The first words of *Hamlet,* spoken by the guard on the fog-shrouded battlements, are "Who's there?" The next-to-last lines of the two acts of *Waiting for Godot* are also questions—the same question, in fact:

ESTRAGON: Well, shall we go?
VLADIMIR: Yes, let's go.

They do not move. Curtain. (Act I)

. . . .

VLADIMIR: Well? Shall we go?
ESTRAGON: Yes, let's go.

They do not move. Curtain. (Act II)

In a special sense, theatre is a searching for answers about human nature and society. It is also a way of disclosing what it means to be a human being in certain situations and under certain conditions. In Sophocles' *Oedipus the King,* Oedipus searches for the cause of the plague and discovers his own identity. In Bertolt Brecht's *The Caucasian Chalk Circle,* Grusha seeks her own humanity in the protection of a child and is rewarded. In Samuel Beckett's *Waiting for Godot,* Vladimir and Estragon keep their appointment with the absent Godot and reveal their natures in the empty gesture.

15

Figure 1-5. Waiting for Godot.
Tom Ewell as Vladimir (center)
and Bert Lahr as Estragon
(right) in the 1956 Cocoanut
Grove Playhouse (Miami)
production of Waiting for
Godot. *This first American*
production of Samuel Beckett's
play was directed by Alan
Schneider (see Figure 4-4).
(Photo from The New York
Public Library at Lincoln
Center, courtesy of Alan
Schneider.)

Figure 1-6. Grusha baptizes the child at the river. Actress Zoe Caldwell as Grusha baptizes a rag doll (Michael) in the 1965 production of Bertolt Brecht's The Caucasian Chalk Circle, *directed by Edward Payson Call, at The Guthrie Theater, Minneapolis. (Photo courtesy of The Guthrie Theater.)*

The Caucasian Chalk Circle was written by German playwright Bertolt Brecht in 1943–45. The play begins in 1945 with two Soviet villages disputing the ownership of a fertile valley.

Before they decide the issue, a singer entertains them with a Chinese parable, the story of the chalk circle. The scene changes to a Georgian city being overthrown by a nobles' revolt. The governor is killed, and his wife abandons their son Michael in order to escape. Grusha, a peasant girl, rescues the child and flees to the mountains. She marries a supposedly dying peasant in order to give the child a name and status. When the revolt ends, the governor's wife sends soldiers to get the child. The scene shifts again, to the story of Azdak, a rogue made village judge by the rebellious soldiers. He is corrupt and prepares to judge the case of Grusha versus the governor's wife for possession of Michael. He uses the test of the chalk circle to identify the child's true mother, but reverses the outcome: The child is given to Grusha because she will *not* engage in the tug-of-war that is supposed to end in the child's being pulled out of the circle by maternal affection. He also gives Grusha a divorce so that she can return to her soldier fiancé, Simon. Brecht's moral is that things—children, wagons, valleys—should go to those who serve them best.

SUMMARY

Theatre, like life, happens within the present moment. It occurs when one or more human beings present themselves in a story before others. Most effectively of all the arts, theatre captures the experience of what it means to be human because human beings are both its medium and its subject. Theatre begins in that empty space where we see and hear the performance.

Types of Contemporary Theatres

Today's theatres are to be found in large cities like New York, London, Paris, Minneapolis, and Washington, D.C., and in small towns like Canada's Stratford-on-Avon, the site of the Canadian Shakespeare Festival Theatre. Just as their locations are diverse, so theatre buildings and stages differ in size and shape.

Figure 1-7a. London's National Theatre, located on the south bank of the Thames River, was completed in 1976. It is a huge complex containing three theatres. The Olivier (named for the famous English actor Sir Laurence Olivier) has an open stage. The 1150 seats are in a bowl-like configuration; the audience encircles the stage and has its attention focused on the playing area. The Lyttleton

Theatre, seating 890, has a conventional proscenium stage; the proscenium opening can be altered by changing its width and height. The Cottesloe Theatre, a workshop theatre, is a rectangular box holding up to 400 people. In addition to three theatres, the complex contains rehearsal rooms, workshops, offices, restaurants, and foyers. (Photo courtesy of The National Theatre of Great Britain.)

Figure 1-7b. The photo of The Guthrie Theater, Minneapolis, built in 1963, shows the large auditorium (1441 seats) encircling the unique seven-sided **thrust stage**. No seat is more than fifty-two feet from the center of the stage. The photo shows the audience's relationship to the actors and stage. (Photo by Robert Ashley Wilson, courtesy of The Guthrie Theater.)

Figure 1-7c and 1-7d. In the Arena Stage, built in 1960 in Washington, D.C., the audience completely surrounds the stage action. Lighting instruments are visible above the stage, and scenery and furniture are minimal. Actors enter and exit through alleyways visible in the photo. (Photos courtesy of Arena Stage, Washington, D.C.)

Figure 1-7e. The Oregon Shakespearean Festival Theatre in Ashland (founded in 1935) is an open-air theatre. The audience sits in front of a platform stage. A multilevel building serves as a permanent background for plays by Shakespeare and other great playwrights. Compare this photo with the picture of Shakespeare's Globe on page 41. (Photo courtesy of Hank Kranzler of The Oregon Shakespearean Festival.)

Figure 1-7f. The Performance Garage, located at 33 Wooster Street, New York City, was converted in 1967 by director Richard Schechner and designer Jerry N. Rojo from a garage into an environmental theatre. The photo shows the garage's interior, with scaffolding surrounding a central acting area. The actors are rehearsing Dionysus in 69. In environmental theatre all the available space is shaped to each production's needs. Unlike the other theatres shown here, The Performance Garage makes no clear division between acting and audience areas. Environmental theatre uses the entire space and mingles actor with audience during the performance. (Photo by Frederick Eberstadt, courtesy of Richard Schechner.)

QUESTIONS FOR STUDY

1. How does theatre differ from other art forms, such as film, music, dance, and painting?

2. What did the ancient Greeks mean when they called their theatre a "seeing place" or *theatron*?

3. What types of theatres are we likely to find today on our campuses and in our cities?

4. What is special about theatrical space?

5. Why are the actor and the audience the theatre's two unchanging components?

6. What do we mean when we say that on each night in the theatre there is an "illusion of the first time"?

7. How did Thespis create dialogue, according to legend?

8. What do we mean when we say that theatre is an *immediate* art?

9. How does the theatre's quality of entertainment differ from the entertainment of a sports event like basketball or football?

10. What do we mean when we say that theatre is a *collaborative* art?

11. What kinds of *audience feedback* are we likely to experience in the theatre?

12. How are human beings both theatre's subject and its means of expression?

13. What did Shakespeare mean by writing in *Hamlet* that a performance is like a mirror held up to nature?

14. Describe the type of theatre found on your campus.

2

The Seeing Place: Traditional Spaces

Since its beginnings, theatre has been a place for seeing—for viewing, presenting, perceiving, understanding. Places for theatre to happen are found in all societies, ancient and modern. Throughout history the theatre space has been arranged so that audiences can see and performers can be seen.

There are, for example, privileged places, qualitatively different from all others—a man's birthplace, or the scenes of his first love, or certain places in the first foreign city he visited in youth. . . . as if it were in such spots that he had received the revelation of a reality *other* than that in which he participates through his ordinary daily life.

Mircea Eliade, *The Sacred and the Profane: The Nature of Religion*

Let us begin the discovery of theatre in the theatrical space—with the stages and auditoriums where it all happens. Let us start by studying familiar and traditional spaces. All cultures, no matter how primitive or sophisticated, have theatrical performances and places for *seeing* these events.

RITUAL AND THEATRE

The Special Place

When we examine the origins of ritual and theatre, we discover that the actors, however primitive, always perform in a special or privileged place. The priest, the guru, the dancer, or the actor is in a hut, a building, or an enclosure that is shared with the onlooker or audience. In some ritual spaces a circular area is surrounded by spectators. In others, special buildings are constructed for the occasion and destroyed at the end of the rite. Some groups move from place to place.

Early Theatre and Fertility Rituals

Since the publication of Sir James Frazer's *The Golden Bough* in 1890, theatre historians have connected the origins of theatre with vegetation and fertility rites. Primitive people staged mock battles between death and life in which the king of the old year, representing death, perished in a duel with the champion of the new year. In these rituals we can see possible precursors to theatre as we know it. They are enactment, imitation, and seasonal performance.

There are also dramatic overtones to ceremonies designed to win favor from supernatural powers. The rain-dance ceremonies of the American Southwest Indians were ways to ensure that the tribal gods would send rain to make crops grow. Early societies acted out seasonal changes—patterns of life, death, and rebirth—until their ceremonies became formalized dramatic rituals. Harvest rituals, for example, celebrate abundant food supplies. Imitation, costume, makeup, gesture, and pantomime were the theatrical elements in these early rituals.

The Shaman's Healing Ritual

Another kind of ritual performance was the ceremony conducted by the shaman, or master of spirits, to cure illness. The shaman performs in a trance; while he is curing the patient, a supernatural presence manifests itself to the patient and onlookers.

Anthropologists and historians conjecture that theatre owes a debt to the thousands of unknown magicians who carved their enemies' faces on tree trunks, performed voodoo spells, and threatened or wooed bad and good spirits. But though the two activities have much in common, theatre is profoundly different from this kind of magical ritual. Theatre's most common objective is to please and entertain rather than to pacify or heal. Theatre's creators are more likely to be talented hard workers than inspired practitioners of magic tricks. And its audiences are not secondary to what's going on onstage, as they may very well be in the practice of ritual magic. Theatre's audiences are central and indispensable to the theatrical experience.

Theatre and the Human Condition

Primitive ritual was concerned with the protection of the tribe. Theatre, on the other hand, deals with the mystery, history, and ambiguity of human events. Plays speak to us of individuals, as well as of groups. They hold the mirror up to our joys and our sorrows, to our questions about life. Theatre aims to provoke thought while entertaining us, rather than to provide answers. We spoke in the previous chapter about the playwright's concern for the human condition. Shakespeare demonstrates the sensitivity of a supreme dramatic artist in this speech by Hamlet:

What a piece of work is a man, how noble in reason, how infinite in faculties; in form and moving how express and admirable, in action how like an angel, in apprehension how like a god: the beauty of the world, the paragon of animals! And yet to me what is this quintessence of dust? (II, ii)

Hamlet speaks about himself, but he also speaks in universal terms about all of us. He raises questions about human nature; insights are there for those who want them. But even so, the play's essential function is to entertain. For without diversion, all else in the theatre must inevitably fail.

Although ritual performances are often entertaining, their objective is largely practical: Crops will grow, the hunt will succeed, warring tribes will be placated. In ritual, entertainment is a bonus for the onlooker; in theatre it's the name of the game.

What Is Theatrical Space?

Theatre differs from ritual in several ways. Unlike participants in a ritual, actors create fictional characters. Actors also present themselves on a stage, or in a special place, using the playwright's words to create an illusion of a real world. That the actor appears *on a stage* is important not only for an actor, and for the other artists and technicians involved, but also for the audience. Theatrical space has two components: the stage and the auditorium.

Stage and Auditorium   The ratio between the size of the playhouse and its performance area affects the conventions of staging, the styles of acting and production, and even the plays performed there. Most important is the degree to which the aesthetic experience, for performer and for audience, is molded by this environment. We discussed the theatrical "seeing place" in the first chapter. Let's follow this up by discussing performance spaces and spectator areas in various places at various times, beginning with the *Nanda* initiation rite in Fiji.

The Nanda Ritual

Anthropologist Mircea Eliade describes a Fiji initiation rite called *Nanda:*

The ritual began with the construction of a stone enclosure, sometimes a hundred feet long and fifty wide, at a great distance from the village. The stone wall might reach a height of three feet. The structure was called Nanda, literally "bed." . . . The Nanda obviously represents the sacred ground. Two years pass between its building and the first initiation, and two more years between the latter and the second ceremony. Some time before the second ceremony large quantities of food are stored up and cabins are built near the Nanda.

On a particular day the novices, led by a priest, proceed to the Nanda in single file, with a club in one hand and a lance in the other. The old men await them in front of the walls, singing. The novices drop their weapons at the old men's feet, as symbols of gifts, and then withdraw to the cabins. On the fifth day, again led by the priests, they once more proceed to the sacred enclosure, but this time the old men are not awaiting them by the walls. They are then taken into the Nanda. There "lie a row of dead men, covered with blood, their bodies apparently cut open and their entrails protruding." The priest-guide walks over the corpses and the terrified novices follow him to the other end of the enclosure, where the chief priest awaits them. "Suddenly he blurts out a great yell, whereupon the dead men start to their feet, and run down to the river to cleanse themselves from the blood and filth with which they are besmeared."[1]

The mysteries of death and rebirth underlie the *Nanda* ritual. The ritual is enacted in a sacred place, and the spatial arrangements of the event are important.

Events Shape the Space Four years before the ceremony, a temporary building is erected. The initiates enter the privileged place to discover what the building has concealed: the actor-corpses. After the novices have participated in the spectacle of death, the pretend-dead rise and rush to the river. The initiates are left by themselves in the enclosed space. You will notice how much this ritual has in common with modern theatre:

> The space is special and is arranged for the event.
>
> The performers within the enclosed space pretend to be other than what they are.
>
> The audience-participants enter the enclosed space and discover a formerly concealed special place.
>
> The dramatic action ends when the performers leave the special place.
>
> When the performers exit from the enclosed space, the audience-participants are left to themselves (to find their way out).

The shaman of early hunting cultures was both a healer and an artist. Andreas Lommel in Shamanism: The Beginnings of Art (1967) distinguishes between the medicine man and the shaman in the following way: Unlike the medicine man, the shaman acts under an inner compulsion. This compulsion takes the form of artistic productivity: dancing, mime, singing, magic tricks, and so on.

Although he functions as a priest, spiritual guide, and doctor, the shaman always acts in a state of self-induced trance. He engenders psychic phenomena, such as telepathy, clairvoyance, and mysterious disappearance and reappearance. The shaman is a creative healer who puts the individual and the tribe in touch with its mythology, spiritual powers, and world view.

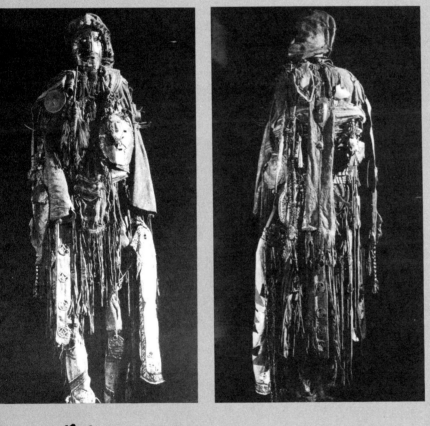

Figure 2-1a.   As well as heal the sick, the shaman brings psychic calm and confidence to the tribe by revitalizing and intensifying its notions of the world. The annual hunting rites carried out by the shaman are a good example. The photos show a Siberian shaman's coat and mask (front and back).

Figure 2-1b.   The shaman's role in energizing the successful hunting life of the tribe is shown in rock paintings. This cave painting below shows reindeer and a shaman in a bison mask. An important part of the shaman's effectiveness is his artistic ability. He employs his dramatic gifts and theatrical effects (mime, masks, costume, drum-beating) to give the tribe superior power over animals and success in the hunt. (Photos courtesy of Staatliches Museum Für Völkerkunde.)

As the *Nanda* ritual suggests, the interplay between space, time, performer, activity, and audience is a common factor of ritual and theatre.

Did Theatre Begin with Tribal Ritual? Anthropologists and historians agree that it may have, in part. What is certain is that theatre, as we know it now, is a kind of ritual act performed not in a tent or other temporary structure that will be dismantled after the ceremony, but in a permanent building that will be used again and again. The first such permanent theatre building we know of in our culture stands in the curve of a hillside in Greece.

THE GREEK THEATRE

The most celebrated theatre of fifth-century Athens, called the Theatre of Dionysus in honor of the fertility god, was an open-air structure located on the slope of the hill below the Acropolis.

There were two performance areas cradled within the curve of the hillside: the dancing circle (or *orchestra*), and the area backed by the scene building (or *skene*). The chorus, usually portraying ordinary human society, performed in the dancing area. One actor (later three) portrayed mythical and historical characters in front of the rectangular scene building, which formed a background. A late addition to the theatre was the wooden scene building erected on a stone foundation. The actors may also have performed in the orchestra, although no one knows for sure. The chorus, actors, and audience all entered the theatre through passageways called *parodoi,* and the audience stood, or were seated on wooden or stone benches, on the hillside "auditorium."

In the ancient Greek theatre there were no barriers between the performing area and the auditorium. The audience on the hillside had an unbroken view of actor and chorus. The spectators in the lower tiers, in fact, were so near the chorus that they were practically an extension of it.

31

The three photos show the ruins of the Theatre at Delphi and a modern performance of an ancient Greek play in the Theatre at Epidaurus.

Figure 2-2a. The Theatre at Delphi (right) is typical of ancient Greek theatres. It is built on a hillside with seats on three sides surrounding the stage. The temple of Apollo is in the background. Eventually scene buildings were built behind the playing area. Audiences could look past the stage to the mountains or the sea in the distance. The photo shows the stone benches placed on the hillside for the audience, the flat dancing circle or stage at the foot of the hill, and the remains of the stone foundation of the scene building.

Figure 2-2b. The Epidaurus Festival Theatre (left) is the best preserved of the Greek amphitheatres. In the photo we can see the relationship of the theatre to its natural environment. The scene building is of recent construction; the entrance ways, or parodoi, are clearly marked.

Figure 2-2c. The National Theatre Company of Greece performs today in the Epidaurus Festival Theatre. The photo shows the chorus in the orchestra and the actor standing above them on the stone steps leading into the modern scene building, or skene. (Photos courtesy of the Greek National Tourist Organization.)

The Chorus as Spectator

The Greek chorus shared the audience's reactions to events and characters, and sometimes interacted with the actor. The actor, representing a heroic figure like Oedipus or Creon, stood apart in the performance space, just as he stood apart from ordinary mortals in life. Thus the dancing circle and the chorus formed a kind of bridge between actor and audience.

Theatre as Social Commentary

The arrangement of spaces in the Greek theatre made a statement about how the Greeks saw their world: Classes

---

Aeschylus (525/4–456 B.C.), Sophocles, Euripides, and Aristophanes are four Greek playwrights whose work has survived today. Aeschylus began at an early age to write tragedies for the festivals, winning thirteen first prizes during his lifetime. He wrote over seventy plays, seven of which we have. These are *The Suppliants, The Persians, The Seven Against Thebes, Prometheus Bound, Agamemnon, The Libation Bearers,* and *The Eumenides.* The *Oresteia (Agamemnon, The Libation Bearers,* and *The Eumenides)* was presented by Aeschylus in 458 B.C. It is the only surviving Greek trilogy, or sequence of three tragedies. Only its satyr play, a comic burlesque of Greek myth performed with the trilogy, is missing.

Sometime before or during Aeschylus' career, the features of Greek tragedy became fixed: At an Athenian festival, three groups of players, each consisting of a chorus and two (later three) actors, competed in acting four sets of plays. Each set contained three tragedies and a satyr play for comic relief. The plays were based on Greek legend, epic poems, or history. Costumes were formal, masks elaborate, physical action restrained; violent scenes occurred offstage. The playwright expanded and interpreted the characters and stories of legend or history.

We know little about Aeschylus as a person except that he fought at Marathon (490 B.C.) during the Persian Wars and probably at Salamis (480 B.C.). His epitaph, which he wrote himself, shows that he was most proud of his military record:

Under this monument lies Aeschylus the Athenian, Euphorion's son, who died in the wheatlands of Gela. The grove of Marathon with its glories can speak of his valor in battle. The long-haired Persian remembers and can speak of it too.

separated physically by space and social status found themselves on common ground when faced with spectacles of terror and misfortune. They found common comfort in being part of a cosmology of beings dominated by gods and heroes. Sophocles' *Oedipus the King* speaks to master and slave when the chorus concludes: "Count no man happy until he has passed the final limit of his life secure from pain."

From the Minoan to the Hellenistic period the Greek theatre underwent changes: Wooden seats were replaced by stone; the addition of the scene building made the actors' area more complex, providing a scenic background and dressing area; a raised stage was added for the actors to perform on. But the theatres remained in the open air with well-defined places for the audience to sit and for the actors and chorus to perform. As we shall discover in a later chapter, the rigid division of space dictated the structure of the plays performed there. For example, the playwright had to use the chorus in the Dionysian Festival theatre. And the plays of Aeschylus, Sophocles, Euripides, and Aristophanes were shaped by the theatre's conventions.

MEDIEVAL THEATRE

The medieval theatre (c. 1300–1500) began in churches with Latin playlets performed by priests. (An early example is the *Quem Quaeritis* trope mentioned in Chapter 1.) Gradually, the religious gave way to the secular. Performances moved out of the churches into the marketplaces. Lay performers replaced priests; scripts grew longer and more complex.

Like the Greek and Roman amphitheatres, the medieval European theatre was an open-air festival theatre. There were few permanent structures. The plays (called *cycles*) dealt with Biblical events and ranged from the creation to the destruction of the world. They were performed in spring and summer months on religious holidays such as Corpus Christi, Easter, and Whitsuntide. Productions were sponsored by town councils, often with the help of local priests. Religious confraternities or secular trade guilds usually produced them; they hired a director or stage manager and recruited actors from the local population, which turned out en masse to become part of the event.

Two Types of Medieval Staging

Elements of the medieval *fixed stage* are to be found in the permanent Greek and Roman theatres. The *movable stage* had its beginnings in the medieval processions that celebrated religious and state occasions. We can see the influence of the medieval theatre on our own fixed and movable stages, open-air theatre buildings, street theatre, festival theatre, and holiday parades.

The Fixed Stage   One of the best-known fixed stages was constructed in 1547 for the Valenciennes Passion Play (France). Other important medieval fixed stages include the Roman amphitheatres, the "rounds" in Cornwall, and the stages set up in public squares in Mons and Lucerne.

The fixed stage at Valenciennes was a rectangular platform with two chief areas. One contained the "mansions," or huts, which depicted specific locales; the other was the *platea,* an extended playing space. There were no scene changes as we know them in our theatre. The actor merely went from hut to hut to indicate change in locale. Heaven and hell were usually represented on each end of the fixed stage, with earthly scenes of humor, travail, and so on, occurring between them. The fixed stage made it possible to present numerous scenes and actors, along with the necessary costumes, **properties,** and special effects.

In the Roman and Cornish amphitheatres the audience probably viewed the action from two or three sides. When the stage was the platform type, viewers might be grouped around three sides of the playing areas. Or they might gather at the front only. Whichever way, the fixed stage was always in the open air; there was a definite performing space for the actors and a definite audience area. The actor was close to the audience, and performances sometimes continued from dawn to dusk.

The Pageant Wagon   While fixed stages were common in many parts of Europe, theatrical space sometimes took on

Figure 2-3a. A Cornish circular amphitheatre (fixed stage). A typical permanent open-air theatre in Cornwall (also called a round) was made out of earth with circular turf benches surrounding a level area 130 feet in diameter. Openings on two sides of the earthen mound provided entrances and exits. This diagram (of the fourteenth-century theatre at Perranzabulo) shows the staging for a Biblical cycle called The Resurrection of Our Lord Jesus Christ. There are eight scaffolds located in the round's center. Action requiring a specific locale took place on the scaffolds, progressing from one scaffold to another around the circle. The audience, seated on the earthen tiers of seats, could follow the scenes with ease. (Diagram courtesy of Columbia University Press.)

Figure 2-3b (below). The fixed stage used for the Valenciennes (France) Passion Play in 1547. The mansions or huts represent (from left to right) specific locations: paradise, Nazareth, the temple, Jerusalem, the palace, the golden door, the sea, and hell's mouth. (From a manuscript in the Bibliothèque Nationale, Paris.)

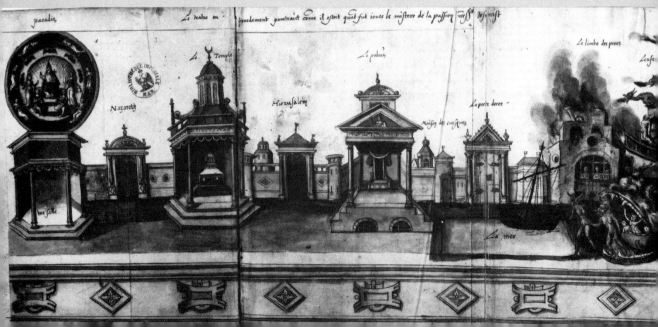

Figure 2-3c. *The English pageant wagon or processional stage (right). Glynne Wickham's drawing is a reconstruction of an English pageant wagon and ground plan of the overall playing arrangement. The drawing shows the essential features of what was to be the Elizabethan playhouse: a platform acting area, a tiring house with a recessed area (the loca) for interior scenes and costume changes, and an area above the cart for machinery.* (From Early English Stages, Vol. 1 (1959), *reprinted by permission of Glynne Wickham, Routledge & Kegan Paul, and Columbia University Press.*)

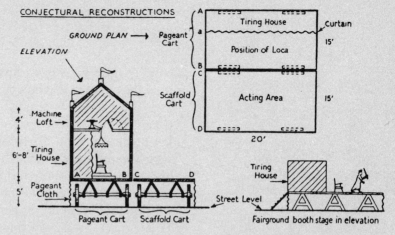

CONJECTURAL RECONSTRUCTIONS

Figure 2-3d (below). *A Mardi Gras parade float (modern processional stage). This colorful float appeared around 1937 in a Mardi Gras parade in New Orleans. It was entitled "You Are My Mardi Gras Valentine." The platform base of the float rests on a cart drawn by horses or mules. The masked riders, called the "Krew," throw inexpensive trinkets, usually beads and doubloons, to crowds waiting along the parade route. The flambeaux carriers (bottom center) light the way for the floats.* (Photo by Charles Genella from The Historic New Orleans Collection.)

entirely different forms. Spain and England, for example, used the pageant wagon and processional, or portable staging. The pageant wagon was a platform on wheels, something like our modern parade float. It was a portable playing area with a hut or tiring house on top for the actors, which could also serve as a scenic background or acting area. No one is certain of the wagons' dimensions, but they had to move through the narrow streets of medieval towns. The wagons stopped for performances at a number of different places and may have been used individually or in groups.

Each cycle contained as many as forty-two plays. The audience stood around the wagon to watch, so the actors were very close to the audience, just as they were on the fixed stage. The flexible playing space encouraged vigorous action; episodic, loose-knit plot structure; and some sort of scenic element to fix locale. *The Second Shepherd's Play*, one of thirty-two surviving plays of the English Wakefield Cycle, requires continuous action, change of locale from a field to a hut, and the annunciation of the heavenly angel to the shepherds.

THE ELIZABETHAN THEATRE

By the late sixteenth century permanent structures were being built in England and on the continent to house a new kind of theatrical entertainment, one that was losing its ceremonial or festive quality. In 1576, James Burbage built London's first theatre. He called it simply "The Theatre." It was an open-air structure that adopted features from various places of entertainment: inn yards, pageant wagons, banquet halls, fixed platforms, and portable booth-stages.

Shakespeare's Globe

In 1599, Richard Burbage built the Globe Theatre which became a showcase for Shakespeare's talents as actor and playwright. The Globe was an open-air building. There was a flat area in the middle for the stage, which was surrounded by a large enclosed balcony with one or two smaller roofed galleries over it. The stage was an open platform backed by a multilevel facade. On the stage level there were places for hiding and discovering people and things. The audience stood around the platform or sat in the galleries. Like the medieval audience, they were never far removed from the performers.

With little scenery and few properties, the Elizabethan theatre encouraged both playwright and actor to create unlimited illusions, transporting the audience from Juliet's tomb in one play to a raging storm at sea in another.

William Shakespeare (1564–1616) was an Elizabethan playwright of unsurpassed achievement. Born in Stratford-on-Avon, he received a grammar-school education and married a twenty-six-year-old woman when he was eighteen. He became the father of three children, Susanna and twins Judith and Hamnet. Few other facts about Shakespeare's life have been established. By 1587–88 he had moved to London, where he remained until 1611, except for occasional visits to his Stratford home. He appears to have found work almost at once in the London theatre as an actor and a writer. By 1592 he was regarded as a promising playwright; by 1594 he had won the patronage of the Earl of Southampton for two poems, *Venus and Adonis* and *The Rape of Lucrece.* In 1594–95 he joined James Burbage's theatrical company, The Lord Chamberlain's Men, as an actor and a playwright; later he became a company shareholder and part owner of the Globe and Blackfriars theatres. He wrote some thirty-seven plays for this company, suiting them to the talents of the great tragic actor Richard Burbage (James Burbage's son) and other members of the troupe. Near the end of his life he retired to Stratford as a well-to-do country gentleman. Shakespeare wrote sonnets, tragedies, comedies, history plays, and tragicomedies, including some of the greatest plays written in English: *Hamlet, King Lear, The Tempest, Macbeth,* and *Othello.*

Theatrical Influences

The Elizabethan theatre, like that of Greece and medieval Europe, was a festival theatre depicting cosmic drama that touched all people, peasant, artist, and noble. Its architecture, as we shall see, affected the structure of the plays written for it. Yet it all happened so long ago. Why

In The Globe Restored *(1968) C. Walter Hodges describes the Elizabethan theatre as self-contained, adjustable, and independent of any surroundings other than its audience.*

Figure 2-4a (right).   The drawing of the Swan Theatre in London dates from about 1596; it is the first picture we have of the interior of an Elizabethan theatre.

Figure 2-4b (below left).   It is generally agreed that the tiring house (the area around and within the house wall at the back of the stage) was divided off from the stage by hangings of some sort, usually curtains opening in the middle.

Figure 2-4c (below right).   The inner stage is thought to be a small, recessed area with curtains in the tiring house wall. Hodges shows a discovery area surrounded by curtains. The permanent upper level or upper stage is a characteristic feature of the Elizabethan stage; it was used for scenes like Juliet's balcony scene in Romeo and Juliet. Hodges's reconstruction of the inner and upper stages brings them forward into the main acting area.

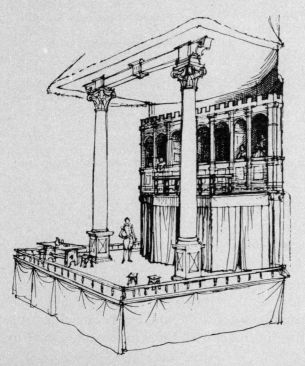

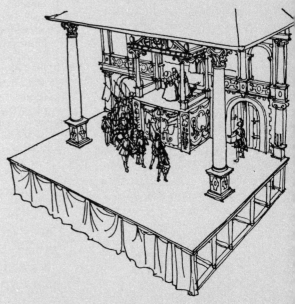

Figure 2-4d (right). Hodges's detailed reconstruction of the Globe Playhouse (1599–1613) shows the building's super-structure, with galleries, yard, and railed stage. Notice the trapdoor in the stage, stage doors, curtained inner and upper stages, tiring house (as backstage area with workrooms and storage areas), hut with machines, the "heavens," and playhouse flag. (Reprinted by permission of Oxford University Press.)

Figure 2-4e (below). The Oregon Shakespearean Festival Theatre is a modern recon-struction similar to The Fortune Theatre of Shakespeare's London, which was built in 1599. Although the seating and lighting facilities are modern, the stage and tiring house are patterned after the earlier theatre. (Photo courtesy of Hank Kranzler of The Oregon Shakespearean Festival.)

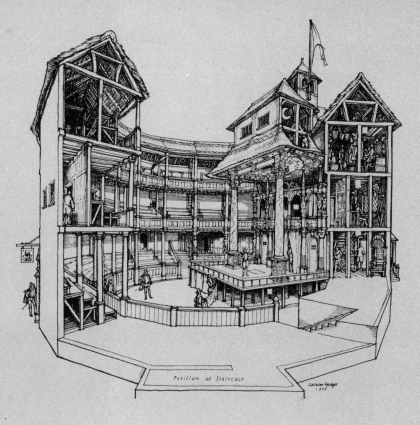

Position of Staircase

Figure 2-5. Outdoor drama. The Lost Colony *is produced annually by the Roanoke Island Historical Association in North Carolina. The 2000-seat amphitheatre has a thrust stage that enables the audience to be in the middle of the action. The theatre is surrounded by a high wooden palisade reminiscent of the fortifications used by early colonists and native Indians. (Photo by J. Foster Scott, Dare County Tourist Bureau.)*

do we study these ancient modes of theatre, whose traditions are often so hard to trace? Do they really tell us anything about our own theatre? Are they related to the buildings and performance spaces that we think of as being so modern?

The answer is yes, and you will agree next time you see a Mardi Gras or mummers' float or an open-air theatre designed for summer productions of Shakespeare. The open-air theatre is alive and well today. In large parks (often known as theme parks), plays with historical and period themes are performed for audiences looking for family entertainment; touring companies travel widely to college campuses with portable stages, costumes, and **props** to present plays with current social and political messages.

Figure 2-6.   An early proscenium theatre. Our modern proscenium theatre with perspective scenery had its origins in Italy. Between 1500 and 1650, a typical theatre was developed with an auditorium, painted scenery, proscenium, curtain, and musicians' pit. Spectacle and entertainment were its primary purpose. The Farnese Theatre was one of the earliest with a permanent proscenium arch.

THE PROSCENIUM THEATRE

The proscenium theatre dates back to the Italian Renaissance. The Farnese Theatre built in 1618 at Parma was one of the early proscenium theatres (Figure 2-6). An ornamental facade framed the stage and separated the audience from the actors and scene.

The invention of the proscenium brought with it innovative scenery techniques. Renaissance architects painted perspective scenery on large canvas pieces placed on a raked or slanted stage. In the seventeenth century, an architect named Giambattista Aleotti created a new system for changing scenery with movable, two-dimensional wings painted in perspective. This method, now called a wing-in-groove system (because grooves were placed in the stage floor to hold the scenery), replaced the raked stage.

Figure 2-7. Scenic illusion. The principles of perspective painting were introduced to theatrical scene design in the sixteenth century. Perspective scenery was painted to create the illusion of large streets or town squares, with houses, churches, roofs, doorways, arches, and balconies all designed to appear exactly as they would seem to a person at a single point. This kind of painted background was designed to give a sense of depth to the scene. In his book Architettura, *Sebastiano Serlio (1475–1554) explained the construction and painting of scenery for* comedy, *including the houses, tavern, and church shown in the drawing.*

Most of the theatres built in the Western world over the last 350 years are proscenium theatres. The concern of scenic designers working within the **picture-frame stage** was to use perspective scenery and mobile scenic pieces to achieve the effect of life being lived within the picture frame. The result was literally to frame the actor so that an audience, sitting in an enclosed, darkened space, could observe the actor in his or her setting. Playgoers were confined to the tiered galleries or to the orchestra, as the ground-level seats were called.

Eighteenth- and Nineteenth-Century Theatres

As audiences grew larger and the playhouses became more profitable, the auditoriums of public theatres increased steadily in size. And as the auditoriums grew larger, theatre architects added boxes for the affluent and cheap seats for the less well-off. In the nineteenth century the proscenium opening was enlarged to exploit the pictorial possibilities of the stage space. The auditorium was made shallower so that the audience was drawn closer to the stage, where they could see the actors' emotions and the details of their environment.

Figure 2-8. The proscenium stage. In Ibsen's Ghosts *the audience looks in upon the desperate lives of characters constrained by Victorian morality. Left to right, Marti Maraden is Regina, Nicholas Pennell is Oswald, Margaret Tyzack is Mrs. Alving, and William Hutt is Pastor Manders in the 1977 Stratford (Ontario) Festival Theatre Production. (Photo by Robert C. Ragsdale, courtesy of the Stratford Festival, Ontario, Canada.)*

The Proscenium Theatre Today

Today our proscenium theatres (many built in the late 1800s) contain a framed *stage* with scenery, machines, and lighting equipment; an *auditorium* (possibly with balconies) seating 500 to 600; and *auxiliary rooms*, including foyers, workrooms, and storage space.

The function of the proscenium theatre is to create illusion. In this complex, designers, director, playwright, and actors work in collaboration to create make-believe worlds. For instance, the **box-set** drawing room of Henrik Ibsen's *Ghosts* (1881) contains the world of the play; the setting's walls, like the pressures of Ibsen's nineteenth-century society, enclose Mrs. Alving's life and destroy her son's.

Ghosts, written by Henrik Ibsen in 1881, is the story of the Alving family. Mrs. Alving, widow of the admired and respected Captain Alving, has been living alone on her husband's estate with her maid Regina, carrying on her husband's philanthropic projects. Her son, Oswald, has returned from Paris for the dedication of an orphanage she has built.

The play opens with a conversation between the carpenter Jacob Engstrand and his supposed daughter, Regina. He tries to convince the girl to do her duty to her father and become the "hostess" of a sailors' hostel, which he plans to open with his savings. Regina refuses; she hopes for a more genteel life. Pastor Manders, a longtime friend of the family, arrives to dedicate the orphanage. He and Oswald heatedly discuss new moral codes. Oswald goes into the dining room, where sounds of his advances to Regina are heard. Mrs. Alving remarks that the "ghosts" of the past have risen to haunt her.

In Act II, Mrs. Alving explains that Regina is actually Captain Alving's daughter by a serving girl, and that his upstanding reputation has been falsely derived from her own good works. At the end of Act II the orphanage burns to the ground as a result of Engstrand's carelessness.

In Act III, it is revealed that Manders's fear of scandal has led him to bribe Engstrand. (Engstrand has convinced Manders that Manders himself started the fire.) Engstrand goes off with Regina to open the sailors' "home." Oswald confesses that he suffers from a venereal disease inherited from his father—another ghost. Mrs. Alving promises to give him a deadly drug should he become insane as the disease progresses. As the play ends, Oswald's mind disintegrates under a final seizure, and Mrs. Alving must decide whether to administer the drug as she has promised or to let her son live as a helpless invalid. The curtain falls as she tries to decide.

The Audience Discovers the Play

In the proscenium theatre the stage is usually hidden by a curtain until the play begins and it is time for the play's world to be "discovered" by the audience. Staging, scenery, lighting, and production style all work together to suggest that what's going on inside the proscenium arch is a self-contained world. The room often looks like a typical living room. The street, garden, factory, or railway station resemble places the audience would know. But in the proscenium theatre the audience is intentionally kept at a distance. They are primarily onlookers or witnesses to an event.

Figure 2-9. Stratford's thrust stage. The thrust stage at Stratford's (Ontario) Festival Theatre has a permanent facade or background resembling Shakespeare's theatre (see Figure 2-4d). In contrast, The Guthrie Theater in Minneapolis is a proscenium-thrust stage utilizing changeable, perspective scenery as background for the actor (see Figure 1-7b). (Photo by Robert C. Ragsdale, courtesy of the Stratford Festival, Ontario, Canada.)

The Thrust or Open Stage

Variations of the proscenium theatre often adopt features from Elizabethan inn-theatres and open stages. Today's proscenium open or thrust stage is an example. Thrust stages were largely designed to utilize perspective scenery without distancing the actor physically and psychologically from the audience. The idea here, as in many open, postwar theatres, was to minimize the separation of actor and audience created by the proscenium arch and the recessed stage. The actor performs on a platform that thrusts into the audience and has immediate contact with persons seated in the first several rows of seats.

Figure 2-10a (left). Drottningholm Court Theatre, located near Stockholm, was built in 1764–1766 for the entertainment of the Swedish Royal Court. This eighteenth-century proscenium theatre is unique today. The original decor, stage sets, machinery, and costumes have survived and are functional. The photo shows the interior of the Court Theatre. (Photos of Drottningholm Court Theatre courtesy of The Swedish Information Service.)

Figure 2-10b (below left). Today, eighteenth-century plays are given at the Court Theatre during the summer months. The photo shows a modern performance with stage setting and musicians.

Figure 2-10c (below). Underneath the Court Theatre's stage a giant windlass that is functional is operated by four men and changes the scenery noiselessly in ten seconds.

Figures 2-10d and 2-10e. Booth's Theatre, a formal proscenium theatre in New York, was built in 1869. The illustrations of exterior and interior are from a contemporary magazine. The interior is typical of elaborate proscenium theatres of the era in America and Europe. It features elegant decor, tiers of boxes around the sides and back of the auditorium, orchestra seats on the main floor, a musicians' pit, and a picture-frame stage. The elaborate perspective scenery towers above the actress onstage. (Photos from Harvard Theatre Collection.)

49

Figures 2-10f to 2-10h. Modern proscenium stages. (Photos courtesy of The John F. Kennedy Center for the Performing Arts.)

Figure 2-10f.   The John F. Kennedy Center for the Performing Arts, Washington, D.C., towers above the Potomac River and houses two proscenium theatres used exclusively for plays.

Figure 2-10g.   The Eisenhower Theatre, seating 1100, is used as a touring house and also for shows specially mounted for production at the Kennedy Center.

Figure 2-10h.   The Terrace Theatre was a bicentennial gift from the Japanese government to the American people. Opening in 1979, it seats 500 and has a mauve and silver interior. The American College Theatre Festival holds its annual spring festival of plays in this small proscenium theatre.

THE JAPANESE NOH THEATRE

Until this century, the theatrical traditions of Eastern cultures have been curiously removed from the West. The Japanese Noh Theatre hasn't changed since the seventeenth century, but it has only recently influenced Western directors and actors.

Japanese Noh developed in the late fourteenth century. Unlike Western drama it is highly stylized, and it depends heavily on music and mime for its effectiveness.

The Noh Stage

The stage is situated in a corner of a building at the audience's right hand. A temple roof rises above the stage floor, which is divided into two areas: the stage proper *(butai)* and the bridge *(hashigakari)*. All elements on this stage, including the four columns supporting the roof, have names and significance during performance.

The stage proper is divided into three areas: The largest is about eighteen feet square and marked off by four pillars and roof; at the rear of the stage are the musicians—a flute player and two or three drummers; and to the left of the main area sits the six-to-ten-member chorus. The stage's two entrances are the bridge, a railed gangway that leads from the dressing room to the stage and is used for all important entrances, and the "hurry door." Only three feet high, the hurry door is used by minor characters, musicians, chorus, and stage assistants. Three small pine trees in front of the bridge symbolize heaven, earth, and man. Another pine tree, symbolizing the play's earthly setting, is painted on the center wall behind the musicians. This wall forms the scenic background for all Noh performances.

The Performers

Like the stage, all features of a Noh performance are carefully controlled and fixed by tradition. The principal character *(shite)* is usually an aristocrat, ghost, lady, or supernatural being. This actor performs facing the column

Figure 2-11a.   The Noh stage (above) is a square, polished cedar platform open on three sides; it has a temple roof above and a back wall with a painted pine tree. In this photo the National Theatre of Japan performs for a modern audience. The musicians and chorus surround the principal actor (shite) on two sides; the audience is seated in front and to the left of the stage. (Photo courtesy of the Japan National Tourist Organization.)

Figure 2-11b.   The painted, wooden Noh mask (right) was made by hand; the secret process was handed down from one generation to the next. The purity and simplicity of the mask reflects the highly formal theatrical tradition of which it is a part. (Photo from Rizzoli International Publications, Inc.; U. Bar Verlag; photographer Fred Mayer.)

Figure 2-11c. Bertolt Brecht's
production in 1954 of The
Caucasian Chalk Circle *at the
Theater am Schiffbauerdamm,
East Berlin, shows the influence
of Eastern theatre. In the photo,
Grusha journeys with the child
to the mountains. On a bare
stage she mimes her long
journey before a simple white
curtain with pine trees in the
center. (Photo courtesy of The
Berliner Ensemble, East Berlin.)*

Figures 2-11d. Harold Prince directed an elaborate Broadway musical, Pacific Overtures (1975),
with lyrics by Stephen Sondheim, scenery by Boris Aronson, and costumes by Florence Klotz, in
the style of the Japanese Kabuki theatre. The settings and costumes for Kabuki are elaborate and
dazzling. Some settings extend the entire length of the stage, like the Aronson set. (Photo by
Martha Swope.)*

Figure 2-11e.   Kabuki actors are skilled in dancing, acting, singing, and playing musical instruments. Kabuki costumes, like the one worn by this principal actor in Pacific Overtures, *are made of layers of richly embroidered, hand-painted kimonos. (Photo by Martha Swope.)*

at the downstage (nearest the audience) right corner. The downstage left column is associated with the secondary character *(waki)*.

The conventions of performance are handed down from one generation of actors *(all male)* to the next. Every movement of the hands and feet and every vocal intonation follow a set rule. The orchestra supplies a musical setting and controls the timing of the action. The chorus sings the actor's lines while he is dancing, and narrates many of the play's events. Song and dialogue outline circumstances.

Some Noh actors wear painted wooden masks that designate basic types—men, women, aged people, deities, monsters, spirits. The silk costumes and headdresses are rich in color and design.

ORIENTAL THEATRE IN THE WEST

In recent years, Western scholars, directors, and actors have become interested in several Eastern theatrical practices: minimal staging; fixed conventions of movement, style, and dress; symbolic properties, dress, and masks; and visible musicians and stage assistants. In addition, the main forms of Oriental theatre—The Peking Opera (China); Noh theatre, Bunraku or doll theatre, and Kabuki theatre (Japan); shadow puppets (Malaysia); Balinese dance theatre (Bali); and Kathakali dancers (India)—have influenced Western producer-directors such as Gordon Craig, William Butler Yeats, Vsevelod Myerhold, Bertolt Brecht, Jerzy Grotowski, and Harold Prince.

SUMMARY

In Western and Eastern theatre, traditional spaces are divided into stage and auditorium. Dating back to ritual performances in early societies, the theatrical space is special. Theatre seeks out a place—a hillside, a street, a building—to engage audiences in the experience of seeing life imitated by actors.

QUESTIONS FOR STUDY

1. What are the two essential components of theatrical space?

2. In what sense are *enactment, imitation,* and *seasonal rites* forerunners of today's theatre?

3. What are the essential features of the ancient Greek theatre?

4. In what sense is the medieval European theatre a *festival theatre*?

5. How are the medieval theatre's *fixed* and *processional* stages related to our own theatre practices?

6. How did the features of Shakespeare's stage influence his use of space in such plays as *Hamlet* and *Othello*?

7. What are the principal features of the proscenium theatre?

8. How are the acting and audience spaces related in theatres designed to create an illusion of recognizable places, people, and events?

9. How does the modern proscenium-thrust stage, or open stage, combine features of the Elizabethan theatre and of the picture-frame stage?

10. What are the fixed traditions of the Japanese Noh theatre?

11. Modern directors are interested in Japanese Noh theatre because it does not attempt to create an illusion of life being lived before us. How does a Noh performance differ from the Western realistic theatre of Henrik Ibsen or Tennessee Williams?

12. How have the physical relationships between actor and audience changed throughout theatrical history?

NOTE

[1]Mircea Eliade, *Birth and Rebirth: The Religious Meanings of Initiation in Human Culture,* trans. Willard R. Trask (New York: Harper & Row, 1958), pp. 34–35.

3

The Seeing Place: Nontraditional Spaces

Recent efforts to find new kinds of theatrical space have created different ways of seeing theatre. Jerzy Grotowski in Poland and Richard Schechner in New York have rearranged theatrical space to bring audiences and actors closer together. As audiences, we are part of the staged action, seeing both as spectators and as participants.

The elimination of the stage-auditorium dichotomy is not the important thing—that simply creates a bare laboratory situation, an appropriate area for investigation. The essential concern is finding the proper spectator-actor relationship for each type of performance and embodying the decision in physical arrangements.

Jerzy Grotowski, *Towards A Poor Theatre*

During the last forty years some theatre directors and designers totally rejected the traditions of the picture-frame stage, and looked for new theatrical spaces. In warehouses, lofts, and halls they began reshaping *all* of the space available to audience and actor. They sought to bring the audience into direct contact with the actor, and to make it a more obvious part of the theatrical event.

This chapter is a brief discussion of two of these nontraditional approaches to the use of theatrical space: The Polish Laboratory Theatre and The Performance Group.

THE POLISH LABORATORY THEATRE

Grotowski's Poor Theatre

Jerzy Grotowski founded The Polish Laboratory Theatre in 1959. He set out to answer the question: What is theatre? Grotowski evolved a concept that he called poor theatre, which he opposed to rich theatre. For him, theatre's essentials are the actor and the audience in a bare space. He found that theatre could happen without costume, scenery, makeup, stage lighting, and sound effects; all it needed was the actor and audience in live communion. Grotowski writes:

I propose poverty in theatre. We have resigned from the stage-and-auditorium plant: for each production, a new space is designed for the actors and spectators. . . . The essential concern is finding the proper spectator-actor relationship for each type of performance and embodying the decision in physical arrangements.[1]

Environments

In his production of *Akropolis* (1962), the actors built structures among the spectators, subjecting them to a sense of congested space. In *The Constant Prince* (1965), the audience was separated from the actors by a high fence. They looked down on the actors like medical students watching a surgical operation. In *Dr. Faustus* (1963), the entire space became a monastery dining hall, and the spectators were guests at a banquet during which Faustus offered them entertaining episodes from his life.

Jerzy Grotowski (b. 1933) is founder and director of The Polish Laboratory Theatre, an experimental company located in Wroclaw. Not a theatre in the usual sense, The Laboratory Theatre has become an institute for research into acting. Under Grotowski's leadership, it conducts applied research into theatre art in general and the actor's art in particular. In addition, the laboratory also undertakes performances for audiences and instruction of actors, producers, students (many of them foreigners), and people from other fields. The plays performed are based on Polish and international classics. In recent years Grotowski's productions of Stanislaw Wyspianski's *Akropolis*, Shakespeare's *Hamlet*, Marlowe's *Dr. Faustus*, and Calderon's *The Constant Prince* have attracted worldwide attention. His closest collaborators are actor Ryszard Cieslak and literary advisor Ludwik Flaszen. Grotowski lectures in many countries, including the United States; he has written about his methods in *Towards a Poor Theatre* (1968).

Figure 3-1. The drawing shows the room at the beginning of the performance of Akropolis. *Note that the wire struts above the audience are empty.*

Figure 3-2. The room at the end of Akropolis. *The actors have disappeared, leaving the stovepipes hanging from the wire struts as gruesome reminders of the events in the concentration camps.*

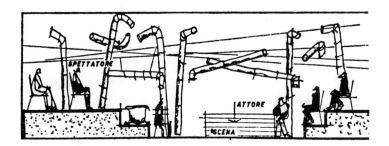

Figure 3-3. A view of the scenic action for Grotowski's production of Dr. Faustus, *based on the Elizabethan text by Christopher Marlowe. One hour before his death, Faustus offers a last supper to his friends (the audience) seated at the refectory tables. The theatrical space has been converted into a monastery dining hall.*

Figure 3-4. A view of the scenic action for The Constant Prince, *based on the seventeenth-century Spanish text by Pedro Caldéron de la Barca. The audience, seated behind a barrier, looks down on a forbidden act. Their positioning suggests a surgical operating theatre or a bullring. (Line drawings courtesy of H. M. Berg, Odin Teatret, Denmark.)*

Holy Theatre

Within the whole space, Grotowski creates what he calls holy theatre: The performance is a semireligious act in which the actor, prepared by years of training and discipline, undergoes a psycho-spiritual experience. Grotowski sets about to engage the audience in this act, and thus to engage both actor and audience in a deeper understanding of personal and social truths.

Akropolis

In *Akropolis,* Grotowski adapted a text of Polish playwright Stanislaw Wyspianski that was written in 1904. In the original, statues and paintings in Cracow Cathedral come to life on the eve of Easter Sunday. The statues reenact scenes from the Old Testament and antiquity. But Grotowski shifted the action to an extermination camp, Auschwitz, in wartime Poland. In the new setting he contrasted the Western ideal of human dignity with the human degradation of the camp.

The Setting   Akropolis takes place in a large room. Spectators are seated on platforms, and passageways for the actors are created between the platforms. Wire struts are strung across the ceiling. In the middle of the room is a large, boxlike platform for the actors. Rusty pieces of

The rule of The Laboratory Theatre is to distribute the action all over the room and among the spectators. There are no sets or props in the usual sense. The value of each object resides in its use. The stovepipes and metal junk are used as setting and as three-dimensional, functional metaphors. The wheelbarrows, tools for daily work, become hearses for carrying corpses to the crematorium.

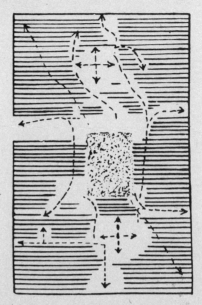

Figure 3-5a (right). The diagram shows Grotowski's use of space for *Akropolis.* The lines with arrows indicate the actors' movements and areas of action; the straight lines show audience areas. The central playing space is a boxlike "mansion" where pipes are assembled and into which the actors disappear at the end of the performance.

Figure 3-5b (below). The character Esau (played by Ryszard Cieslak) sings of the freedom of a hunter's life while enmeshed in the wire struts.

Figure 3-5c (below). This photo is called a "dialogue between two monuments." The metal stovepipe and the human leg with boot make a visual statement about the way human beings can be treated as objects. This is one of many statements in the performance about man's inhumanity to man throughout history. The two actors are Rena Mirecka and Zbigniew Cynkutis. (Photos and drawing courtesy of H. M. Berg, Odin Teatret, Denmark.)

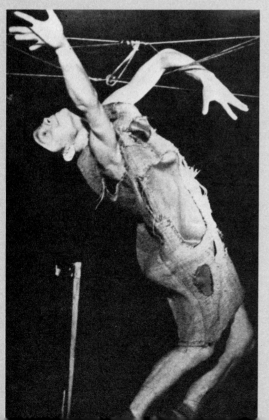

metal are heaped on top of the box: stovepipes, a wheel-barrow, a bathtub, nails, hammers. With these objects the actors build a civilization of gas chambers. They wear a version of a camp uniform—ragged costumes, heavy wooden shoes, and anonymous berets.

The Action   Grotowski juxtaposes Biblical and Homeric scenes and heroes against the grotesque reality of the modern death camp. The love of Paris and Helen, for instance, is played out between two men to the accompaniment of the laughter of the assembled prisoners; Jacob's bride is a stovepipe with a rag for a veil. *Akropolis* ends with a procession around the box in the center of the room led by a Singer carrying the headless corpse of the Savior. Grotowski describes it:

The procession evokes the religious crowds of the Middle Ages, the flagellants, the haunting beggars. . . . the procession reaches the end of its peregrination. The Singer lets out a pious yell, opens a hole in the box, and crawls into it dragging after him the corpse of the Savior. The inmates follow him one by one, singing fanatically. . . . When the last of the condemned men has disappeared, the lid of the box slams shut. The silence is very sudden; then after awhile a calm, matter-of-fact voice is heard. It says simply, "They are gone, and the smoke rises in spirals." The joyful delirium has found its fulfillment in the crematorium. The end.[2]

Grotowski's poor theatre returns to the essentials of theatre: actor, audience, space. Stage and auditorium are no longer separate units. As Grotowski says, "The essential concern is finding the proper spectator-actor relationship for each type of performance and embodying the decision in physical arrangements."[3]

THE PERFORMANCE GROUP

Much of the work of Jerzy Grotowski (The Polish Laboratory Theatre), Peter Brook (International Centre for Theatre Research), Ariane Mnouchkine (Théâtre du Soleil), Julian Beck and Judith Malina (The Living Theatre), Joe Chaikin (The Open Theatre), André Gregory (Manhat-

Richard Schechner (b. 1934) is an American producer, director, writer, and teacher. He founded The Performance Group in 1967. He has produced and directed *Dionysus in 69* (1968), *Makbeth* (1969), *Commune* (1970), *The Tooth of Crime* (1973), *Mother Courage and Her Children* (1974), *The Marilyn Project* (1975), *Oedipus* (1977), and *Cops* (1978). Author of *Public Domain* (1969) and *Environmental Theater* (1973), he teaches at the School of the Arts, New York University.

Schechner's writings on environmental theatre have changed our ways of thinking about theatre spaces.

tan Project), and Peter Schumann (The Bread and Puppet Theater) is labeled *environmental theatre*. Richard Schechner, founder of The Performance Group in New York City, has worked with environmental productions as a particular way of creating theatre.

Environmental Theatre

Environmental theatre uses all the space within a room, hall, garage, or loft, and transforms the area into a total performance environment. Actor and audience are intermingled during the performance. Schechner writes: "The thing about environmental theatre space is not just a matter of how you end up using space. It is an attitude. *Start with all the space there is and then decide what to use, what not to use, and how to use what you use.*"[4] Schechner founded The Performance Group in a garage (known today as The Performance Garage) at 33 Wooster Street, New York City. Like The Polish Laboratory Theatre, The Performance Group ordinarily uses the same space for each new production, but constructs a different environment in it.

Dionysus in 69, performed in 1968–69, was the group's first work. It was based on Euripides' *The Bacchae*, a play about the seduction and death of Pentheus at the instigation of the god Dionysus. The environment within The Performance Garage was roughly fifty feet by thirty-five feet in extent and twenty feet high. There were two dominant towers and a central area marked by black rubber mats. The audience arranged themselves on the carpeted floor, the platforms, and the towers, and the actors moved among them horizontally on the floor and platforms, and vertically on the towers.

Dionysus's birth and Pentheus' seduction and death took place on the black mats. After Pentheus was killed, the women in the company rushed into the audience and all at once told of their part in the murder. At the play's end, and weather permitting, the large overhead garage door at the end of the room was opened and all the performers marched out into Wooster Street, often followed by the audience.

Euripides' *The Bacchae* is the story of the phenomena of religious ecstasy that we call Dionysiac (after the god), and of the young man Pentheus, King of Thebes, who dies as a scapegoat for rejecting Dionysus (also called Bacchus).

The play pits young god against young king. As the chorus of worshippers of Dionysus (women called maenads) endorses the new religion, Pentheus, ignoring the warnings of Cadmus (his grandfather) and Teiresias (the seer), decides to stamp it out. The play becomes a confrontation between two powers—human and divine—and the god proves superior. In a rite of religious fervor, a group of Theban women that includes Pentheus' mother, Agave, celebrates the god's mysteries in a secret place. Pentheus dresses as a woman to spy on them and is torn to pieces by the women, who are in a state of drunken madness. Returning from the rite, Agave holds up the head of her dismembered son and the chorus is moved to horror and pity. At the play's end, the sufferings of Agave and Cadmus have led them to discover compassion for the nature of humankind.

Based on Euripides' The Bacchae, Dionysus in 69 *became a paradigm of environmental theatre production. The photos illustrate three separate events in the performance.*

Figure 3-6a. *The birth ritual. The god Dionysus is born through the collective efforts of the actors who, as chorus, represent society. A birth-ritual canal is formed by the line of bodies, and the actor who plays Dionysus is pushed through and born as the god. (Photo © Max Waldman 1969.)*

Figure 3-6b. Pentheus announcing his presence. The photo shows the space designed by Michael Kirby and Jerry N. Rojo populated with platforms and towers. There is no clearly defined stage. The spectators sit just about anywhere. The action goes on around and among them. In this scene Pentheus speaks from the tower through the bullhorn seen in the photo; he announces, "I am Pentheus, son of Echion and Agave, and King of Thebes." (Photo by Frederick Eberstadt, courtesy of Richard Schechner.)

Figure 3-6c. Dionysus' exit. On some occasions spectators and actors merge, carrying Dionysus through the open garage door into Wooster Street at the performance's end. (Photo by Frederick Eberstadt, courtesy of Richard Schechner.)

Performance Style

As we see from the description of *Dionysus in 69,* environmental theatre requires a different attitude toward performance, text, action, and the intermingling of actors and audience. The actor and the audience are not separated from each other by architecture or scenery—they are both contained within a whole space. Moreover, the style of performance draws them together visually, physically, and psychically. In *Dionysus in 69* the actors, for example, ask the audience to help murder Pentheus. The script was not written, in the usual sense, by a playwright, but was developed in rehearsals by the company as a whole. The group reduced Euripides' play from 1300 lines to 600; actors wrote some of their own dialogue; and Euripides' story took on new meaning—it became an enactment of rituals of birth and death.

SUMMARY

Another way of thinking about theatrical spaces is to consider what Carlos Castaneda says about special places in *The Teachings of Don Juan: A Yaqui Way of Knowledge* (1968). Don Juan instructs him to find a special place by using his eyes, and he explores the porch of Don Juan's house searching for a "personal" spot to sit upon. After many hours, he senses the correct place and settles into it, filling and shaping it.

Approaches to nontraditional theatre are similar to Castaneda's experience with space. Each member of the audience seeks out and finds a space as special and particular as that occupied by the actors. Environmental theatre rejects conventional seating and arranges the audience as part of the playing space. Like the actors, they become part of what is seen and done; they are both seeing and seen. In contrast, traditional theatre arranges the audience *before* a stage, where they see and hear at a comfortable remove.

The 1973–74 production of *Candide* was one of Broadway's early environmental efforts. Originating with the Chelsea Theatre, Brooklyn, and directed by Harold Prince, *Candide* was designed by Eugene and Franne Lee, who collaborated to transform the Broadway Theatre into an environment for musical comedy. The story was adapted from Voltaire by Hugh Wheeler with lyrics by Richard Wilbur, Stephen Sondheim, and John Latouche.

When the play was moved from the 180-seat Chelsea Theatre, where it had a limited, six-week run, to the large Broadway Theatre, seats were removed, the balcony closed off, and the ground floor renovated. The orchestra seating was divided to make two audience groups. One group was seated around the periphery of the main performing areas. The other, seated in the center, was actually part of the production. (Photos by Martha Swope.)

Figure 3-7a. The photo of the Broadway Theatre's interior shows ramps, platforms, and runways, with actors performing throughout the space. The audience is seated around the circumference and in the center. The musicians are scattered throughout the space.

Figure 3-7b (above). When
Candide is about to set off for
the new world, he needs a boat
and one is brought out. The
small stage at one end of the
theatre onto which the boat is
pulled is less important than the
ramps, runways, and trapdoors
all over the theatre. The
environmental design allows the
audience to participate in the
inventive freedom of the
performance.

Figure 3-7c. Candide and his
beloved Cunegonde talk to each
other across the audience. The
photo gives a sense of the close
contact between actors and
audience.

Figure 3-7d. *The photo of the* finale *indicates the intimate relationship between audience, actors, musicians, and space in this environmental production.*

QUESTIONS FOR STUDY

1. How does Jerzy Grotowski define "poor theatre"?

2. Why is the work of The Polish Laboratory Theatre important?

3. What are the social and moral objectives of Grotowski's Laboratory Theatre?

4. How does Grotowski's production of *Akropolis* portray these objectives?

5. What is *environmental theatre*?

6. What seating arrangements are used in environmental productions?

7. Explain how Richard Schechner's *Dionysus in 69* is an environmental production.

8. What is the actor-audience relationship in The Performance Garage's production of *Dionysus in 69*? Study the photographs to arrive at your answer.

9. What theories of environmental theatre are at work in producer-director Harold Prince's Broadway production of *Candide*?

10. How was the Broadway Theatre renovated to create an environment for *Candide*?

11. What solutions have the new directors arrived at in their efforts to discover the proper audience-actor relationship for each production?

12. Are there any created or "found" spaces used for theatrical productions on your campus or in your community?

NOTES

[1]Jerzy Grotowski, *Towards a Poor Theatre* (New York: Clarion Press, 1968), pp. 19–20.

[2]Ibid., p. 75.

[3]Ibid., p. 20.

[4]Richard Schechner, *Environmental Theater* (New York: Hawthorn, 1973), p. 25.

4

The Image Makers:
Playwright and Director

The playwright envisions the play's world. The director, with the help of many others, transposes it into the theatre's space for us to see and hear.

☙

Perhaps without knowing it I have stumbled on a definition of art in the theatre; all art in the theatre should be, not descriptive, but evocative.
Robert Edmond Jones,
The Dramatic Imagination

Chapter Four

Who fills the theatrical space? Who is seen in the space? What methods and materials are used to create the stage environment, what a famous designer called "the machine for acting"? In theatre we are continually exposed to the idea of building. Actors speak of building a character. Technicians build the set and costumers build costumes. The director "blocks" the play. The word *playwright* is formed in the same way as *wheelwright* or *shipwright:* It means "playbuilder." Theatre is the collaborative effort of all these builders; the whole is greater than the sum of its parts. The American scene designer Robert Edmond Jones refers to this wholeness when he speaks of theatre as an *evocation.* The stage as medium evokes for us the imaginary world created by the theatre's artists. The efforts of many artists using various methods and materials fill the theatrical space. In the next three chapters we consider the working methods of the *playwright, director, actor,* and *designer.*

THE PLAYWRIGHT

A Personal Vision

The playwright writes a play to express some aspect of reality, some measure of experience, some vision or conviction about the world. Like any artist, the playwright shapes a personal vision of many experiences into an organized, meaningful whole. Thus a script is more than words on a page—it is the playwright's *architecture* of a special kind of experience created to appeal as much to the eye as to the ear. All in all, playwriting is the search for the truth of human experience as the playwright perceives it.

Playwrights such as Henrik Ibsen write plays to expose truths about the realities of social injustice. Other playwrights, like Bertolt Brecht, have political or economic statements to make about men and governments. These writers frequently use the theatre as a vehicle for a message or ideology. Other writers turn their personal experiences, wishes, and dreams into drama. For American playwright Adrienne Kennedy, writing is an outlet for inner, psychological confusion and questions stemming from

Figure 4-1.   A page from Edward Albee's typescript of Who's Afraid of Virginia Woolf? *with the playwright's handwritten corrections. (From the manuscript in the New York Public Library at Lincoln Center; reproduced by permission of Edward Albee.)*

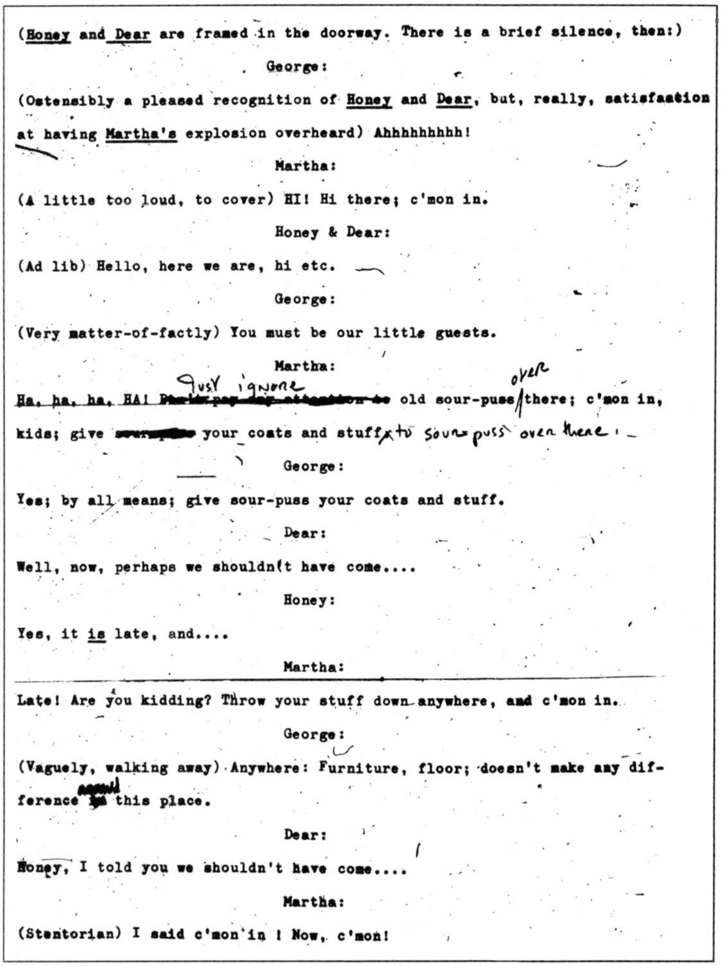

childhood. Other writers, like Eugene Ionesco, ridicule the conventions of theatre and certain kinds of human behavior to persuade us to see the world differently.

How the Playwright Works

The playwright creates on paper an image or sense of life being lived before us. The playwright's script is of major importance in the theatre because it is the usual starting point for the theatrical production.

Playwrights start with an idea, theme, or notes and work out an action; or begin with an unusual character or a real person and develop an action around that character;

or start with a situation based on a personal experience, their reading, or an anecdote. Other writers working with groups evolve scenarios with actors and arrange a final script from the group's improvisations, situations, dialogue, and movement. Some write from scenarios or plot summaries; others write from outline, crisis scene, images, dreams, myth, or imagined environment.

Bertolt Brecht usually worked from a story outline, which he called the draft plan. Next, he summarized the story's social and political ideas before developing scenes based on the outline. Some playwrights claim their characters talk to them and develop themselves; others claim they hear the play's voices and sounds in their heads. Some playwrights speak lines out loud before writing them down, or work from visions of their characters moving and talking.

The Broadway Option

When the play is finished, the playwright usually sends it to an *agent* who contacts producers (persons responsible for financing productions) and sells the play for a commission. Another approach is to send the script directly to a regional theatre or university theatre department in the hope that the play can interest a director in producing an original script. Today, university, regional, and off-Broadway theatres often produce new plays and many Broadway hits are first seen elsewhere.

When a commercial producer options or buys the exclusive rights to a play for a Broadway production, the playwright then is asked to rewrite parts of the script during rehearsals and out-of-town tryouts. Tryouts and previews are the testing ground for commercial production. On the basis of critical notices and audience response during this period, the play is reworked and sometimes completely rewritten before the official opening. There is enormous pressure on the playwright to satisfy various interest groups, including director and producer. Once produced, the script is published—usually by Samuel French Publishers or Dramatists' Play Service—and made available to commercial and noncommercial producers.

Edward Albee (b. 1928), American playwright and director, was born in Washington, D.C., and adopted by Mr. and Mrs. Reed A. Albee of the Keith-Albee theatre chain. He attended Hartford's Trinity College but left after a year and a half to work at odd jobs: radio copywriter, waiter, telegram messenger. In 1958 he wrote *Zoo Story,* a one-act play, and in 1960 *The Death of Bessie Smith;* both were produced abroad and acclaimed by critics before they premiered in New York. In 1962 Albee made a successful Broadway debut with *Who's Afraid of Virginia Woolf?* This full-length play established him as a major playwright. More recently, Albee has written *Tiny Alice* (1964), *A Delicate Balance* (1966), *All Over* (1971), *Seascape* (1974), *The Lady from Dubuque* (1979), and directed the 1976 New York revival of *Who's Afraid of Virginia Woolf?*

THE DIRECTOR

Background

Emerging as a force in the nineteenth century, the director is the most recent addition to the list of principal theatre artists. Before the director became part of theatre, leading actors, theatre managers, and sometimes playwrights set the actors' movements, dictated production, and took care of financial matters. Nineteenth-century advances in technology made stage machinery and lighting more complex, and changing social and political thought so altered the theatre's subjects, characters, and staging that a *coordinating specialist* became necessary.

Figure 4-2. Playwright Edward Albee directs the 1976 New York revival of Who's Afraid of Virginia Woolf? *Albee is a successful stage director as well as a playwright; in 1977 he formed a touring company to bring performances of his one-act plays to college and university campuses. (Photo by Joseph Abeles.)*

In the 1860s in Europe the practice of a single person guiding all aspects of the production process began to emerge. During the first half of the nineteenth century, actor-managers (following the tradition of James Burbage in England and Moliere in France) functioned more like the modern director. Nevertheless, the actor-manager was still first of all an actor and considered the production from the perspective of the role he was playing. David Garrick (1717–1779), for example, was one of England's successful actor-managers (see Figure 5-3). While the theatre between 1750 and 1850 was immensely popular in Europe, most actor-managers—Garrick was an exception

Figure 4-3. Colleen Dewhurst as Martha shouts at husband George (left) played by Ben Gazzara in the 1976 New York revival of Who's Afraid of Virginia Woolf? *Richard Kelton (right) plays Nick, the biology professor who joins George and Martha for a late night party. (Photo by Joseph Abeles.)*

—maintained inferior artistic standards in their pursuit of large box-office receipts. This general condition in the theatre began to concern a growing number of theatre people who reexamined the production process. With the formation in 1860 of the company of Duke George II of Saxe-Meiningen in Germany (known as the Meiningen Players), the director in the modern sense of the term began to emerge. His efforts to shape the director's role were followed by those of André Antoine in France and Constantin Stanislavsky in Russia. Under their influence the modern stage director's role took shape in Europe: someone who understood all theatre arts and devoted full energies to bringing them together in a unified, artistic whole.

Duke of Saxe-Meiningen, George II (1826–1914) transformed the Duchy of Meiningen (Germany) court theatre into an example of scenic historical accuracy and lifelike acting. As producer-director, the duke designed all costumes, scenery, and properties for historically authentic style, and worked for **ensemble acting.** The Meiningen Players were noted throughout Europe for their crowd scenes, in which each member of the crowd had individual traits and specific lines. In rehearsals the actors were divided into small groups, each under the charge of an experienced actor. This practice was in keeping with the company's rule against actors being stars, and was the beginning of the new movement in 1874 toward unified production under the director's control. Saxe-Meiningen's example of the *single creative authority* in charge of the total production influenced Antoine and Stanislavsky.

How the Director Works

The director collaborates with the playwright, actors, and designers to create on stage a carefully selected imitation of life—a special mirror. Responsible for what is seen and heard, the director works with the actors and designers to interpret the playwright's world, characters, and events. In addition, the director chooses sound effects, music, makeup, **stage** and **hand properties,** and sometimes attends to publicity, theatre programs, and box-office details.

Figure 4-4.   The director at work. Alan Schneider, Broadway director, directing at Stanford University in California. He directed the first American production of Samuel Beckett's Waiting for Godot in Miami in 1956, as well as the New York premiere of Edward Albee's Who's Afraid of Virginia Woolf? in 1962. (Photo courtesy of Alan Schneider.)

Basically, the director has six responsibilities: (1) selecting the script, especially in colleges and universities; (2) deciding upon the script's interpretation; (3) casting actors in the various parts; (4) working with other theatre artists to plan the production; (5) rehearsing the actors; (6) coordinating all elements into the final stage performance.

André Antoine (1858–1943) was producer-director of the Théâtre Libre, or "Free Theatre," in France. Beginning as a part-time actor, Antoine founded in 1887 a theatre and a naturalistic production style that became world famous. The Théâtre Libre was a subscription theatre, one open only to members, and therefore it was exempt from censorship. It became a showcase for new plays (Ibsen's *Ghosts* was one) and new production techniques. Seeking authentic detail, Antoine tried to reproduce exact environments on stage. In one play he hung real beef carcasses on stage. In an effort to stage "real" life, Antoine developed three important principles: realistic environments, ensemble acting, and the director's authority.

Before rehearsals begin, the director *visualizes the play* in space. Since a play involves people living in a world, the director must "see" the actors' movements in their stage lives. Usually beginning with the script, the director takes the play apart to examine its mechanics and ideas, decides upon the play's main action or **"spine,"** and puts it back together again. To analyze the play's organization, including its strengths and weaknesses, the director usually divides the play into *beats* (or short segments).

Characters also have spines, or chief motivating actions. Director Elia Kazan described Blanche DuBois' spine as *the search for protection*. The director studies the spine and function of each character in the play and the physical, vocal, and emotional demands made on the actor playing the part. The script's scenic, costume, and lighting requirements are also considered.

The Audition and Casting

Casting is matching the actor to the role. During auditions the director looks for actors whose physical appearance, personality, and acting style flesh out the director's idea of the characters. In college and university theatres, audition or tryout procedures are more or less standardized. Copies of the play are made available and notices of the audition posted. The director holds private interviews or general tryouts, or a combination of the two. The director usually asks actors to come prepared to illustrate their acting range by performing selections from plays of their own choosing, or provides material at the audition for them to read aloud.

Beginning with the leads, the director narrows the choices for each part and calls back a final group. This group reads together from the play to be produced so that the director can visualize the actors together. It is important to see how they relate to one another, how they work together, and how they complement one another in physical appearance and in vocal and emotional quality. Once the director decides upon the desired ensemble effect, there is a further elimination process, the casting notice is posted, and rehearsals begin.

The Director and Actor

At the most basic level the director helps the actor to find the character's inner life and to project this life vocally and visually to the audience. One basic approach used by some directors is to preplan the actors' movements, and, like a photographer composing a group photograph, arrange the actors in the stage space to show their physical and psychological relationships. The director's emphasis here is upon *stage composition* and *picturization*. Like a photographer, the director composes pictures with actors on stage to convey truths about human relationships and to tell the playwright's story. Each actor-as-character is pictured by the director within the group to show relationships, emotions and attitudes. The first three or four rehearsals are used to block the play. In blocking rehearsals the director goes through each scene line by line, telling the actors when to come in, where to stand or sit, on what lines to move. As they go through the actions, the actors write down the directions and stage business (or specific actions, such as answering a telephone) in their scripts.

Directors vary a great deal in their approach to beginning rehearsals. Some give full directions immediately; others leave much of the detail to be worked out later as the actors try out their lines and reactions to one another. Almost any director makes adjustments in later rehearsals as director and actors discover better ways of moving and reacting.

Constantin Stanislavsky (1863–1938) was producer-director-actor and founder of the Moscow Art Theatre. As a director, Stanislavsky aimed for ensemble acting and the absence of stars; he established such directorial methods as intensive study of the play before rehearsals began, the actor's careful attention to detail, and recreation of the play's milieu after visiting locales or extensive research. The Moscow Art Theatre's success was seen in Anton Chekhov's plays depicting the monotonous and frustrating life of the rural landowning class.

Stanislavsky is remembered most for his attempts to perfect a method of acting. His published writings in English— *My Life in Art* (1924), *An Actor Prepares* (1936), *Building a Character* (1949), and *Creating a Role* (1961)— provide a record of the "Stanislavsky System" as it evolved.

A second basic approach that most modern directors favor is the *collaborative approach*. Often called *organic blocking*, director and actors work together in rehearsals to evolve movement, gestures, character relationships, stage images, and line interpretations. Rather than entering the rehearsal period with entirely preset ideas, the director watches, listens, suggests, and selects as the actors rehearse the play. The methods of German playwright and director Bertolt Brecht (1898–1956) have been described in this way:

During rehearsals Bertolt Brecht sits in the auditorium. His work as a director is unobtrusive. When he intervenes it is almost unnoticeable and always in the "direction of flow." He never interrupts, not even with suggestions for improvement. You do not get the impression that he wants to get the actors to "present some of his ideas"; they are not his instruments.

Instead he searches, together with the actors, for the story which the play tells, and helps each actor to his strength. His work with the actors may be compared to the efforts of a child to direct straws with a twig from a puddle into the river itself, so that they may float.

Brecht is not one of those directors who knows everything better than the actors. He adopts towards the play an attitude of "know-nothingism"; he waits. You get the impression that Brecht does not know his own play, not a single sentence. And he does not want to know what is written, but rather how the written text is to be shown by the actor on the stage. If an actor asks: "Should I stand up at this point?", the reply is often typically Brecht: "I don't know." Brecht really does not know; he only discovers during the rehearsal.[1]

The importance of the rehearsal process is to discover a unity and meaning for the production. Sometime in the rehearsal period, the director sets the performance by selecting from what has evolved in rehearsals. In this second approach, improvisation or gameplaying is an important director's tool.

Improvisation can free the actors' imaginations and bodies for spontaneous story telling. Often the director uses improvisations early in rehearsals to spark the cast's imagination, behavior, reactions, and mood as they begin

Figure 4-5. *Actors improvise movement in* Hair *(a 1967 "American tribal love-rock musical" directed by Tom O'Horgan on Broadway). Improvisation is primarily a rehearsal tool and not a performance technique. How much improvisation is used in rehearsal depends on the director's skill with it and on the actors' needs. Viola Spolin's* Improvisation for the Theatre *(1963) is a good book about this approach to actor training. (Photo by Martha Swope.)*

to work together. In later rehearsals improvisations can increase concentration, discover dramatic action and character relationships, and develop good working relations between actors.

The modern director uses other tools to stimulate the imagination of actors so that they will give life to their roles. The director's *ground plan* defines the space limitations for the story, such as obstacles of furniture, doors, stairs, and so on. As the director physically arranges the actor in the ground plan (sometimes called *composition*), the actor discovers physical relationships with other characters and understands the play's action. As the actor moves about the stage, he or she discovers gestures that further illustrate character and emotion. As the director and actors add story-telling details of gesture and speech, the character's emotional truth is illustrated visually and vocally. The living quality of the play is being communicated.

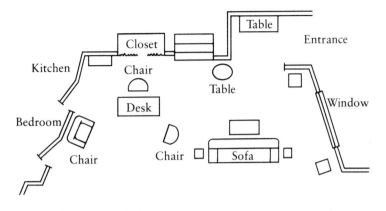

Figure 4-6. The ground plan. Director and designer work out the play's environment, noting where the doorways, windows, steps, levels, walls, and furniture are. These are then outlined in tape on the stage floor so the actor can visualize the environment in rehearsals. (Drawing courtesy of Holt, Rinehart and Winston, Inc.)

The Director's Function

The stage reflects the director's idea of the way the play looks and sounds. This means that the director functions as an interpreter or creator. As an *interpretive artist* the director serves the playwright by translating the script as faithfully as possible into theatrical form. Elia Kazan interpreted Arthur Miller's and Tennessee Williams's plays on Broadway. Edward Albee often directs his own plays.

More recently, the director has become a *creative artist,* one who fashions the script into an original work of art. In this role, the director alters the play—changes the period represented, cuts the text, rearranges the scenes—and practically takes over the role of author. In his recrea-

Elia Kazan (b. 1909 in Istanbul, Turkey) was educated at Williams College and Yale University. He was a member of the Group Theatre and acted in their productions of Clifford Odets's *Waiting for Lefty, Paradise Lost,* and *Golden Boy.*

He is best known today for his direction of plays by Tennessee Williams and Arthur Miller: *A Streetcar Named Desire* (1947), *Death of a Salesman* (1949), *Camino Real* (1953), *Cat On A Hot Tin Roof* (1955), and *Sweet Bird of Youth* (1959). Kazan also directed the films of *A Streetcar Named Desire, On the Waterfront,* and *East of Eden.*

Along with designer Jo Mielziner, Kazan established theatrical realism as the dominant American style during the 1950s. The style combined acting of intense psychological truth with simplified but realistic scenery. Marlon Brando as Stanley Kowalski embodied the style of acting for which Kazan's productions were famous (see Figure 1-1).

Peter Brook (b. 1925) is a British director and founder of the International Centre for Theatre Research in Paris. Born in London and educated at Oxford University, Brook began his directing career in the 1940s. As codirector of England's Royal Shakespeare Company (RSC) from 1962 to 1971, he directed acclaimed productions of *King Lear, The Tempest, Marat/Sade,* and *A Midsummer Night's Dream.* His activities with the Centre include *Orghast* for the Shiraz Festival at Persepolis (Iran), a Central African tour, and *The IK* (based on Colin Turnbull's book *The Mountain People*), which toured London and America. He directed the film of *The Lord of the Flies,* wrote an influential book on theatre, *The Empty Space* (1968), and recently directed Shakespeare's *Antony and Cleopatra* (1978) for the RSC.

Known for his radical adaptations of familiar plays, Brook enjoys an enormous international reputation. His version of *A Midsummer Night's Dream* is not about the romantic fairies and haunted woodlands that Shakespeare imagined. It is an exploration of love performed in a white boxlike set with actors on trapezes and in "mod" clothing and circus costumes (see Figure 4-7).

tion of Shakespeare's *A Midsummer Night's Dream* for the Royal Shakespeare Company (London, 1970), director Peter Brook worked in this way.

Assistants

To prepare a play within a four- to six-week rehearsal period, the modern director has assistants. The *assistant director* attends production meetings, coaches actors, and rehearses special or problem scenes. The *stage manager* compiles the promptbook; records stage business, blocking, lighting, sound, and other cues; makes the rehearsal schedule; takes notes during rehearsals; coordinates rehearsals; and runs the show after it has opened.

SUMMARY

The playwright and director are two of the theatre's most important collaborative artists, although the director has only emerged in the last hundred years. The playwright envisions the play's world—its events, people, and meaning—on paper. The director interprets the playwright's vision, carries that interpretation over into the

After directing critically acclaimed productions in England of Shakespeare's The Tempest *and* King Lear, *and* Peter Weiss's Marat/Sade, *Peter Brook decided to direct Shakespeare's* A Midsummer Night's Dream *using a concept of the actor as acrobat, circus clown, and trapeze artist speaking Shakespeare's verse. The bare, white setting has the three levels of the Elizabethan stage. First there is the audience level, which the cast contacts at the play's close when the audience responds to Puck's request for personal contact and applause: "Give me your hands, if we be friends/And Robin shall restore amends."*

The stage itself is an enclosed white space— a room with doors in the rear wall through which Alan Howard as Theseus and Sara Kestleman as Hippolyta enter; later they reappear as Oberon and Titania, king and queen of the fairies.

For the working out of the premarital dream a third level —equivalent to the Elizabethan stage's balcony—is a catwalk around the top of the white room that is the principal acting area of designer Sally Jacobs's set. (Photos © by Max Waldman 1970.)

Figures 4-7a and 4-7b. The actors as circus artists cavort on trapezes and stilts about the area that serves as Shakespeare's magic forest.

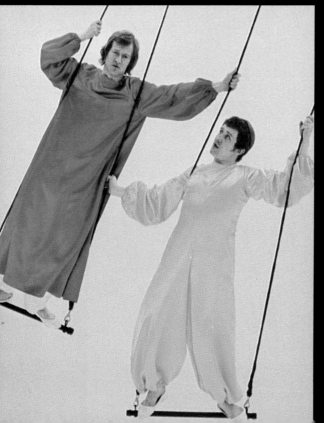

Figure 4-7c (above). In Brook's production there are no woodland fairies and fat, jolly Bottom wearing an ass's head. The directorial influences are circus tricks, puppet theatre, and English music hall. Bottom wears a clown's red nose when under the influence of Puck's magic spell. Bright party streamers simulate the magic forest as Titania, also under Puck's spell, makes love to Bottom.

Figure 4-7d (left). Oberon (Alan Howard) and Puck (John Kane) speak Shakespeare's lines while seated upon trapezes like acrobats.

Figure 4-7e (above). Sara Kestleman as Titania alone in her ostrich-feather bower.

Figure 4-7f (right). The quartet of lovers is caught in the steel coils dangled by the fairies from the catwalk around the top of the room. They manipulate the lovers like marionettes.

Figure 4-7g (above). The "mechanicals" or menial laborers rehearse their parts in the play that they are to perform for the court's entertainment in celebration of the multiple weddings at the play's close. Figure 4-7h (below). The mechanicals performing their amateurish play about Pyramus and Thisbe with Lion "roaring his angry roar" at the audience.

Figure 4-8a. Director's ground plan for a 1976 production of Albee's Who's Afraid of Virginia Woolf? *at the University of Wisconsin, Milwaukee. The director, Ronald A. Gural, has indicated the entrance of George and Martha in Scene One. They enter together at the front door and Martha moves into the living room, stopping between the sofa and chair.*

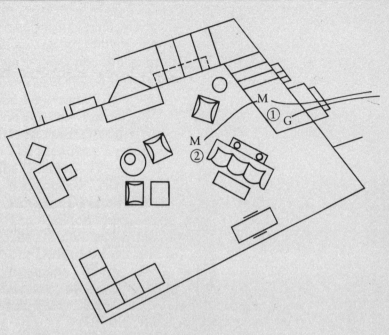

Figure 4-8b. Promptbook page that accompanies the ground plan for Who's Afraid of Virginia Woolf? *The director has indicated movement, attitude, and vocal emphasis. Each page of the script is marked in this way. It is the stage manager's responsibility to keep this record of the performance.*

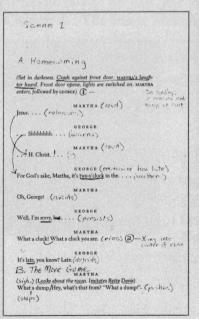

Figure 4-8c. Photo from Who's Afraid of Virginia Woolf? *illustrates the director's ground plan in the stage setting. (Courtesy of Ronald A. Gural.)*

theatre's three-dimensional space, and gives it shape, sound, rhythm, images, and action. Audiences experience the play through the director's eyes, ears, emotions, and intellect, so the director is as distinct a force in the theatre as the playwright.

QUESTIONS FOR STUDY

1. What are some of the ways a play can take shape in a playwright's imagination?

2. What was Brecht's *draft plan* for writing a play?

3. In what ways are auditions important for a director?

4. What does a director look for in casting a play?

5. What are the director's responsibilities? Name *six* major ones.

6. What is a *beat*?

7. What is meant by the play's "spine"?

8. How is *improvisation* a helpful rehearsal tool for director and actor?

9. What are the functions of the assistant director and the stage manager?

10. What is the director's *ground plan*?

11. What information is given in a Samuel French acting edition of a play?

12. What is a director's *promptbook*?

13. What is the difference between the *interpretive* director and the *creative* director?

14. Study the photographs of Peter Brook's production of *A Midsummer Night's Dream* on page 89. In what sense is Peter Brook a creative director?

NOTE

[1]Hubert Witt, ed., *Brecht: As They Knew Him* (New York: International Publishers, 1974), p. 126.

5

The Image Makers: The Actor

Acting is the belief and technique by which the actor brings human presence into the theatre. Theatre is, after all, the art human beings make out of themselves. It doesn't require scenery, costumes, or lighting. It does not even require a play text. It requires only people acting and people watching them act.

Astonish me . . .

Sergei Pavlovich Diaghilev

We discovered in earlier chapters the modern trend to re-
duce the theatrical experience to essentials. Grotowski's
"poor theatre" is perhaps the most widely publicized
example of this trend today. However, in the American
theatre, the trend has its roots in director Jed Harris's 1938
production of Thornton Wilder's *Our Town*. Harris took
Wilder's straightforward play about recognizable towns-
people in Grover's Corner, U.S.A., and placed the actors
on a bare stage framed simply by the theatre's back wall.
Virtually no scenery was used, costumes were muted, and
hand properties were minimal. Even stage furniture was
done away with. The actors told the story using only those
properties, such as chairs and umbrellas, that they could
move on and off stage for themselves. But there was one
element of the theatrical experience that remained essential in this revolutionary production: *the actor*.

*Figure 5-1. Minimal staging.
This photo from Jed Harris's
1938 New York production of
Thornton Wilder's* Our Town
*shows the back wall of the
theatre. Chairs and umbrellas
are the only properties. The
photo reveals two essential
theatrical elements: stage space
and actors. (Photo Vandamm
Collection, New York Public
Library at Lincoln Center.)*

Not only could the actor not be dispensed with (as Grotowski tells us again thirty years later), but Harris's approach to staging placed even greater responsibility on the actor. For forty years actors have recreated Wilder's play following the original stage directions, and they have discovered that a new experience occurs for actor and audience when the stage has no scenery or properties. When the only object of the audience's focus is the actor, the modern audience *rediscovers* the actor's presence and art. In this chapter we investigate what acting is all about.

Figure 5-2. The actor's presence. American actress Irene Worth portrays an unhappy moment for Madame Ranevsky in Anton Chekhov's The Cherry Orchard. *This 1977 New York Shakespeare Festival production was directed by Andrei Serban at the Vivian Beaumont Theatre, Lincoln Center. (Photo by George E. Joseph.)*

THE ASTONISHING ART

Acting does not begin with performing on stage before an audience. It begins with the process of observation—with the eyes and ears, with sensitivity, selection, and memory of what the actor has seen, heard, and felt.

The body, voice, emotions, and the mind are the actor's tools. They must be flexible, disciplined, and expressive to communicate a wide range of attitudes, traits, emotions, and situations. In training and rehearsals, the actor works to understand the body and voice: how to control them; how to release psychological tensions and blocks that inhibit them; how to increase powers of imagination, observation, and concentration; and how to integrate them with the demands of the script and the director. In using these tools, the actor combines an inner belief in the role with external performance techniques. Successful acting combines belief and technique to create a sense of life taking place on stage as if for the first time.

Internal belief and *external technique* are fundamental aspects of stage acting. Although over the years the two tasks have been separated for reasons of analysis, the successful actor aims to integrate these components into a perfect alignment that, in performance, makes acting an astonishing art.

THE ACTOR'S REALITY

Reduced to its simplest terms, the actor's problem is how to tell the character's *situation* in the play as effectively as possible. The actor works in rehearsals to behave as a person would in the situation existing among the play's characters. The actor must concentrate on the character's behavior in this context—not on the performance or the theatre itself.

Like the football or baseball player, the actor comes to believe in what he or she is doing on stage regardless of the reasons for first doing so. To understand better the actor's reality (and stage reality), let us compare the situation in a play with that in an event on the sports field. Like baseball, for example, a play has its own rules and regulations, the set dimensions of the playing area, and a set number of persons on the field. The interactions among the players are real, vital, and intense. For the playing time, the field is the players' whole universe. The game, like a play, has its own reality that is frequently "more real" and vibrant than everyday reality. Sometimes our experiences in the theatre are remembered and treasured moments of our lives, establishing models for what life's peak experiences should be.

THE ACTOR'S TRAINING

Throughout stage history actors have used both external technique and internal belief to create their staged reality. Technique and belief are the fundamentals of their training. Sometimes however, one has been favored over the other.

External Technique

External technique (or external acting) is that activity by which one person imitates another. The mimetic actor chooses to imitate or illustrate the character's behavior. He or she approaches a role through a deep and passionate study of human behavior *in all its outward forms,* with an eye toward reproducing them in a disciplined and sensitive way.

The English actor David Garrick approached acting as an imitation of life—he called acting *mimical behavior.* To prepare for the role of King Lear, for example, he studied the appearance and behavior of a friend who had been driven mad by his child's death. By his accurate reproduction of such behavior on stage, Garrick introduced naturalistic acting into the English theatre. He believed that the actor could produce emotions by a convincing imitation and skilled projection of those emotions being imitated. He did not believe that the actor should experience anger or sadness or joy to project these emotions to an audience. The following words are ascribed to him: ". . . that a man was incapable of becoming an actor who was not absolutely independent of circumstances calculated to excite emotion, adding that for his own part he could

Figure 5-3. Garrick's Macbeth which he played in a contemporary military uniform. He was famous for the dagger scene—his contemporaries praised him for his ability to project the fact that he was "seeing" the dagger before him. It has been said that Garrick's "face was a language." (Courtesy of Theatre Museum, Victoria and Albert Museum.)

speak to a post with the same feelings and expression as to the loveliest Juliet under the heaven."[1] His contemporaries wrote that on occasion he would delight them in relaxed moments with his face alone, without any outward motivation or any inward feeling of personal emotion.

Many actors, particularly in England and elsewhere, have followed Garrick's approach. Richard Boleslavski, one of Stanislavsky's students, wrote a classic book for the beginning actor called *Acting: The First Six Lessons* (1933) in which he sums up the importance of mimetic behavior for the actor. He says that just as children must crawl before they run, so beginning actors must be capable of observation and mimicry before they can project emotional experience onstage.

English actor John Gielgud (b. 1904)—counted among the three greatest actors of his generation (Laurence Olivier and Ralph Richardson are the others)—says of his early days in the theatre that he imitated other actors.

I imitated all the actors I admired when I was young, particularly Claude Rains, who was my teacher at dramatic school. I admired him very much. I remember seeing him play Dubedat in *The Doctor's Dilemma,* especially his death scene, in which he wore a rich dressing gown and hung his hands—made up very white—over the arms of his wheelchair. And then I understudied him. I also understudied Noel Coward, whom I felt I had to imitate because he was so individual in his style. I followed him in *The Vortex* and, naturally, the only way to say the lines was to say them as near to the way he said them as possible because they suited his style. It was, after all, written by him for him. Of course, it got me into some rather mannered habits. . . . [And Komisarjevsky, the Russian director] was an enormous influence in teaching me not to act from outside, not to seize on obvious, showy effects and histrionics, not so much to exhibit myself as to be within myself trying to impersonate a character who is not aware of the audience, to try to absorb the atmosphere of the play and the background of the character, to build it outward so that it came to life naturally. . . .[2]

Internal Belief

For many years European and American actors were trained in the theatre. A young man or woman who showed ability would be hired to play small parts in a provincial stock company. The older actors would coach the young person, prescribing voice and body exercises that had been handed down for generations. This kind of external training developed a voice capable of being heard in large theatres, exaggerated gestures, and skill in speaking Shakespeare. If actors showed talent, they would be given longer parts and eventually invited to join the company.

When realism came into fashion late in the nineteenth century, this "large" style of acting came to seem exaggerated and unconvincing. As the stage came to be thought of not as a symbolic world—a place that symbolized the universe the audience lived in (such as Shakespeare's "Globe" theatre)—but as a place with a reality that corresponded to what people observed with their own senses, both scene design and acting styles changed. The play's world—the environment and characters—were to be represented as directly and as lifelike as possible. A street, houses, and living rooms represented on a stage were to look like streets, houses, and living rooms outside the theatre. Actors as stage characters were to be dressed like the

Figure 5-4.   Stanislavsky as Gaev. Constantin Stanislavsky played Gaev, Madame Ranevsky's brother, in the 1904 Moscow Art Theatre production of Chekhov's The Cherry Orchard. *(Photo from New York Public Library at Lincoln Center.)*

middle-class businessmen or menial laborers that they were playing and that the audience encountered outside the theatre. So, too, the actor was called upon to set aside declamation and artificial gestures for the speech, walk, and behavior of such a person outside the theatre. To capture on stage and before an audience this sense of life being lived as it actually is, new methods for training actors had to be developed.

Figure 5-5. The character's objective. The photo shows the moment when Hamlet (played by Sam Waterston in the 1976 New York Shakespeare Festival production at the Delacorte Theatre) has come upon Claudius and drawn his sword, but decides not to kill him. This is Hamlet's first clear opportunity to kill Claudius and revenge his father's ghost, but Claudius is at prayer and if he dies at this moment he could go to heaven, not hell. The situation sets up inner conflict— an opportunity to kill the king and also the knowledge that Claudius, at prayer, is in a state of grace and will go to heaven should he die at this moment. (Photo by George E. Joseph.)

Constantin Stanislavsky, the Russian actor-director, set about developing a systematic approach (later called "the method") to train actors *to work from the inside outward.* Stanislavsky's method teaches the actor to feel personal emotions during performance and to project them to the audience. Stanislavsky wanted to develop a systematic means whereby the actor would not only represent reality, but would also create a subjective reality of his or her own—an inner truth of feeling and experience. Speaking of external acting, Stanislavsky said that "the difference between my art and that is the difference between 'seeming' and 'being.' "[3]

What distinguished Stanislavsky's theory was the emphasis on the purpose and objectives of human behavior. For Stanislavsky, stage acting rested on the actor's discovery of the objectives and purpose of his character and the successful "playing" of those objectives or goals.

Stanislavsky developed rehearsal methods by which the actor would "live life" onstage. He developed a set of

Figure 5-6. Actor James Earl Jones plays Othello in the 1964 New York Shakespeare Festival Theatre production, Delacorte Theatre. (Photo by George E. Joseph.)

exercises and principles designed to help the actor involve personal feelings and experiences in the creation of the role. This aspect of his training was called the "psycho-technique." Through the development of self-discipline, life observation, and total concentration, his actors learned to recall emotions from their own lives that were analogous to those experienced by the characters they played. They learned to experience what their characters experienced *as if* it were actually happening to them. Stanislavsky called this "the magic if" by which the actor thinks, "If I were in Othello's situation what would I do?" Not, "If I were Othello, what would I do?" By "becoming" a person in the character's situation, the actor's performance became a real experience, not merely the imitation of a fiction.

The Subtext

For Stanislavsky, the actor's preparation involved understanding the text and the subtext, or hidden level, as well. The actor's job is to portray the many levels of what the play's character is about. For example, the character may be saying one thing while thinking or feeling the opposite. Stanislavsky called this real meaning of the line the subtext. As an example of subtext, read the passage from *The Adventures of Sherlock Holmes* which follows. Sir Arthur Conan Doyle was fond of writing this kind of passage to illustrate Sherlock Holmes's keen perception. But the fact is that the unspoken meanings surrounding events and speeches are a part of our own perception of the life around us. What is going on in Dr. Watson's mind is not revealed in talk or dialogue. So, too, in a play the character's speech may be unrelated to what the character is thinking and feeling. Stanislavsky called this nonverbal layer of meaning the subtext; the character's verbal expression made up the text. It is the actor's job to project both to the audience. The following passage is from "The Adventure of the Cardboard Box."

Finding that Holmes was too absorbed for conversation I had tossed aside the barren paper and, leaning back in my chair, I fell into a brown study. Suddenly my companion's voice broke in upon my thoughts.

"You are right, Watson," said he. "It does seem a most preposterous way of settling a dispute."

"Most preposterous!" I exclaimed, and then suddenly realizing how he had echoed the inmost thought of my soul, I sat up in my chair and stared at him in blank amazement.

"What is this, Holmes?" I cried. "This is beyond anything which I could have imagined."

He laughed heartily at my perplexity.

"You remember," said he, "that some little time ago when I read you the passage in one of Poe's sketches in which a close reasoner follows the unspoken thoughts of his companion, you were inclined to treat the matter as a mere *tour-de-force* of the author. On my remarking that I was constantly in the habit of doing the same thing you expressed incredulity."

"Oh, no!"

"Perhaps not with your tongue, my dear Watson, but certainly with your eyebrows. So when I saw you throw down your paper and enter upon a train of thought, I was very happy to have the opportunity of reading it off, and eventually of breaking into it, as a proof that I had been in rapport with you."

But I was still far from satisfied. "In the example which you read to me," said I, "the reasoner drew his conclusions from the actions of the man whom he observed. If I remember right, he stumbled over a heap of stones, looked up at the stars, and so on. But I have been seated quietly in my chair, and what clues can I have given you?"

"You do yourself an injustice. The features are given to man as the means by which he shall express his emotions, and yours are faithful servants."

"Do you mean to say that you read my train of thoughts from my features?"

"Your features, and especially your eyes. Perhaps you cannot yourself recall how your reverie commenced?"

"No, I cannot."

"Then I will tell you. After throwing down your paper, which was the action which drew my attention to you, you sat for half a minute with a vacant expression. Then your eyes fixed themselves upon your newly-framed picture of General Gordon, and I saw by the alteration in your face that a train of thought had been started. But it did not lead very far. Your eyes flashed across to the unframed portrait of Henry Ward Beecher which stands upon the top of your books. You then glanced up at the wall, and of course your meaning was obvious. You were thinking that if the portrait were framed, it would just cover that bare space and correspond with Gordon's picture over there."

"You have followed me wonderfully!" I exclaimed.

"So far I could hardly have gone astray. But now your thoughts went back to Beecher, and you looked hard across as if you were studying the character in his features. Then your eyes ceased to pucker, but you continued to look across, and your face was thoughtful. You were recalling the incidents of Beecher's career. I was well aware that you could not do this without thinking of the mission which he undertook on behalf of the North at the time of the Civil War, for I remember your expressing your passionate indignation at the way in which he was received by the more turbulent of our people. You felt so strongly about it, that I knew you could not think of Beecher without thinking of that also. When a moment later I saw your eyes wander away from the picture, I suspected that your mind had now turned to the Civil War, and when I observed that your lips set, your eyes sparkled, and your hands clenched, I was positive that you were indeed thinking of the gallantry which was shown by both sides in that desperate struggle. But then, again, your face grew sadder; you shook your head. You were dwelling upon the sadness and horror and useless waste of life. Your hand stole towards your own old wound and a smile quivered on your lips, which showed me that the ridiculous side of this method of settling international questions had forced itself upon your mind. At this point I agreed with you that it was preposterous, and was glad to find that all my deductions had been correct."

"Absolutely!" said I. "And now that you have explained it, I confess that I am as amazed as before."

Recalling Emotions

How does the actor induce emotion at the moment of performance night after night? One of the first methods developed by Stanislavsky was "emotional recall" or "affective memory" in which the actor recalled a situation in his or her own life to stimulate an emotional display during the course of the performance. Julie Harris tells us that she conjures up something in her own life that produces tears when she is called upon to cry. Not only will the actor think of something sad (for example, a relative's death or something connected with the sad event), but the actor will try to recreate in the mind's eye all of the surrounding circumstances, the sensory and emotional details that were part of the experience. Actress Uta Hagen (b. 1919) writes

Figure 5-7. Julie Harris as Emily Dickinson. *The actress creates the role of American poetess Emily Dickinson in the 1976 New York production of* The Belle of Amherst, *a one-woman show. (Photo by Sy Friedman.)*

American actress Julie Harris (b. 1925) talks about acting and "the method" in *Talks to Young Actors* (1971). She says, "As much as I would like to, I can't respond to every moment onstage through the character alone. I often have to go outside the character and into my own life. This is *my* method. It I have to cry, for example, I can't always feel the emotion through the character. I have to conjure up something in my own life that produces tears."[4]

about working on the part of Blanche DuBois in Tennessee Williams's *A Streetcar Named Desire*:

Suppose I am going to work on the part of Blanche DuBois in *A Streetcar Named Desire*. I have to hunt for an understanding of—and an identification with—the character's main needs: a need for perfection (and always *when* and *how* have I needed these things); a romantic need for beauty; a desire for gentleness, tenderness, delicacy, elegance, decorum; a need to be loved and protected; a strong sensual need; a need for delusion when things go wrong, etc.

If I return to my cliché image of myself—the earthy, frank, gusty child of nature—I'm in trouble and there will be an enormous distance between Blanche and myself. If, on the other hand, I remember myself preparing for an evening at the opera (bathing and oiling and perfuming my body, soothing my skin, brushing my hair until it shines, artfully applying makeup until the little creases are hidden and my eyes look larger and I feel younger, spending hours over a silky elegant wardrobe, and a

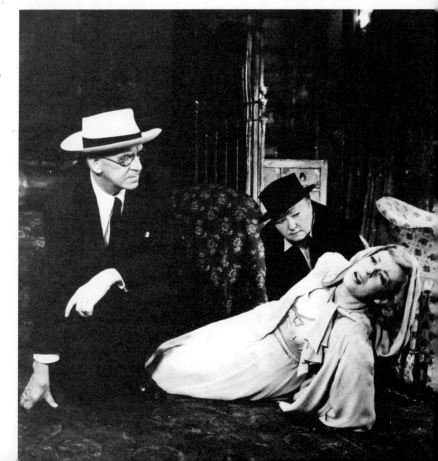

Figure 5-8. Uta Hagen as Blanche DuBois. Uta Hagen succeeded Jessica Tandy as Blanche DuBois in A Streetcar Named Desire *in 1948. She also created the role of Martha in Edward Albee's* Who's Afraid of Virginia Woolf? *(see Figure 11-3a). (Photo Vandamm Collection, New York Public Library at Lincoln Center.)*

day over the meal I will serve before the opera, setting out my freshest linen, my best crystal and polished silver among dainty flowers); if I recall how I weep over a lovely poem by Rilke or Donne or Browning, how my flesh tingles when I hear Schubert chamber music, how tender I feel at a soft twilight, how I respond to someone pulling out a chair for me at the table or opening a car door for me or offering me their arm for a walk in the park—*then* I am beginning to find within myself realities connected with Blanche DuBois' needs.

I was not raised on an elegant plantation like Belle Reve, nor have I lived in Laurel, Mississippi, *but* I have visited elegant mansions in the East, I have seen many photographs of Faulkner country and estates, I have toured some of the South, and from a conglomerate of these experiences I can now make *my* Belle Reve and start to build a reality for my life there before the play's beginning.

Unfortunately, I have never been in New Orleans or the French Quarter, but I have read a great deal, seen many films and newsreels. I have even related the French Quarter of New Orleans, in a way, to a little section of the Left Bank in Paris where I once lived to make it real to myself.

The Kowalski apartment itself, which is dictated for me by the playwright, the designer and the director, must, nevertheless, be made real to me by substitutions from my own life. It is *I* who must make the sense of cramped space, the lack of privacy, the disorder and sleaziness, the empty beer cans and stale cigarette butts, the harsh street noises all move in on me chaotically and frighteningly. Each object or thing that I see or come in contact with must be made particular so that it will serve the new me and bring about the psychological and sensory experiences necessary to animate my actions.[5]

Many actors build an emotion through the substitution of remembered sensory and emotional details. But the actor does not stop there. In the theatre the emotional impact must be produced night after night with precise timing, on cue, and with a minimum of conscious thought during performance.

REHEARSALS AND PERFORMANCE

This task of creating an emotional impact through the careful reconstruction of one's life experience and then relating those emotions to the character and the situation is carried out in rehearsals. The work of rehearsals is to condition the actor's responses so that during performance emotions flow from the actor's concentration upon the material—the character's situation and objectives.

In rehearsals the actor works with the director and other actors to "set" movement and interpretation. Not until dress rehearsal, as a rule, is an actor able to work with a complete set of properties, settings, costumes, makeup, and stage lighting. However, special rehearsal clothes and properties are provided if they are significantly different from ordinary dress and objects.

On each night of the play's run, the actor recreates the character's situation for the audience. Everything the actor

The actor's vocabulary is a language that has developed over the years between director and actor to communicate quickly to each other in rehearsals. It is a kind of stage shorthand in which *all directions are to the actor's left or right.*

Upstage means toward the rear of the acting area. *Downstage* means toward the front. *Stage right* and *stage left* refer to the performer's right or left when he or she is facing the audience. The stage floor is frequently spoken of as though it were divided into sections: *up right, up center, up left, down right, down center, down left.*

Body positions are also designated for work on the proscenium stage. The director may ask the actor *to turn out,* meaning to turn toward the side of the stage. Or *to turn in,* meaning to turn toward the stage's center. Two actors are sometimes told *to share a scene,* or to play in a profile position so that they are equally visible to the audience. An actor may be told *to dress the stage,* or to move to balance the stage picture. Experienced actors take directions with ease and frequently make such moves almost automatically.

In the audience we are almost never aware that the actor is taking a rehearsed position or focusing upon another actor or prop. But the actor's movements control what we see and hear onstage.

Figure 5-9. Stage areas. All stage directions are to the actor's left or right. At times directors and actors divide the stage with imaginary lines into the six basic parts shown here.

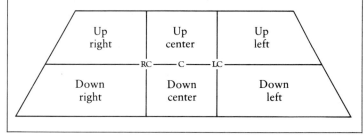

Irene Worth (b. 1916) has had an extraordinary career on American and English stages. She has created roles in plays by American playwrights Edward Albee, Lillian Hellman, and Tennessee Williams. In England and Canada she has appeared on the stages of the Old Vic Company, Royal Shakespeare Company, and the Shakespeare Festival Theatre.

In an interview with the New York Times (Feb. 5, 1976) she talks about the actor's art: "You know what a salmon does when it goes upstream? It feels about for the point of maximum energy in the water, the point where the water whirls round and round and generates a terrific centrifugal force. It looks for that point, and it finds it, and the water quadruples the salmon's own natural strength, and then it can jump. That's what an actor has to do with the text. The point of maximum energy is always there, but it takes finding."

Figure 5-10a.   Irene Worth as Hedda Gabler in Henrik Ibsen's play at the Shakespeare Festival Theatre (Stratford, Ontario), 1970. (Photo by Robert C. Ragsdale.)

Figure 5-10b.   The actress creates the role of Princess Kosmonopolis with Christopher Walken as Chance Wayne in Tennessee Williams's Sweet Bird of Youth directed by Edwin Sherwin at the Brooklyn Academy of Music, 1975. (Photo courtesy of the New York Public Library at Lincoln Center.)

Figure 5-10c. As Madame Ranevsky in Chekhov's The Cherry Orchard *produced by the New York Shakespeare Festival at the Vivian Beaumont Theatre, Lincoln Center, New York City, 1977. (Photo by George E. Joseph.)*

Figure 5-10d.   Irene Worth as Winnie sits in sand buried to her waist in Beckett's Happy Days, *produced (1979) by Joseph Papp at the Public Theatre, New York, and directed by Andrei Serban. (Photo by George E. Joseph.)*

has set or memorized in rehearsals—objectives, mannerisms, movements—stays (or should stay) much the same. But the actor's creativity continues within the boundaries set in rehearsal—this is the actor's art. Each performance requires the actor to give fresh life onstage to the character's situation—to concentrate anew on the character's speech, behavior, and theatrical effectiveness.

SUMMARY

The actor brings human presence onto the stage. The audience sees the actor thinking, planning, working and acting. He or she must also be seen to do all of these things, not in the context of the theatre, but in the situation shared with the other actors onstage. The actor must be continually redefining relationships with other characters, and must be seen as striving to achieve some goal or objective within the play's situation. Only if this happens will the actor be able to create his or her life as a new, living character onstage.

QUESTIONS FOR STUDY

1. Study the photo of *Our Town*—how is the stage stripped down to essentials?

2. What is the actor's *external technique*? Think of an example.

3. What is a character's *situation*? What is Hamlet's situation?

4. What is *subtext*?

5. How does the passage from Sir Arthur Conan Doyle's "The Adventure of the Cardboard Box" reveal *subtext*?

6. The following terms were used by Stanislavsky: "the magic if," "psycho-technique," character's "objectives," "emotional recall." What does each mean?

7. What is the purpose of a *dress rehearsal*?

8. Select a scene from *A Streetcar Named Desire* in which Blanche DuBois appears. What is her objective in the scene? What is her *objective* for the entire play?

9. Memorize Hamlet's speech (III, iii, 73–96) and play it to an imaginary Claudius. What was your *objective* in the speech?

10. What do we mean when we say that *acting is the art of human presence*?

NOTES

[1]Toby Cole and Helen K. Chinoy, eds., *Actors on Acting: The Theories, Techniques, and Practices of the Great Actors of All Times as Told in Their Own Words* (New York: Crown, 1959), p. 132.

[2]Lewis Funke and John E. Booth, eds., *Actors Talk About Acting* (New York: Random House, 1961), p. 14.

[3]Constantin Stanislavski, *An Actor's Handbook,* ed. and trans. Elizabeth Reynolds Hapgood (New York: Theatre Arts, 1963), p. 100.

[4]Julie Harris with Barry Tarshis, *Julie Harris Talks to Young Actors* (New York: Lothrop, Lee & Shepard, 1971), p. 82.

[5]Uta Hagen with Haskel Frankel, *Respect for Acting* (New York: Macmillan, 1973), pp. 37–38.

6

The Image Makers:
The Designers

Theatre artists—actors, directors, and designers—create the play onstage in concrete visual terms. Designers of scenery, costumes, and lighting realize the playwright's intentions graphically and visually in the theatrical space.

Stage-designing should be addressed to this eye
of the mind. There is an outer eye that observes,
and there is an inner eye that sees.
                                    Robert Edmond Jones,
                                    The Dramatic Imagination

Designers shape and fill the stage space. They create the actor's environment and make the play's world *visible* and *interesting* to us. Designers *collaborate* with the director to focus the audience's attention on the actor in a special environment—the stage. Sometimes one person (the **scenographer**) designs scenery, lighting, and costumes. But since scene, costume, and light design are three different arts, we will look at each of them separately.

THE SCENE DESIGNER

Background

The scene (or stage) designer entered the American theatre about sixty-five years ago. The designer's nineteenth-century counterpart was the resident *scenic artist,* who painted the large scenic pieces for the theatre manager. Scenery's main function in those days was to indicate time and place and to give the actor a painted background. Scenic studios (staffed with specialized artists) were even set up to turn out scenery on demand. These studios frequently conducted a large mail-order business for standard backdrops and scenic pieces. By the turn of the century, realism had come into the theatre and the job of making the stage look real became more complex.

Theatre in the late nineteenth century was dominated by a naturalistic philosophy that proclaimed that life could be explained by forces of environment, heredity, economics, society, and the psyche. This being the case, theatre had to present these forces as carefully and effectively as possible. If environment (including economic factors) really did govern people's lives, then it needed to be shown as we actually see it. The responsibility for creating this stage environment shifted from the playwright and actor to the designer. The demands of stage realism called for the stage to look like a living room (or the actual place where the play's action takes place).

Realism has been the dominant convention of the theatre in our time. However, many new and exciting movements in the modern theatre have come about as reactions to this direct representation of reality, which pretends that the stage is not a stage but someone's actual living room and that the audience (seated in a dark auditorium) is really not there beyond the invisible "fourth wall," observing the play. Prophets of many new theatre movements have argued that the stage living room and box-set were also unnatural; they set about pioneering a special kind of theatrical reality for the stage.

Before World War I in Europe, Adolphe Appia and Gordon Craig became self-proclaimed prophets of a new movement in theatre design and lighting. They were concerned with creating mood and atmosphere, opening up the stage for movement, and unifying visual ideas; they assaulted the illusion of stage realism and led the way to a rethinking of theatrical design. In his *Music and Stage Setting* (1899), Appia called for theatrical art to be expressive. And today, in the same spirit, many modern set designers use pipes, ramps, light, platforms, and steps to *express* the play's atmosphere and imaginative life instead of attempting to reproduce the details of its time and place realistically.

Adolphe Appia (1862–1928) and Edward Gordon Craig (1872–1966) built the theoretical foundations of modern expressionistic theatrical practice. For the Swiss-born Appia, *artistic unity* was the basic goal of theatrical production. He disliked the contradiction in the three-dimensional actor performing before painted two-dimensional scenery, and he advocated the replacement of flat settings with steps, ramps, and platforms. He thought the role of lighting was to fuse all visual elements into a unified whole. His *Music and Stage Setting* (1899) and *The Work of Living Art* (1921) are the basic source books for modern stage-lighting practices.

Gordon Craig was born into an English theatrical family (he was the son of Ellen Terry and Edward Godwin) and began his career as an actor in Henry Irving's company. The 1902 exhibit of his work as a stage designer and the publication of his *The Art of the Theatre* in 1905 created controversy throughout Europe, and his entire theatrical life was a storm of controversy. He thought of theatre as an independent art that welded action, words, line, color, and rhythm into an artistic whole created by the single, autonomous artist. Many of his ideas on simplified decor, three-dimensional settings, moving scenery, and directional lighting prevailed in the new stagecraft that emerged after World War I.

Figure 6-1a. Tennessee Williams's A Streetcar Named Desire *was designed in 1947 by Jo Mielziner. (Photo Vandamm Collection, New York Public Library at Lincoln Center.)*

Figure 6-1b. Boris Aronson designed the 1975 New York musical comedy Pacific Overtures. *(Photo by Martha Swope.)*

Figure 6-1c. Ming Cho Lee designed Ntozake Shange's 1976 poetic dance-drama, For Colored Girls Who Have Considered Suicide When the Rainbow Is Enuf. *(Photo by Martha Swope.)*

Appia and Craig influenced the young American designers Robert Edmond Jones, Lee Simonson, and Norman Bel Geddes, who were dedicated to bringing the new stagecraft to Broadway. Two generations of American scene designers have followed their lead. Prominent among them are Jo Mielziner, who designed *Death of a Salesman, A Streetcar Named Desire,* and *The King and I;* Boris Aronson, the designer of *Cabaret, Company,* and *Pacific Overtures;* Oliver Smith, designer of *Brigadoon, The Sound of Music,* and *Plaza Suite;* and Ming Cho Lee, designer of *Hair, Much Ado about Nothing,* and *For Colored Girls Who Have Considered Suicide When the Rainbow Is Enuf.*

The Designer's Training

Sixty years ago the designer, like the actor, was trained in stock and repertory theatres. The scenic artist, with only a rough knowledge of theatrical settings, was concerned almost solely with painting. Design training consisted of an apprenticeship in a scenic studio. With the emergence of the director as artistic coordinator, the concept of the stage designer as a collaborative, interpretive artist with responsibility for all visual and technical elements also developed. In America, the entire groundwork for teaching the new discipline had to be developed. In the 1920s universities became the training ground for the new theatre artists—the scene, costume, and lighting designers.

Designing for the Theatre

Scene designers use one of five basic methods to design stage settings. Some designers start with a real room or place, select from it, change the dimensions, and reshape it for a particular stage. Others start with the actors and the play's most important events and then add platforms, shapes, and voids around them. Some designers start with the play's mood and find the lines, shapes, and colors that will reflect it. Others design the scene as an idea or metaphor—in the 1920s the expressionists in Germany sought to reflect the nightmarish outlook of the disturbed mind in their stage settings. Another group organizes the entire space, including actor and audience, as environment. The environmentalist begins with the notion that the production will both develop from and totally take place in a given space. There is no effort to create an illusion or imitation; rather, the performer and audience, space and materials, exist as what they are: people, ramps, platforms, ladders, stairs, mazes.

The design process may take months. The designer usually begins by studying the script in much the same way as the director, visualizing details of place, movement, and objects in space. The designer asks certain basic questions about the script's requirements: Where does the play take place? How does the play proceed in time and seasons? What kinds of movements do the characters make? What elements from life are essential parts of the play's world? What is the play's spatial relationship to the audience? Is it close up or far away? Are the play and the audience in the same space? How are character relationships expressed in the space? What is the play's historical period? How much playing space is needed? Is the action to be violent or sedate? What is the play's mood? How many exits, properties, and essential pieces of furniture are needed? What is the director's concept?

Figure 6-2. Designer's elevation. A designer's elevation is a two-dimensional drawing that shows no perspective. The elevation for the unit of scenery at right shows overall dimensions, as well as the dimensions of a door.

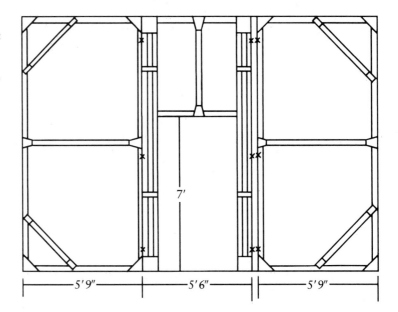

Figure 6-3. The scene painter—in nonprofessional theatres usually the designer—is a specialized artist-craftsman who paints the scenery following painter's elevations and model provided by the designer. Conjoined with lighting, the scene painter's art creates onstage color, perspective, depth, shape, and texture. (Photos from Little, Brown and Company.)

As the designer visualizes the space, details are established in *sketches,* a *ground plan,* and a *model.* Sketches (or rough pencil drawings) are made in the early period when both the director and the designer are visualizing the stage floor. When their ideas have reached some degree of concreteness, they confer and agree upon the ground plan: entrances, exits, and major scenic elements.

127

The designer also researches the play's historical period, background, and style, including architecture, furniture, and decor. Over the next several weeks, sketches, color renderings (watercolor paintings of the stage with scenery), and a model follow until the director and designer have agreed upon the look and details of the setting. The designer then drafts plans, front elevations (two-dimensional drawings outlining the object as it appears to the eye), and paint elevations to give to the technical director or shop foreman who converts them into technical drawings. The scenic elements are built from these drawings and moved onto the stage at the appointed time. (This is commonly called "put-in.") The designer's drawings detail the profile and outer dimensions of all scenic elements, showing where and how they function, and the order in which they will appear onstage.

Scenery is basically two- or three-dimensional, framed or unframed. It is built in a scene shop from the technical director's working drawings of each set unit. The drawings show the scenic pieces to be constructed, materials, and dimensions.

Because of its use, scenery must be strong, portable, and dependable. As we look at a set we are usually not aware of types of scenery, how it fits together, how it is moved about during scene changes—unless the moving is done for theatrical effect.

THE COSTUME DESIGNER

Costume design has been compared by Patricia Zipprodt, an American designer, to a car trip in which unpredictables of life pop up—the unavailable fabric, the inadequate budget, or the temperamental actor. The designer, like the car's driver, is in a constant state of problem solving.

The Costume

Costumes include all the actor's garments, all the character's accessories (purse, jewelry, handkerchief), all items related to hairdressing, and everything associated with face and body makeup including masks, if they substitute for facial makeup.

A costume tells us many things about the character and about the nature, mood, and style of the play. It is a visual signal adding color, style, and meaning to the play's environment. Costumes establish period, social class, economic status, occupation, age, geography, weather, and time of day. They help to clarify the relationships and relative importance of various characters. Ornament, line, and color can tie together members of a family, group, faction, or party. Changes in costume can indicate alteration in relationships among characters or in a character's psychological outlook. Similarities and contrasts in costumes can show sympathetic or antagonistic relationships. Hamlet's black costume, for instance, is contrasted with the bright colors worn by the court and speaks more eloquently than words of his altered attitude toward the court.

Figure 6-4. Hamlet's "inky cloak." The black costume worn by actor Sam Waterston as Hamlet in the 1976 New York Shakespeare Festival production visually sets him apart from the other members of the Court. (Photo by George E. Joseph.)

The Design Conference

Scene and costume designers work with the director to make visible the world in which the play's characters live. They explore verbally and with rough sketches the many different approaches and ideas that might bring the script into dramatic focus onstage. The designers supplement visually the director's concepts, and, in so doing, often inspire the director to a new way of thinking about the play.

Like the director and the scene designer, the costume designer begins by studying the script and taking note of the story, mood, characterization, visual effects, atmosphere, geography, period, and season. Then the designer asks the practical questions: What actors have been cast? How many costumes (including changes) and accessories are needed? What is the costume budget? What stage actions, such as fighting, will affect the construction or wear of the costumes?

The overall concept and plan of the production is worked out in the design conference. The costume designer brings sketches, color plates, costume charts, accessory lists, and fabric swatches to these meetings to make his or her visual concept clear to the director and scene designer. The designer must be specific to avoid later misunderstandings and costly last-minute changes.

The costume designer is another of the new theatre artists. Years ago, the actor, director, or person in charge of stage wardrobe was responsible for costumes. But in the last sixty years, the new stagecraft has required costume designers trained in the visual arts to select and control the visual elements with far more attention to detail. Costume design has become an industry. Professional designers work in film, fashion, theatre, opera, television, dance, commercials, and extravaganzas (ice shows, nightclubs, circuses, and dance revues). Many people are involved in costume research and in sketching, choosing fabric, cutting, fitting, sewing, and making accessories. The large New York costume houses, such as Brooks Van Horn and Eaves Costume House, buy stage costumes from closing shows, build costumes on demand, and rent garments to regional, community, and university theatres. A visit to their vast warehouses to select costumes for a play in production is not only an exciting adventure in itself, but also may be a tour through the history of theatre design.

Patricia Zipprodt (b. 1925),
American costume designer,
studied at Wellesley College
and the Fashion Institute of
Technology (New York). She
has designed costumes for
many Broadway musicals and
plays, including *Fiddler on the
Roof, Cabaret, The Little
Foxes, 1776, Pippin,* and
Chicago. She has also designed
costumes for operas, for Jerome
Robbins's ballets *Les Noces*
and *Dybbuk Variations,* and
for such films as *The Graduate,
1776,* and *The Glass
Menagerie.*

*Figure 6-5. The strolling
players. Patricia Zipprodt's off-
white and beige costumes for
the musical* Pippin *(1972) are
seen in this photo from the
original New York production.
(Photo by Martha Swope.)*

Sometimes a brilliant costume design develops through trial and error. While designing the costumes for the Broadway production of *Pippin* (1972), Patricia Zipprodt and director Bob Fosse had difficulty deciding on the right look for the strolling players. The script said, "Enter strolling players of an indeterminate period." She remembers:

Now, to me, this meant exactly nothing. I did a lot of sketches, which everybody seemed to like. On the day I was supposed to present finished sketches, time ran short. Instead of fully coloring the costumes of the strolling players as was planned and expected, I just painted beige and off-white washes so that Fosse could read the sketches more easily. I put the whole group of 14 or 15 in front of him and was just about to apologize for not getting the color done when he said, "That's just brilliant, exactly the colors they should be. How clever of you." The minute he said it, I knew he was right. By looking at those off-white costumes, we all recognized who those "strolling players of an indeterminate period" were. The whole show started to come closer into focus.[1]

But more often, the selection is made only after numerous alternatives have been explored.

Costume Construction

When sketches and plans have been approved, the director turns full attention to rehearsals, and the costume designer arranges for purchase, rental, or construction of costumes. The designer sets fitting dates with the actors. If the costumes are being constructed in the theatre's shop (as is most often the case in college and university productions), actors are measured, patterns cut, garments constructed, dyeing and painting done, and accessories built or purchased. After several fittings with the actors, the costumes are ready for *the dress parade,* during which designer and director examine the costumes on the actors before the dress rehearsal begins.

To accomplish this work the designer may have an assistant designer, shop supervisor, crew head, and crew to cut, sew, dye, and make hats, footwear, and wigs. Often this personnel doubles up on the responsibilities.

Dress Rehearsal

The dress parade and rehearsal (where the costumes, masks, and makeup are worn onstage in front of scenery and under lights) take place usually a week before opening night. It is not unusual to discover that a costume is inappropriate, or that a color does not work under the lights or against the scenery. In this event, the designer may redesign the garment, select another fabric or color (or both), and have the costume reconstructed or dyed almost overnight and ready for the next rehearsal or opening performance.

Wardrobe Personnel

A wardrobe crew takes over the costume shop to handle costume problems during dress rehearsals and production. Once costumes and accessories are finished, the costumes leave the shop and usually a new group (the wardrobe crew) takes charge of them. Their responsibility is to mend, iron, clean, and generally maintain the costumes for the play's run. Although in the professional theatre there is a clear-cut division between these two

The makeup for The Everyman Players' 1972 production of Shakespeare's The Tempest was designed by Irene Corey. The director's concept established the setting as a sunken Atlantis island where Prospero's extraordinary powers sustained the life force of the creatures living there, and brought into this watery realm the shipwrecked survivors from the mainland.

All visual elements for the production were inspired by the shapes of underwater sea forms. The designer's idea of "brain coral," for example, combined with the image of phosphorescent lights glowing inside transparent jelly fish to suggest the intricate, magical workings of Prospero's mind. Corey achieved the realization of her makeup design for Prospero by

by placing electric lights inside a dome made of melted gelatin and framed with coral encrustation and tentacles, and mounting the structure on Prospero's elongated forehead.

The stylized makeup for Prospero illustrated here creates the effect of a penetrating gaze from deep-set eyes, suggestive of psychic powers.

Figure 6-6a. Irene Corey's original design for Prospero's makeup.

Figure 6-6b. This photo shows the designer's progress from the original design plate (left) to the wig and false forehead. The wig is made of nylon tricot and ostrich feathers, the forehead of organdy padded with dacron.

Figure 6-6c. Prospero's makeup
chart (left) is followed by actor
Hal Proske to apply makeup.

Figure 6-6d. Proske combines
the wig and false forehead with
the makeup.

*Figure 6-6e. Actor Proske in completed
Prospero costume, headdress,
and makeup. (Photos by Irene Corey.)*

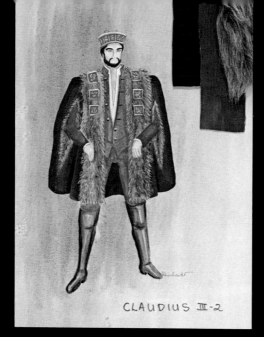

CLAUDIUS III-2

Figure 6-6f. Costume designer Paul D. Reinhardt's rendering of Claudius' costume for the 1976 production of Hamlet at the University of Texas, Austin. The cloth swatches at the right-hand corner of the rendering suggest the texture and color of the fabric to be used in construction of the garment.

Figure 6-6g. The photo shows the fully realized design of the Claudius costume worn by actor Stephen Coleman (center) in the University of Texas production directed by James Mollat. (Rendering and photo courtesy of Paul D. Reinhardt.)

groups, in college and university theatres the construction and wardrobe crews may be many of the same people.

The wardrobe supervisor (sometimes called the wardrobe master or mistress) or crew head makes a list of the costumes and accessories worn by each actor before dress rehearsals begin. These lists are used by crew members and actors to check that each costume is complete. The wardrobe "running" crew helps each actor to dress and is responsible for the costumes before, during, and after each performance. Wardrobe routines are established during the dress rehearsal period and are followed during the production. The crew is also responsible for "striking" the costumes when the production closes. Costumes are cleaned, laundered, and placed in storage along with accessories, such as hats, wigs, shoes, and jewelry.

Makeup

Makeup helps the actor and completes the costume. It is essential to the actor's visibility. In a large theatre, distance and lighting can make an actor's features without makeup colorless and indistinct. And makeup, like the costume, helps the actor to reveal character by stressing the character's physical appearance—personality, age, background, race, health, environment.

Makeup is classified as *straight* and *character*. Straight makeup highlights an actor's normal features and coloring for distinctness and visibility. Character makeup transforms the actor's features to reveal age or attitude. Noses, eyepouches, eyebrows, teeth, hair, and beards can be added to change the actor's appearance. Makeup can also be misused and can destroy the actor's characterization by giving an external "look" that conflicts with the character's inner life. The actor must know, then, the basics of makeup as an art and how to work with hair and wigs.

Most frequently, makeup is designed and applied by the actor (especially in the professional theatre), although in fantasy productions makeup may be designed by someone else. How does the actor make up? There is no substi-

Figure 6-7. "Fly" design by Irene Corey for The Butterfly, *a Persian fantasy, by Bijan Mofid. The mask of sculptured wire and fabric-covered foam gives the actor facial mobility and expression while resembling the insect. (Photo by Irene Corey.)*

tute for practice with a basic makeup kit; every actor comes to know his or her face in a new way as soon as practice begins. Each face is different, catching and reflecting light in a different way. Each character presents a new set of challenges in which greasepaint, nose putty, and wig are used to accent the character's expressions and attitudes. For this reason, the actor should apply his or her own makeup since the actor knows best the expressions, lines, and shadows the character uses.

Masks

In the early theatre masks had many uses. They enlarged the actor's facial features so that the character's basic image would be apparent at great distances. The Greek masks expressed basic moods: grief, anger, horror, sadness, pity. But most important for us today, the masked actor created an altogether different *presence* onstage than the actor without a mask. Although a masked actor may lose something in subtlety of expression, the presence the actor creates can be stately, heroic, awesome, or mysterious; the actor may move the audience simply by standing onstage and reflecting light. Nor is the masked actor totally deprived of the facial subtlety available to the actor

Figure 6-8.   Masked actor. The headdress of the governor's wife in The Caucasian Chalk Circle *reflects light and lends her awesome stature in the Guthrie Theater production in Minneapolis. (Photo courtesy of The Guthrie Theater.)*

whose facial muscles move and change expression. By changing the mask's position (if the mask is made with this effect in mind), by angling the head and catching the light, different emotional responses can be produced in the audience.

Mask-making is an ancient art dating from early cultures where masks were objects of fear; they were thought to have supernatural powers. Masks were used in the Greek and Roman theatres, by the *commedia dell'arte* in Renaissance Italy, and in the modern theatre. The study of masks can fill up a lifetime as it did for Wladyslaw Benda, a great mask-maker of the twentieth century. In addition to an artful exterior, a mask must be comfortable, strong, light, and molded to the contours of the actor's face. Today, in college and university theatres, the costume designer makes the masks as part of the costume, designing for color, durability, and expressiveness.

THE LIGHTING DESIGNER

Light affects what we see, how we see, how we feel, and even how we hear. It is essential to the modern stage's theatrical effectiveness. It is also one of the most powerful tools the director has to control the audience's focus of attention and to enhance their understanding.

Although artificial lighting (first candles and then gas) has been used to illuminate the stage since the seventeenth century, the invention of electric light in 1879 transformed overall possibilities for design in the theatre. It made possible complete control of a range of intensities and colors; it could be used flexibly to light or darken different areas of the stage; it provided a source of mood and atmosphere for the actor.

Swiss designer Adolphe Appia (see page 123) understood the artistic possibilities of light in the theatre. In his book *Music and Stage Setting* (1899) he argued that light should be the guiding principle of all design. He believed that light could unify or bring into harmony all production elements, including two- and three-dimensional objects,

Jean Rosenthal (1912–1969), American lighting designer, was born in New York and trained at the Neighborhood Playhouse and the Yale Drama School. The growth of the light designer's profession in America spans her career.

She began in the 1930s and pioneered design theory and practice while working with the Federal Theatre Project and the Mercury Theatre in association with Orson Welles and John Houseman. For thirty years she designed for the Broadway theatre; her credits include *Carousel, The Sound of Music, Fiddler on the Roof, Cabaret, Hello Dolly, The King and I, Plaza Suite,* and *West Side Story.* She pioneered dance lighting while working for George Balanchine, Jerome Robbins, and Martha Graham. Of her work she said, "If I leave anything to posterity, it will be, I think, most importantly in the field of dance lighting."[2]

living and inanimate people, shapes, and things. Appia established light as an artistic medium for the theatre designer.

The Art of Light

Designer Jean Rosenthal defined, lighting design as "the imposing of quality on the scarcely visible air through which objects and people are seen." One rule of lighting maintains that *visibility* and *ambience* (the surrounding atmosphere) must be inherent to the total theatrical design, including scenery and costumes. The light designer's tools, other than the instruments themselves, are *form* (the shape of the lighting's pattern), *color* (the lighting's mood achieved by gelatins or by varying degrees of intensity, or by both), and *movement* (the changes of form and color by means of dimmers and switchboards located in the light booth).

Plotting and Cueing

The lighting designer reads the script and confers with the scene designer and director. There are basic questions to be answered: What degree of reality does the director want to suggest? Where are the important scenes placed within the set? What restrictions are there? What forms, moods, color patterns, and movements does the play require?

With answers to these questions, the designer sketches out a preliminary "light plot," starting with a simple sketch of the stage and theatre building as it would be seen from directly above. On this basic plan (see Figure 6-9) the designer marks the location of the lighting instruments that will be needed. There are no set rules that any particular instrument may or may not be used in any location. The only limitations in light design are those imposed by the director, by the physical nature of the theatre, and by safety.

The designer's finished lighting plot shows: (1) the location of each lighting instrument to be used; (2) the type of instrument, wattage, and color medium (called *gels*); (3) the general area to be lighted by the instrument; (4) circuitry necessary to operate the instruments; (5) any other details necessary for the electrical operation of the lighting. For example, if a wall fixture is needed onstage so that an actor can turn on a light, the position of this fixture is shown on the light plot.

After the instruments are angled, focused, and circuited, the designer is ready to cue the show. A written cue sheet (or chart of the control board indicating instrument settings and color) may be provided in advance to the crew at the control board, or a series of rehearsals may be called during which the designer asks for various intensities of light and makes changes until satisfied. For each change of stage lighting (or light cue), a notation is made that tells how to set the control board and at what point in the stage action to change the lighting's intensity or color. Successful stage lighting complements and unifies the whole without calling attention to itself. It contributes to the play's interpretation with visibility and ambience—controlling what we see and the way we see it.

Figure 6-9. Light plot. Jean Rosenthal's light plot for playwright Neil Simon's comedy Plaza Suite *(1968) shows the configuration of the theatre building and stage as seen from directly above. The various lighting instruments are marked along with circuitry and other electrical details. Working from the light plot, the light crew hangs and focuses the instruments. (Photo from Little, Brown and Company.)*

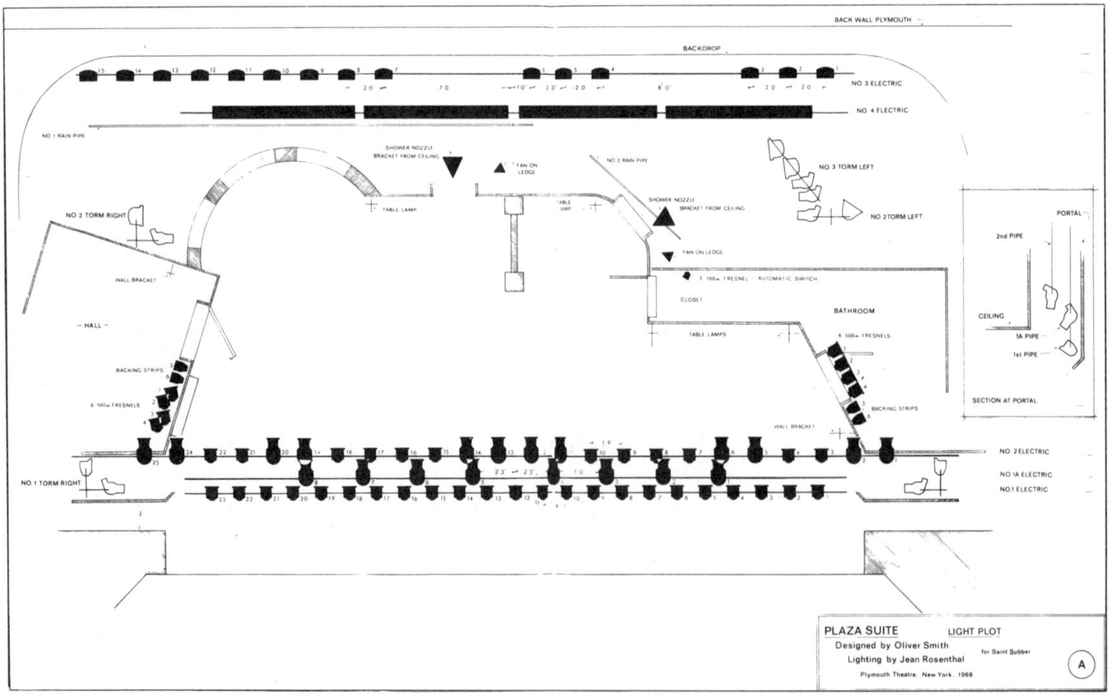

SUMMARY

Theatre artists—actors, directors, designers—create the play onstage in *concrete visual terms.* They translate the playwright's words and concepts into a total evocation whose parts are acting, costume, scenery, and light—a visual and aural equivalent onstage for what occurs in the script. The designer's job (and there may be one or several) is to transform the stage space into the world of the play. The designer transforms what British director Peter Brook refers to as the "empty space" into theatre's special world with its color, lights, sounds, scenery, makeup, masks, and actors. Central to the play's world is the actor, and all good stage design enhances the actor's presence in the space. Moreover, all design elements (scenery, costumes, and lighting) must serve the play's dramatic action—developing, visualizing, and enriching it—without distracting the audience.

Figure 6-10. Stage lighting controls what we see. Jennifer Tipton's lighting for the 1977 production of Agamemnon *at the Vivian Beaumont Theater, Lincoln Center, New York, creates a somber atmosphere while calling attention to the bodies of Agamemnon and Cassandra lying before the palace doors. (Photo by George E. Joseph.)*

These instruments are the primary devices used for theatrical lighting, but there are others designed specifically for stage use. Textbooks on stage lighting introduce students to a variety of instruments. Television and film have developed lighting instruments with very intense and even light especially suited to their needs; these lights are occasionally used onstage. Some obsolete instruments, such as footlights, have qualities that are right for some special effects and period plays. Even instruments that are not specifically theatrical are frequently useful to lighting designers. Movie and slide projectors, for instance, play an important role in many modern plays.

Selection of the proper instrument is based on the designer's long experience with and technical knowledge of the qualities and potentials of each. An instrument is selected only after full consideration is given to the technical and artistic purpose to be served, as well as to the physical potential and limitation of each situation.

Figure 6-11a.   The Fresnel spotlight. Named for the Fresnel lens, the instrument concentrates light in a desired direction. The Fresnel light pattern is very bright over a controllable, large area; beyond that area brightness fades rapidly to near black with no discernible edge. This instrument is used whenever blending between areas is important, or when sharp edges of light would be distracting. The light beam can be further controlled and shaped by using a set of shutters (called "barn doors") placed on the instrument's front. The Fresnel is not well suited for positions over the audience that point toward the stage unless some illumination of the audience is acceptable.

Figure 6-11b.   The ellipsoidal reflector spotlight. This is the most commonly used instrument for any "throw" (or the distance from the light to the object to be illuminated) when a fine control of the light pattern is important. The edges of the light pattern of a well-focused ellipsoidal (or "Leko") are sharp, but the instrument may deliberately be kept slightly out of focus to facilitate blending between areas. The beam of light, which is normally circular, can be decreased in size by using an iris or changed by using shutters.

Figure 6-11c. The beam projector. This instrument is a small version of the searchlight seen in World War II movies and on the street outside movie premieres. It does not have a lens, so its use is limited to situations requiring a concentrated shaft of light of a fixed diameter. It is used most often in dance productions for lighting directly across the stage or along very long diagonals.

Figure 6-11d. The strip light (x-ray). This is a long (about eight feet), narrow instrument containing a number of separate lamp compartments each with its own reflector. The strip light is capable of creating a wash-of-light with a broad point of origin. The compartments are wired so that one third of the lights may be operated by three separate control circuits. By giving each set of lamps a different color, a wide range of intermediate colors can be achieved by blending any two or three circuits at different intensities. The strip is used to color a cyclorama (or neutral background), to indicate time of day, or to tone the acting space with a color desired for its effect on mood.

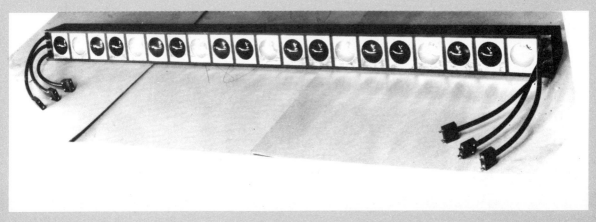

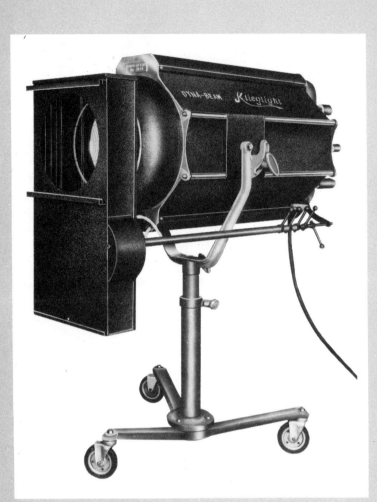

Figure 6-11e. The follow spot. An expected part of the lighting scheme for most American musicals, this blatantly theatrical instrument is used to hold the attention of the audience on a point of interest, such as a leading singer or dancer. Ice shows and other extravaganzas also make good use of follow spots; their moving pools of light enhance mood and create an ever-changing environment. (Photos courtesy of Kliegl Bros. Lighting, Inc.)

QUESTIONS FOR STUDY

1. What are five methods used by scene designers to design stage settings?

2. How does a designer study a script?

3. Why were Adolphe Appia and Edward Gordon Craig important scenic artists?

4. Why are *ground plans, models,* and *renderings* important in the design process?

5. What is the *technical director's* job?

6. What is a *costume*?

7. How does a costume establish aspects of character, social class, age, or weather?

8. What is a design conference? Why is it important?

9. How does the costume designer study a script? What questions do costume designers ask about the script?

10. Why is the dress rehearsal important for designers and directors?

11. What is the function of stage makeup?

12. What is the difference between *straight* and *character* makeup?

13. Why are masks effective onstage?

14. What are the light designer's tools?

15. What is a light plot?

16. Study the photo of *For Colored Girls Who Have Considered Suicide When the Rainbow Is Enuf* on page 124. How do scenery, costume, and lighting enhance the actors' work?

NOTES

[1]Patricia Zipprodt, "Designing Costumes," in *Contemporary Stage Design U.S.A.* (Middletown, Conn.: Wesleyan University Press, 1974), p. 29.

[2]Jean Rosenthal and Lael Wertenbaker, *The Magic of Light* (Boston: Little, Brown, 1972), p. 115.

7

Structures of Seeing

To read drama, the printed page of a script, is to experience much of the playwright's art. Drama has the potential for becoming human speech, action, sound, and movement. Different types of play structures and dramatic conventions help playwrights shape their materials into potential theatrical experiences for us to share.

In the theatre, every form once born is mortal; every form must be reconceived, and its new conception will bear the marks of all the influences that surround it.

Peter Brook, *The Empty Space*

DRAMA

Drama is another way of seeing in the theatre—it is the playwright's art. It takes its name from the Greek verb *dran,* meaning "to do" or "to act." In the best sense, drama is a pattern of words and actions having the potential for "doing" or becoming living words and actions. It is the source of what we see and hear in the theatre.

On the printed page drama is mainly *dialogue*— words arranged in sequence to be spoken by actors. Often stage dialogue is similar to the dialogue we speak in conversation with friends. Often, as with Shakespeare's blank verse or the complex verse forms of the Greek plays, dialogue is more formal. But stage dialogue differs from ordinary conversation in one important way: The play-

Figure 7-1. The elements of drama are words, symbols, signals, signs, plot, action, character, gesture, space, time, and meaning. Together, they make up a pattern for doing. In the theatre, drama's elements become living words and actions.

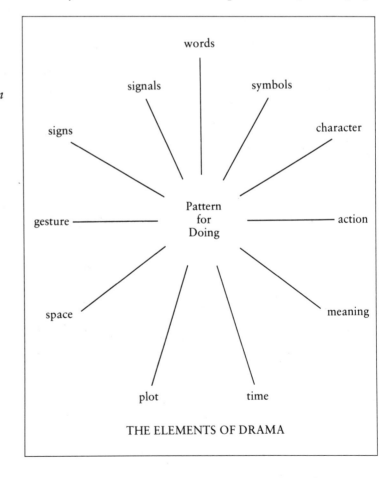

THE ELEMENTS OF DRAMA

wright creates it and the actor speaks it. *Performability* is the link between the playwright's words and the actor's speech.

Let us begin to think about drama as a way of seeing by discussing *play*.

Childhood Games

Every child at some time has been a playwright. Cowboys, doctor, hide-and-seek, cops and robbers, all the games that children *play* are ways of acting out reality. Children play to entertain themselves, to imitate adult behavior, and to help fit themselves into an unfamiliar world. Children try out and learn roles they will "play" in their adult lives—they develop what the American psychiatrist Eric Berne calls *life-scripts*.

Play and Drama

Play and drama have much in common: The child playing hide-and-seek or an actor playing *Hamlet* must start with a scenario or script, imagined situation, dialogue, and locale. The primary role of each is to imitate and entertain. They contribute to a sense of well-being and to an understanding of human behavior. Play and drama have their own fixed rules. And, like the play of children, drama is *an imitation of human events*.

Drama as Imitation

In the fourth century B.C., the Greek philosopher Aristotle described drama as *mimesis*—the imitation of human beings in action. His mimetic theory has been important in the development of Western drama for 2500 years. In his *Poetics*, he showed that the playwright uses certain devices to turn written material into human action: plot, action, character, language, meaning, music, and visual elements. From our modern perspective, we could add time and space to Aristotle's list of dramatic elements.

The Elements of Drama

Plot is an arranged sequence of events or incidents usually having a beginning, middle, and end. These incidents spring from an action, or motive. *Action* is the more difficult concept, since it embodies all the physical, psychological, and spiritual gestures and motivations that result in the *visible behavior* of the characters. It is the source of the play's outward and visible deeds. The American scholar Francis Fergusson defines *action* as "the focus or aim of psychic life from which the events, in that situation, result." In this sense, the action of Oedipus is to find the killer of Laius, the former Theban King, and to purify the city by punishing the guilty man. During his investigation of the plague's cause, Oedipus discovers that he is the guilty man, that he unwittingly killed his father and married his mother. In a deeper sense, for that reason, the action of *Oedipus the King* is really man's attempt to *know himself.*

Character includes the physiological and psychological makeup of the persons in the play. *Language* is the spoken word, including symbols and signs. The play's *meaning* is its underlying idea—its general and particular truths about human experience. Today, we frequently use the word *theme* when we talk about a play's meaning. A play may have more than one basic theme. *Othello,* as we pointed out, is a play about false appearances, errors of judgment, social differences, passion without reason, and the nature of evil.

Aristotle used the word *spectacle* to take in all visual and aural elements: costumes, settings, music, and sound. In the modern theatre we add stage lighting to this list.

A play's *time* is a more recent concern, though many early critics were concerned that a play's *actual time*—the "running time" it takes to see the show—be the same as the number of hours covered in the story. *Symbolic time* is integral to the play's world and events, and may be spread out over hours, days, or years. *Hamlet* frequently takes four hours to perform, although the story covers many months. In Henrik Ibsen's *Ghosts,* we are asked to believe that the incidents take place in a little more than twenty-four hours.

The "happenings" of the 1960s introduced *event time* into American theatre. Allan Kaprow's happening called *Self-Service* (1967) was created to be done over a summer, during which the participants could do the tasks on any weekend. Kaprow roughly combined actual time (the summer months) with event time (the task). (See page 161 for a discussion of happenings.)

PLAY STRUCTURE

In Western drama, plot and action are based on a central *conflict* and organized usually in the following progression: confrontation—crisis—climax—resolution. This generalization is true for plays written by Shakespeare, Ibsen, or Edward Albee. As members of the audience (or readers), we experience characters moving through confrontations to crises to resolutions. The way the playwright varies this pattern determines the play's structure. There are three general ways to structure or organize plays: *climactic, episodic,* and *situational.* And recently, entirely new structures such as happenings have been devised.

Henrik Ibsen (1828–1906), Norwegian playwright, is frequently considered the most influential playwright since Shakespeare. He published his first play, *Catiline,* a verse tragedy, in 1850. His early plays celebrating his country's past glories were poorly received. As stage manager and playwright with the National Stage in Bergen, and later artistic director of the Norwegian Theatre in Oslo, he developed a knowledge of stagecraft. After years of failure and poverty, Ibsen immigrated to Italy where he wrote *Brand* (1865), which brought him immediate fame. For twenty-seven years he remained with his family in self-imposed exile in Rome, Dresden, and Munich. During this time he wrote such plays as *A Doll's House, Ghosts, An Enemy of the People, The Wild Duck, Rosmersholm,* and *Hedda Gabler.* These plays changed the direction of the nineteenth-century theatre. In 1891 he returned to Norway, and in 1899 completed *When We Dead Awaken,* the play that James Joyce considered his finest. He died there in 1906.

Called the father of modern drama, Ibsen wrote plays dealing with problems of contemporary life, particularly those of the individual caught in a repressive society. Although his social doctrines, radical and shocking in his own day, are no longer revolutionary, his portraits of humanity are timeless.

Climactic Play Structure

Found in classical and modern plays, climactic structure confines the characters' activities and intensifies the pressures on the characters until they are forced into irreversible acts—the climax. As the action develops, the characters' range of choices is reduced. Frequently, they are aware that their choices are being limited and that they are being moved toward a crisis and turning point. Climactic structure is a *cause-to-effect* arrangement of incidents ending in a climax and quick resolution.

Mrs. Alving in Ibsen's *Ghosts* is methodically shown that the "ghosts" of her past are the cause of the present situation. Her son "looks like" his father; like his father, he makes advances to the serving girl; he also carries his father's moral corruption within him as a physical disease; and Mrs. Alving is conditioned to do what society dictates is proper and dutiful.

As Mrs. Alving faces her terminally ill son, she must decide whether or not to kill him. She has two alternatives at the play's end. She must choose *one*.

Figure 7-2. Climactic play structure. Ghosts, *like the classical plays* Agamemnon *and* Oedipus the King, *begins late in the story, near the crisis and climax. All the events of the story's past (to the left of the vertical line) occur before the play begins and are revealed in exposition. Each act of Ibsen's play ends with a climax, building to the highest point of tension—Oswald's collapse. Since a climactic plot begins late in the story, the period of time covered is usually limited. The classical play usually takes place in a few hours.* Ghosts *begins in the afternoon and ends at sunrise the following day.*

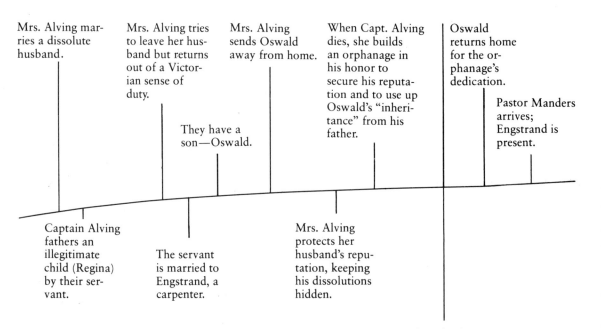

Mrs. Alving marries a dissolute husband.

Mrs. Alving tries to leave her husband but returns out of a Victorian sense of duty.

Mrs. Alving sends Oswald away from home.

When Capt. Alving dies, she builds an orphanage in his honor to secure his reputation and to use up Oswald's "inheritance" from his father.

Oswald returns home for the orphanage's dedication.

They have a son—Oswald.

Pastor Manders arrives; Engstrand is present.

Captain Alving fathers an illegitimate child (Regina) by their servant.

The servant is married to Engstrand, a carpenter.

Mrs. Alving protects her husband's reputation, keeping his dissolutions hidden.

Act I begins.

Figure 7-3. Climactic drama. Oswald and Mrs. Alving face the crisis in their lives. In climactic drama the characters are confined within time and space. There is usually a limited number of characters, and locale and events are restricted. Ghosts has five characters and takes place in Mrs. Alving's living room. As the pressures of the past go to work in the present, the action develops, limiting the choices the characters have open to them. An explosive confrontation becomes inevitable. In the photo Mrs. Alving (Margaret Tyzack) learns the truth from Oswald (Nicholas Pennell) about his disease in the 1977 Stratford Festival Theatre, Ontario, production of Ghosts. (Photo by Robert C. Ragsdale, courtesy of the Stratford Festival Theatre, Ontario, Canada.)

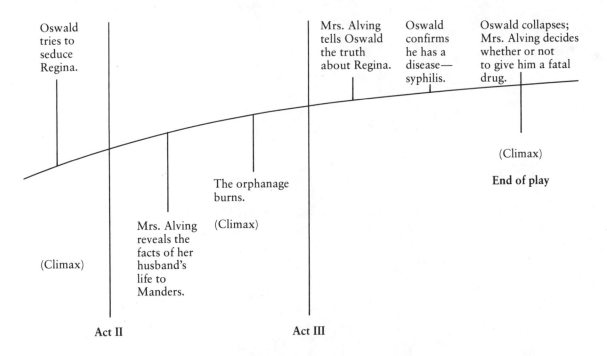

Prologue	Narrator tells	She flees with	She bargains	The soldiers capture
1945— people from two valleys dispute the land's ownership.	the story of Grusha, a peasant girl, saving the governor's child in the midst of a revolution.	the child Michael to the mountains, leaving her fiancé behind.	to feed the child, escapes pursuing soldiers, and marries to provide food and shelter for Michael.	Grusha and Michael; they are returned to the city.

Grusha's story

Figure 7-4.   *Episodic play structure (above). It begins early in the story and involves many characters and events. The action is a journey of some kind, and place and event do not confine the characters. Instead, the plot expands to include a variety of events and activities. The Shakespearean episodic play usually has a double plot to contrast events and people. Brecht's* The Caucasian Chalk Circle *is made up of two stories, Grusha's and Azdak's. The expanding plot moves in a linear fashion, telling the two seemingly unrelated stories until Brecht combines them in the chalk circle test to make his point about decent people caught in the injustices of a corrupt political system.*

Figure 7-5.   *Azdak the judge. In Bertolt Brecht's 1954 production of* The Caucasian Chalk Circle *by his company, The Berliner Ensemble, in East Berlin, the child sits at the feet of actor Ernst Busch as Azdak. (Photo courtesy of The Berliner Ensemble.)*

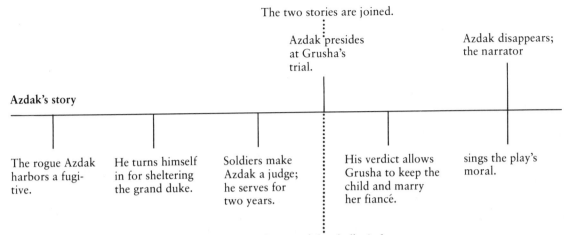

The two stories are joined.

Azdak presides at Grusha's trial.

Azdak disappears; the narrator

Azdak's story

The rogue Azdak harbors a fugitive.

He turns himself in for sheltering the grand duke.

Soldiers make Azdak a judge; he serves for two years.

His verdict allows Grusha to keep the child and marry her fiancé.

sings the play's moral.

The test of the chalk circle

Episodic Play Structure

We associate episodic play structure with Shakespeare and Brecht. Episodic structure traces the characters through a *journey* of sorts to a final action, and to an understanding of what the journey meant. It can always take a new turn. In Shakespeare's plays, persons are not forced into unmaneuverable positions. Possibilities of action are always open to them. Events do not accumulate to confine the characters because the play takes in large amounts of time and distance. *Hamlet* takes place over several years and countries. Also, the expanding plot takes in a variety of events and activities. Frequently, Shakespeare used main plots and subplots to contrast events. In this loose structure, characters are not caught in circumstances, but pass through them, as Grusha does in Brecht's *The Caucasian Chalk Circle*. She undergoes a variety of experiences in her efforts to save the governor's child from mercenary soldiers. She *journeys* through the countryside until she is captured and brought before Judge Azdak to be tested by the chalk circle rite. She passes the test and Azdak awards the child to her.

Situational Play Structure

In absurdist plays of the 1950s, *situation* shapes the play, not plot or arrangement of incidents. It takes the place of the journey or the pressurized events. For example, two tramps wait for a person named Godot who never arrives *(Waiting for Godot)*; a husband and wife talk in meaningless clichés as they go about their daily routines *(The Bald Soprano)*.

The situation has its own inner rhythms, which are like the basic rhythms of life: day, night, day; hunger,

Figure 7-6.   Brecht's Chalk Circle. In the 1954 Berliner Ensemble production of The Caucasian Chalk Circle *in East Berlin, directed by Bertolt Brecht, gifts are brought to the governor and his wife. (Photo courtesy of the Berliner Ensemble.)*

thirst, hunger; spring, summer, winter. Although the situation usually remains unchanged, these rhythms move in a cycle.

In *Waiting for Godot*, Vladimir and Estragon grow increasingly frenetic and despairing as they wait; finally, the tension is released in Vladimir's explosion of self-awareness. Vladimir realizes that all they can say for themselves is that they have kept their appointment with the absent Godot. After his outburst, we realize that the situation is unchanged. The two characters are still waiting for Godot. To demonstrate the unchanging situation, Beckett ends the last act in the same way he ends the first. He writes: "They do not move."

In *The Bald Soprano*, Ionesco introduces a fire chief and the Martins into Mr. and Mrs. Smith's typical middle-class English living room. After a series of absurd events, the dialogue crescendos into nonsensical babbling. The words stop abruptly and the play begins again. This time Mr. and Mrs. Martin are seated as the Smiths were at the play's beginning, and repeat the Smiths' lines from the first scene. In the repetition, Ionesco gives a demonstration of the interchangeability of middle-class lives.

Figure 7-7. Situational play structure. Following World War II, "the theatre of the absurd" emerged in Europe. Absurdist plays convey a sense of alienation, of people having lost their bearings in an illogical or ridiculous world. Their structure mirrors this world view.

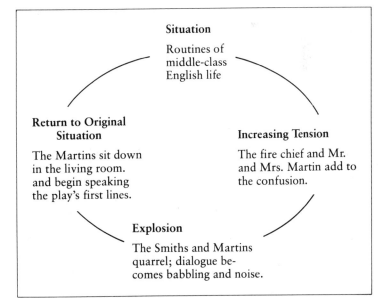

Situation

Routines of middle-class English life

Increasing Tension

The fire chief and Mr. and Mrs. Martin add to the confusion.

Explosion

The Smiths and Martins quarrel; dialogue becomes babbling and noise.

Return to Original Situation

The Martins sit down in the living room. and begin speaking the play's first lines.

The Bald Soprano (produced at the Théâtre de Noctambules, Paris, 1950) is Ionesco's "antiplay" that dramatizes the absurdity of human existence. In 1948, while taking a course in conversational English, Ionesco conceived the idea of using many of the practice sentences to create an absurd atmosphere.

Mr. and Mrs. Smith talk in clichés about the trivia of everyday life. The meaninglessness of their existence is caricatured in dialogue in which each member of a large family, living and dead, regardless of age or sex, is called Bobby Watson. Mr. and Mrs. Martin enter. They converse as strangers but gradually discover that they are both from Manchester, that they arrived in London at the same time, that they live in the same house, sleep in the same bed, and are parents of the same child. The Martins and the Smiths exchange banalities, a clock strikes erratically, and the doorbell rings by itself. A fire chief arrives. Although in a hurry to extinguish all fires in the city, he launches into long-winded, pointless anecdotes. After he leaves, the two couples talk in clichés until language breaks down into basic sounds. The end of the play completes a circle: The Martins replace the Smiths and speak the same lines that opened the play.

Figure 7-8. Ionesco's middle-class English couple. Mr. and Mrs. Smith discuss dinner, the newspaper, and Bobby Watson in the original 1950 Paris production of The Bald Soprano. *(Photo courtesy of Cultural Services of the French Embassy, New York City.)*

Happenings

Happenings in the early 1960s were one among several new trends in the American theatre. First of all, they were an attempt to break down barriers between the arts, as well as between performers and their audiences. American painter Allan Kaprow (b. 1927) became interested in creating environments (that is, use of the entire space, not just the art works on display) of art works at an exhibit to give persons attending the exhibit something to do to involve them with the art.

The name *happening* resulted from Kaprow's use of the word in his presentation called *18 Happenings in 6 Parts* (1959). It soon became a label for task-oriented events in which chance and improvisation played a large part. For instance, Kaprow's *Arrivals,* which was "performed" in 1968 at Nassau Community College in New York, consisted of a set of instructions handed out to the participants:

Unused airstrip

Tarring cracks in airstrip

Painting guidelines on airstrip

Cutting grass at airstrip's edge

Placing mirrors on airstrip

Watching for reflections of planes

The aim of the happening is to permit participants to engage in a task, usually related to our urban society, to encourage them to *perceive* the world's complexity in a new way.

Few happenings engaged our sense of theatre and they declined in popularity in the late 1960s. However, they did contribute to greater reliance in the theatre on improvisation, use of whole space as environment, and a new actor-audience relationship. John Cage, Allan Kaprow, Claus Oldenburg, and Michael Kirby orchestrated happenings in the 1960s. Kirby has written a book on the phenomenon, *Happenings* (1966).

Figure 7-9. Kaprow's happening. Calling, *by Allan Kaprow, was performed in New York City in 1965. It involved an orchestration of cars converging at prearranged points to pick up passengers, wrapping someone in aluminum foil to sit motionless on the back seat of a parked car, and two girls wrapped in muslin to be taken to the information booth at Grand Central Station. The photo shows the two muslin-covered girls, one standing and one seated at lower left corner, unwrapping themselves. They leave the train station and telephone certain numbers. A name is asked for and the person at the other end clicks off. (Photo © 1965 by Peter Moore.)*

The Theatre of Images

The Theatre of Images—a label coined by the American critic Bonnie Marranca in 1976—is the name given to the 1970s work of American writer-director-producers Richard Foreman (Ontological-Hysteric Theater), Robert Wilson (Byrd Hoffman School of Byrds), and Lee Breuer (Mabou Mines). Revolting against words, they create plays dominated by visual and aural images. Stage pictures, illustrations, sounds, and images replace plot, character, and theme. Wilson's *A Letter for Queen Victoria* is composed of bits and pieces of overheard conversations, clichés, newspaper blurbs, colors, radio spot announcements, television images, and film clips. Wilson creates his own *visual language* out of objects, sounds, people, and gestures. In Act II, pilots talk about faraway lands against a background of gunfire sounds and bomb blasts. Instead of discussing American imperialism, the scene projects an *image* of it.

Figures 7-10. Robert Wilson's theatre of images. The photo and portion of the text are from A Letter for Queen Victoria, *which premiered at the 1974 Festival of Two Worlds in Spoleto, Italy. They demonstrate how Wilson "assembles" actors, shapes, words, sounds, light, and shadow to make a theatrical statement. The visual image of the autistic boy, Christopher Knowles, framed in white light against the broken language projected behind him, makes a statement about communication in our computerized society. The theatrical meaning and effect are based on* visual image *rather than verbal communication. (Photo by Johan Elbers; text courtesy of Robert Wilson.)*

```
                                    ACT IV
                                  SECTION 4

(BREAK DROP)

(4 BECOMES 2 FROM ACT I. 3 BECOMES 1 FROM ACT I.)
(PILOTS REENTER)

PILOTS:  I DON'T KNOW HOW TO THANK YOU
             (PAUSE 5 SECONDS)
         SAY
             (PAUSE 4 SECONDS)
         WHAT
             (PAUSE 3 SECONDS)
         CERTAINLY
3        MY KNOWLEDGE ABOUT YOU IS REDUCED TO A HANDFUL OF FACTS


(PILOTS EXIT)

1 AND 2 ALTERNATE  SEEM WHAT
                   SEEMED WHAT
                   SEEM
                   SEEMS THE SAME
                   SEEMED THE SAME
                   SEEMS
                   SIMULTANEOUSITY O'CITY O'VORST
                   WHEEL WHAT WHEN NOW
                   AN ALLIGATOR'S SPAN
                   SEEM WHY
                   SEEM WHAT
                   SEEMED
                   SEEMS
                   SCREEN TELL A VISIONS
                   SCREENED TOLDA VISIONS
                   SCREEN
                   SCREAM
                   A MILLION DANCES

                   (FRAMED IN WHITE LIGHT)

   A          HAP HAT HAP     AAAAAAAAAAAO    CONFORMING     O
   AO         HATH HIP HA     AAAAOAOAOA      VCONFORMIN     OK
   OAOA       HAT HIT HAP     AAAOAOAOA       VECONFORMI     AOKO
   XXXXX      HATH HAP HA     AAOAOAO         VERCONFORM     LAOKOK
   AOAOAOA    HIP HIT HATH    AOAOA           VERYCONFOR     LLAOKOKO
   XXXXXXXXX  HAP HATH HI     OAO             VERYVCONFO     ELLAOKOKOK
   XXXXXXXXXX HAP HI HATH     AO              VERYVECONF     WELLAOKOKO
   OAOAOAOAOAOAO  HI HI HAP HA    O           VERYVERCON     AWELLAOKOKOKO
```

Richard Foreman, an American philosopher-playwright, founded the Ontological-Hysteric Theater in 1968 to create avant-garde theatre based on sounds, images, and illustrations. Stage pictures interrelated with words replace dialogue, characters are social types, sets are constructed before the audience. Foreman has produced, designed, and directed his own plays in a New York City loft.

Lee Breuer, founding member in 1970 of the Mabou Mines, has written and directed theatrical cartoons: *The Red Horse Animation, The B Beaver Animation,* and *The Shaggy Dog Animation.* Breuer's work is a kind of theatrical "action painting." Breuer sculpts an environment with space, light, and sound; uses actors as story tellers; and creates images of people's social behavior.

Robert Wilson founded the Byrd Hoffman School of Byrds in New York in 1970. His productions of *The Life and Times of Joseph Stalin, Einstein on the Beach,* and *A Letter for Queen Victoria* "assemble" actors, sounds, music, light, and shadow to comment on American society and cultural myths. A student of architecture and painting, Wilson creates living pictures on stage—collages of sounds, sculptured forms, and visual images—requiring many hours to experience. His lengthy productions stretch the audience's attention and attempt to alter our perceptual awareness of people, places, and things.

CONVENTIONS OF DRAMA

Over the years playwrights have worked out different dramatic structures to say different things about experience. In addition, they have worked out dramatic conventions, ground rules, to set plot and character in motion. A *convention* is an agreed-upon method of getting something quickly across to an audience. Just as we have social conventions in life to help us meet strangers or answer the telephone, so the playwright has conventions to solve problems, pass along information, develop plot and action, and create interest and suspense. Conventions make it possible for the playwright to use shortcuts to give us information, shorten experiences that in life would require weeks or even years, tell two stories at once, and complicate the stage action without confusing the audience. What follows is a discussion of seven dramatic conventions: exposition, point of attack, complication, crisis, resolution, double plots, and the play-within-the-play.

Exposition

In a play's beginning, we are given certain information about what is going on, what has happened in the past, and who is to be seen. This is *exposition.* In Aeschylus' *Agamemnon,* the watchman tells us that it is the tenth year of the Trojan War. We therefore anticipate the flashing beacon lights and the murders that follow.

Some plays begin with a telephone ringing; the person answering—for instance, a maid in drawing-room comedy—gives the background information by talking to an unseen party about the family, plans, and conflicts.

Other plays begin with informational exchanges of dialogue. *Othello* begins with Iago in conversation with Roderigo. Iago complains that Othello did not promote him and that he plans to serve his "peculiar end" upon Othello in the near future.

Contemporary drama makes fewer demands for information of this kind. Instead of asking who these people are and what is going to happen next, we usually ask: "What's happening now?"

Figure 7-11.   Queen Clytemnestra. Priscilla Smith as Clytemnestra in splendid robes and mask in the 1977 production of Agamemnon *at the Vivien Beaumont Theatre, Lincoln Center, New York City. (Photo by George E. Joseph.)*

Agamemnon, first produced at the Festival Dionysia, Athens, in 458 B.C., is the first play in Aeschylus' trilogy *The Oresteia.* Plotting with her lover, Aegisthus, to kill her husband upon his return from the Trojan War, Queen Clytemnestra has ordered that a guard keep watch from the palace roof at Argos. A succession of beacon fires set on hilltops is to bring the news from Troy when that city is captured by the Greek forces under Agamemnon's command.

The play opens as the watchman waits in the dead of night. As the signal blazes forth, he sends out a cry of joy. The queen gives thanks for Troy's fall. A herald announces Agamemnon's arrival, but tells of sacrilegious acts committed by the Greeks against the gods' temples. Clytemnestra speaks of her love for Agamemnon, but the chorus hints at hypocrisy.

Agamemnon enters with the Trojan princess, Cassandra, also a priestess of Apollo, captured in Troy and made his unwilling mistress. Clytemnestra persuades Agamemnon to walk into the palace on a rich purple carpet. He does so unwillingly, knowing that it constitutes an act of pride.

Cassandra recalls the bloody history of the house of Atreus and predicts Agamemnon's death and her own. They go into the palace and are killed. The palace doors open, revealing Clytemnestra standing over their bodies. She exults in the deed. The chorus predicts her future punishment by Zeus' law, that the doer must suffer the consequences of his deeds, and warns that Agamemnon's son Orestes will avenge his father.

The first play in the trilogy ends with the warning. The story of Clytemnestra, Aegisthus, Orestes, and Electra (his sister) is taken up in *The Libation Bearers* and *The Eumenides.*

Point of Attack

The moment early in the play when the story is taken up is the *point of attack*. In *Othello,* it comes when Iago and Roderigo arouse Desdemona's father to tell him that she has eloped with the Moor.

Complication

The middle of a play is made up of complications and a crisis, or turning point. *Complication* involves the discovery of new information introduced by new characters, unexpected events, or newly disclosed facts. In *Ghosts,* Mrs. Alving overhears Oswald seducing Regina in the dining room. Regina is the child of her husband's affair with a servant and is, therefore, Oswald's half-sister. Mrs. Alving must deal with this complication.

Crisis

A play's complications usually develop into a crisis, or turning point, of the action. The crisis is an event that makes the resolution of the play's conflict inevitable. Othello's murder of Desdemona is the play's crisis. A play's ending usually becomes a matter of resolving the conflict in the climax or highest point of intensity and tying off loose strands of action in the play's resolution. Othello's discovery that he has murdered an innocent wife and been duped by Iago is the crisis that leads to his suicide and the play's climax.

Resolution

The resolution restores balance and satisfies the audience's expectations. Othello has paid for his crime, Iago is punished for his part in the affair, and Cassio becomes governor of Cyprus. In *A Streetcar Named Desire,* Blanche DuBois is taken to an asylum and the Kowalski household

Figure 7-12. Othello's discovery. Paul Robeson as Othello learns the truth about Desdemona's innocence from Margaret Webster as Emilia in the 1944 Theatre Guild production in New York. The play's climax *and* resolution *follow Othello's discovery. (Photo Vandamm Collection, New York Public Library at Lincoln Center.)*

settles back into its routines of poker, beer, and Saturday-night bowling. The absurdist play usually completes a cycle in its resolution, suggesting that the events of the play will repeat themselves over and over again. Some plays end with unanswered questions—for example, will Mrs. Alving in *Ghosts* give Oswald the fatal drug, or won't she?—to stimulate the audience to think about what kind of choice each would make in a similar situation. Whatever the case, the resolution brings about a sense of completed action, of conflicts resolved in probable ways, and of promises fulfilled.

Other dramatic conventions relate past and present events and behavior. *Simultaneous plots* and the *play-within-the-play* are two important conventions used by Renaissance and modern playwrights.

Simultaneous or Double Plots

Figure 7-13. The secondary plot resolved. Hamlet stands above the wounded Laertes near the end of the duel. Laertes' death concludes the story of his family. Albert Finney as Hamlet watches Simon Ward as Laertes in the 1976 production at London's National Theatre, directed by Peter Hall. (Photo by Anthony Crickmay.)

The Elizabethans used double plots to represent life's variety and complexity. Two stories are told concurrently; the lives of one group of characters affect the lives of the other group. *Hamlet,* for instance, is the story of two families: Hamlet-Claudius-Gertrude, Laertes-Polonius-Ophelia. The secondary plot or subplot is always resolved before the main plot to maintain a sense of priority and importance. Laertes, for instance, dies before Hamlet in the duel resolving that family's story.

The Play-within-the-Play

The play-within-the-play was used by Shakespeare and it is still used. In *Hamlet,* the strolling players recreate a second play on stage about the murder of Hamlet's father. Claudius' reaction to it gives Hamlet proof of his guilt.

Modern playwrights use the play-within-the-play in a more complex way: to show that *life is like theatre* and vice versa. In his celebrated play *Marat/Sade (The Persecution and Assassination of Marat as Performed by the Inmates of the Asylum of Charenton under the Direction of the Marquis de Sade)*, Peter Weiss uses the play-within-the-play convention to show that our contemporary world is a madhouse. The inmates of Charenton asylum produce a play in 1808 about Jean-Paul Marat written by the Marquis de Sade (who is author, actor, producer, and inmate).

Weiss uses two plays-within-the-play: (1) the events of July 13, 1793—the historical setting of de Sade's play during the French Revolution—that culminate in the death of Marat; and (2) the frustrations of 1808, when de Sade and other inmates are staging the events of 1793. The play's madhouse world at Charenton reflects the violence and irrationality of our modern world. The plays-within-the-play force us to see the relationships of past and present events: The violence of one era is contrasted with the violence of another, political ideologies of one time with those of another, guillotine with atomic bomb, and so on.

SUMMARY

As words for doing, drama has three functions: (1) It is the playwright's *means* of presenting imagined human behavior and events; (2) it is the actor's *blueprint* for physical and psychological experience; and (3) it is words having the potential for becoming *visible* behavior. That behavior, which the actor brings us, takes many forms depending upon the playwright's attitude and interpretation of experience. Drama's major forms are the subject of the next chapter.

Figure 7-14. Playwright Peter Weiss. (Photo courtesy of Swedish Information Service.)

Peter Weiss (b. 1916) was born in Berlin. He took refuge from the Nazis in Sweden during the 1930s and has lived there since. Weiss attracted the theatre world's attention with the Schiller Theater's Berlin production of *Marat/Sade* in 1964. Subsequently, the play was produced by the Royal Shakespeare Company in London under the direction of Peter Brook, brought to New York, and also filmed. Weiss is author of *The Investigation* (1965), *The Song of the Lusitanian Bogey* (1969), and *The Prozess* (from Kafka's *The Trial,* 1975), and has made documentary films.

Marat/Sade *is an episodic play that uses debate, mime, song, dance, and chanting to comment upon the irrationality of human events. Neither a straightforward account of a revolutionary's death nor a literal account of a theatrical rehearsal, it defies our expectations. Weiss uses theatrical conventions, such as a rehearsal, to place a fundamental issue on stage: how personal viewpoint obscures our perception of reality. In effect, reality is perceived as the sum of any number of personal experiences: neurotic, pathological, philosophical, aesthetic.*

Weiss holds a number of mirrors up to our chaotic world. De Sade's play is taking place in 1808 — Napoleon is about to fall in Europe. But the play is about an event in 1793 — the death of a leading revolutionary, Marat. And we watch Weiss's play about these times from a perspective of 180 years after the French Revolution or Napoleon's reign.

Donald Driver directed this 1967 National Players Company production on Broadway; it was designed by Richard Burbridge, with lighting by Martin Aronstein and costumes by Lewis Brown.

Figure 7-15a. Marat the revolutionary (below). At the play's core is a philosophical argument (written, we must remember, by the Marquis de Sade). The central debate about the possibility of revolution is between Marat and de Sade. Marat defends the classic Marxist viewpoint; that is, the world can be changed only if we impose a rational order by force. "Revolution, now!" is his essential call to the people. But Marat, as seen here writing political treatises while relieving his skin disease by soaking in a bathtub, is an asylum inmate.

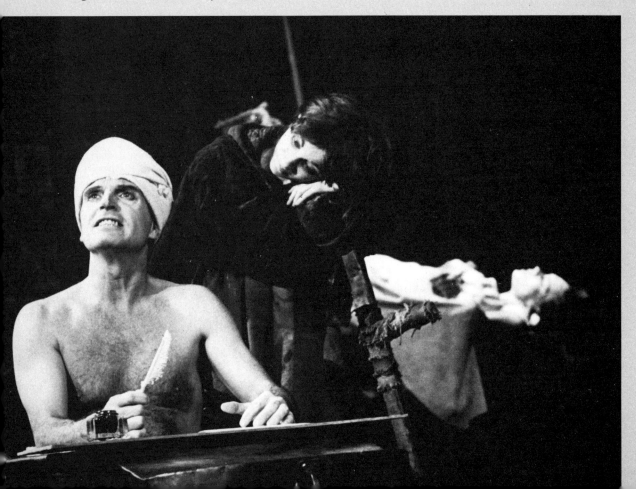

Figure 7-15b.   De Sade and Marat debate issues. The Marquis de Sade, author and director of Weiss's play-within-a-play, is an extreme individualist. Historically, de Sade was a writer who uncovered an unconscious world of violence, torture, evil, and degradation. During the Revolution the authorities confined him to Charenton where he died in 1814. Here he debates political issues with Marat.

Figure 7-15c.   The murder of Marat. De Sade assigns the part of Charlotte Corday, Marat's murderer, to a somnambulist. Within de Sade's play, Corday makes three visits to Marat before killing him. Her journeys, along with the political debates, contribute to the play's episodic structure.

Figure 7-15d. *The inmates. Dressed in rags, the inmates assume the part of actors, chorus, onlookers, revolutionaries, and madmen. At the play's end, they break loose and violently assault their keepers and the audience, calling for "Revolution! Copulation!" This final image of chaos and madness before the curtain falls completes Weiss's comment upon the irrationality of human conduct. (Photos by Joseph Abeles.)*

QUESTIONS FOR STUDY

1. What is *dialogue*?

2. What similarities are there between children at play and theatre?

3. What is *mimesis*?

4. What is the difference between a play's *actual time*, *symbolic time*, and *event time*?

5. What are the basic differences between *climactic, episodic,* and *situational* play structure? Give examples of each.

6. What are *happenings*?

7. Study the photograph and text from Robert Wilson's *A Letter for Queen Victoria*. How do visual images take the place of traditional stage dialogue?

8. What is a dramatic *convention*?

9. Why is *exposition* an important playwright's tool? Give some examples of exposition.

10. Why does *complication* often follow the *point of attack*?

11. How are *crisis* and *climax* related?

12. What does an audience expect at a play's *resolution* or ending?

13. What is the function of a *double plot*?

14. Describe the double plot in *Hamlet*.

15. "The Murder of Gonzago" as performed by the strolling players in *Hamlet* is an example of a play-within-a-play. What is the function of this "inner" play?

16. How has Peter Weiss complicated the play-within-the-play convention?

NOTES

For my understanding of climactic and episodic drama I am indebted to material from Bernard Beckerman, *Dynamics of Drama: Theory and Method of Analysis* (New York: Alfred A. Knopf, 1970).

8

Perspectives and Forms

Playwrights use different dramatic forms to express their understanding of human experience. Tragedy and comedy are the forms most familiar to us, but there are many other ways to classify plays and to label the playwright's **vision**—*the way he or she perceives life in theatrical terms. A study of drama's changing forms is also a study of the playwright's changing perception of the world.*

If art reflects life it does so with special mirrors.
Bertolt Brecht,
A Short Organum for the Theatre

Over the centuries playwrights have developed different forms and styles to mirror the changing intellectual and emotional life of their cultures. This is what Peter Brook means when he says that every theatrical form once born is mortal.[1] Drama's forms change as societies and perceptions of the world change.

Drama's essential forms are ways of seeing human experience. The words *tragedy, comedy,* and *tragicomedy* are not so much ways of classifying plays by their endings as ways of talking about the playwright's vision of experience—of the way he or she perceives life. They provide clues about the play's style and how the play is to be taken. For instance, is the play a serious statement about the difficulties of being human? Or does it hold up to ridicule man's uncompromising postures?

TRAGEDY

It is not altogether simpleminded to say that a tragedy is a play with an unhappy ending. Tragedy, the first of the great dramatic forms in Western drama, makes a special statement about human fallibility.

The Tragic Vision

The writer's "tragic vision" of human experience conceives of people as both vulnerable and invincible, as capable of abject defeat and transcendent greatness.

The great mysteries and paradoxes of our world have been put before us in such plays as *Oedipus the King, Hamlet, Othello, Ghosts,* and *A Streetcar Named Desire.* Tragedy shows the world's injustice, evil, and pain. Tragic heroes, in an exercise of free will, pit themselves against forces represented by other characters or by their physical environment. We witness their suffering, their inevitable defeat, and their personal triumph in the face of defeat. The hero gives meaning to the pain and paradox of our humanity.

In some tragedies we are concerned in the end of the play with the meaning and justice of an ordered world; in others, with humanity's helpless protest against an irra-

Figure 8-1. Tragic suffering. Othello and Desdemona, caught in the web of Iago's plotting, suffer intensely when Othello accuses his wife of being unfaithful. Paul Robeson is Othello and Uta Hagen is Desdemona in Margaret Webster's 1944 New York production for The Theatre Guild. (Photo Vandamm Collection, New York Public Library at Lincoln Center.)

tional universe. In both kinds, the hero, alone and willful, asserts his or her intellect and energy against the ultimate mysteries of an imperfect world.

Tragic Realization

The realization that follows the hero's efforts usually takes one of two directions: We may learn that, despite human suffering and calamity, a world order and eternal laws exist and people can learn from suffering; or we may learn of the futility of human acts and suffering in an indif-

ferent, capricious, or mechanical universe, but at the same time celebrate that protest against the nature of existence. In *Oedipus the King* and *A Streetcar Named Desire* we find examples of these two kinds of tragic realization.

Aristotle on Tragedy

Aristotle spoke of tragedy as "an imitation of an action . . . concerning the fall of a man whose character is good (though not preeminently just or virtuous) . . . whose misfortune is brought about not by vice or depravity but by some error or frailty . . . with incidents arousing pity and fear, wherewith to accomplish the catharsis of these emotions."[2]

Going all the way back to Aristotle and the Greek playwrights, we think of tragedy's action as an imitation of a noble hero who suffers a downfall or of tragedy's subjects as dealing with suffering and death to arouse our emotions and awareness of life's possible defeats and failures.

The heroes of ancient tragedies were often aristocratic to show that even the great among us can suffer from the irremediableness of the human condition. In modern plays the hero's very averageness speaks to us of human kinship in adversity. Whether the hero is aristocratic or ordinary, his fate is influenced by the writer's tragic view (or perception) of life, which centers on the human need to give meaning to our fate despite the fact that we are doomed to failure and defeat.

COMEDY

In the eighteenth century, Horace Walpole said, "The world is a comedy to those that think, a tragedy to those that feel." In comedy the playwright examines the social world, social values, and people as social beings. Frequently, comic action shows the social disorder created by an eccentric, or "blocking," character who deviates from such reasonable and viable values as sensibility, good nature, flexibility, moderation, tolerance, and social intelli-

Molière (Jean Baptiste Poquelin, 1622–1673), French playwright-actor-manager, was the son of Louis XIV's upholsterer. Poquelin spent his early years close to the court and received a gentleman's education. He joined a theatrical troupe in 1643 and became a professional actor with the stage name Molière. Molière helped to found the Illustre Théâtre Company in Paris, which soon failed, and spent twelve years touring the French provinces as an itinerant actor and company playwright. He returned to Paris to become the foremost comedian of his time. Within thirteen years (1659–1673) he wrote and acted in *Tartuffe, The Misanthrope, The Doctor In Spite of Himself, The Miser,* and *The Imaginary Invalid.* Writing during France's golden age, Molière's comedies balance follies of eccentric humanity against society's reasonable good sense.

gence. Deviation is sharply ridiculed in comedy because it threatens to destroy revered social structures like marriage and the family.

The writer's comic vision calls for sanity, reason, and moderation in human behavior so that society can function for the well-being and happiness of its members. In comedy, society survives the threat posed by inflexible or unnatural behavior. Tartuffe's greed is revealed and Orgon's family is returned to a normal, domestic existence. For Molière, the well-being of the family unit is a measure of the well-being of the society as a whole.

At the end of comedy, the life flow is ordinarily symbolized in a wedding, a dance, or a banquet celebrating the harmony and reconciliation of opposing forces: young and old, flexible and inflexible, reasonable and unreasonable. These social ceremonies allow us to see that good sense wins the day and that humanity endures in the vital, the flexible, and the reasonable.

Tartuffe (1664) is Molière's comedy about a hypocrite. Tartuffe disguises himself as a cleric, and his apparent piety ingratiates him with the credulous merchant Orgon and his mother Madame Pernelle. As the play begins Tartuffe has taken over Orgon's house. Both Orgon and his mother believe that Tartuffe's pious example will be good for the family. But everyone else in the family, including the outspoken servant Dorine, is perceptive enough to see through Tartuffe.

Despite the protests of his brother-in-law Cleante and his son Damis, Orgon determines that his daughter Marianne, who is in love with Valere, will marry Tartuffe. When Orgon's wife Elmire begs Tartuffe to refuse Marianne's hand, he tries to seduce her. Damis, who has overheard, denounces Tartuffe. Orgon banishes his son rather than his guest and signs over his property to Tartuffe.

Elmire then plots to expose the hypocrite. She persuades Orgon to conceal himself under a table while she encourages Tartuffe's advances. Orgon's eyes are opened, but it is too late. The imposter realizes he has been discovered and turns Orgon's family out of the house. Then he reports to the authorities that Orgon has a strongbox containing illegal papers and contrives to have Orgon arrested. But, by the king's order, the arresting officer takes Tartuffe to prison instead.

The play ends with Damis reconciled to his father, Orgon reconciled with his family, and Valere and Marianne engaged.

Figure 8-2. Comedy's deviant or blocking character. Tartuffe pretends to be a person of utmost piety to Elmire, Orgon's wife, while plotting to seduce her and to take her husband's property. He disrupts the household and threatens its well-being before being found out and sent to prison for his misdeeds. John Wood is Tartuffe and Tammy Grimes is Elmire in the 1977 Circle-in-the-Square production (New York), directed by Stephen Porter. (Photo by Martha Swope.)

TRAGICOMEDY

Tragicomedy is a mixed form. Up to the end of the seventeenth century in Europe, tragicomedy was defined as a mixture of tragedy, which went from good fortune to bad, and comedy, which reversed the order. Tragicomic plays mixed serious and comic incidents as well as the styles, subject matter, and language proper to tragedy and to comedy, and it mixed characters from all stations of life. The *ending* was its principal feature: Tragicomedies were serious and potentially tragic plays with happy endings, or at least averted catastrophes.

We use the term *modern tragicomedy* to designate plays with mixed moods in which the endings are neither exclusively tragic nor comic, happy nor unhappy. Beckett calls *Waiting for Godot* a tragicomedy. In this play two tramps in Charlie Chaplin bowler hats entertain themselves with comic routines while they wait in a sparse landscape adorned by a single tree for someone named Godot to arrive. Their situation does not change throughout the play—they wait for someone who never comes. As they react to this situation, humor and aliveness are mixed with anguish and despair.

Beckett's play about human endurance and existential despair in an unchanging dramatic situation is characteristic of modern tragicomedy. In the modern form, tragic and comic qualities and behavior are mixed. Playwrights show people laughing at their anxieties and life's contradictions with little effect on their situations. In a sense, Beckett's Vladimir summarizes the form of modern tragicomedy when he says, "The essential doesn't change."

Figure 8-3. Tragedy and comedy emphasize different values, emotions, conditions, and outcomes. The chart helps us understand the different emphases to be found in the dramatic forms.

Oppositions between Tragedy and Comedy

Tragedy	Comedy
Individual	Society
Metaphysical	Social
Death	Endurance
Error	Folly
Suffering	Joy
Pain	Pleasure
Life-Denying	Procreative
Separation	Union/Reunion
Terror	Euphoria
Unhappiness	Happiness
Irremediable	Remediable
Decay	Growth
Destruction	Continuation
Defeat	Survival
Extreme	Moderation
Inflexible	Flexible

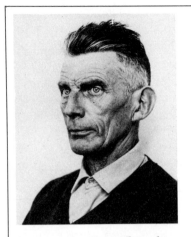

Figure 8-4. Samuel Beckett. (Photo courtesy of French Cultural Services, New York.)

Samuel Beckett (b. 1906), is an expatriate Irishman living in France. Beckett grew up near Dublin and attended Trinity College, where he received two degrees in literature and began a teaching career. In the 1930s Beckett left his teaching position, traveled in Europe, published his first book *(More Pricks Than Kicks),* and wrote poetry in French. During World War II he worked with the French Resistance and barely escaped capture by the Nazis.

Beckett's first major play, *Waiting for Godot,* was written in French and premiered in 1953 in Paris. During the last twenty years he has written some twenty-seven theatrical pieces, including radio plays, mime sketches, monologues, and four full-length plays *(Waiting for Godot, Endgame, Krapp's Last Tape, Happy Days). Endgame,* like *Waiting for Godot,* is a modern classic.

Recently, Beckett's plays have become minimal. *Come and Go* (1965) is a three-minute play and *Breath* (1966) is a thirty-second play. With these brief pieces Beckett constructs a theatrical image of how we come and go on this earth, briefly filling a void with our bodies and voices, and then disappear into darkness without a trace.

Figure 8-5. Modern tragi-comedy. Samuel Beckett's tramps, Vladimir and Estragon, entertain themselves by searching for a missing boot. Although Godot has not kept his appointment with them, the tree has grown leaves between the first and second acts. With Godot's absence and the tree's growth, Beckett juxtaposes despair with hope, loss with gain. The photo is from the 1961 Paris revival of Waiting for Godot *directed by Jean-Marie Serreau with Lucien Raimbourg as Vladimir and Etienne Berg as Estragon. The tree was designed by sculptor Alberto Giacometti. (Photo courtesy Cultural Services of the French Embassy, New York.)*

MELODRAMA

Another mixed form, melodrama, derives its name from the Greek word for music, *melos*. It is a combination of music and drama in which the spoken voice is used against a musical background. Jean Jacques Rousseau, who introduced the word's modern use in 1772, applied it to his *Pygmalion*, a *scène lyrique* in which words and music were linked together in the action.

The term became widely used in the nineteenth century to describe a play having a serious action ordinarily caused by the villainy of an unsympathetic character. Melodrama's characters are clearly divided—either sympathetic or unsympathetic—and the villain's destruction brings about the happy resolution. Melodrama usually shows a main character in circumstances that threaten

Figure 8-6. Melodrama's basic emotions. Paranoia, relief, and despair are the basic emotions of melodrama. In playwright Joseph Walker's The River Niger, *produced by the Negro Ensemble Company (1972) in New York, we feel relief that John Williams (center), played by Douglas Turner Ward, takes control of his life at the moment of his dying. (Photo by Bert Andrews.)*

death or ruin from which he or she is rescued at the last possible moment. Like a film's musical score, music heightens the mood of impending disaster. The term *melodrama* is most often applied to such nineteenth-century plays as Harriet Beecher Stowe's *Uncle Tom's Cabin* (1852) and Dion Boucicault's *The Octoroon* (1859). Today, we apply the term to such diverse plays as Lillian Hellman's *The Little Foxes* (1938), Lorraine Hansberry's *A Raisin In The Sun* (1959), and Joseph Walker's *The River Niger* (1972).

There is a fundamentally melodramatic view of life that sees human beings as whole, not divided; sees them enduring outer conflicts, not inner ones, in a generally hostile world; and sees these conflicts resulting in victory or defeat as they are pressed to extreme conclusions. Melodrama's characters win or lose in the conflict. The endings are clear-cut and extreme. There are no complex and ambiguous resolutions, as when Hamlet wins in losing.

Even though melodrama oversimplifies, exaggerates, and contrives experience, the fact is that we see most of the serious conflicts and crises of our daily lives in melodramatic terms. We take comfort in the fact that our failures are the fault of others and our victories the result of others' help. In short, melodrama is the dramatic form that expresses the truth of the human condition as we perceive it most of the time.

FARCE

Farce is best thought of as comedy of situation. In farce, pies in the face, beatings, mistaken identities, slips on the banana peel—those physical activities growing out of situation—are substituted for comedy's traditional concern for social values. The writer of farce presents life as mechanical, aggressive, and coincidental, and entertains us with seemingly endless variations on a single situation. For instance, a typical farce situation is the bedroom crowded with concealed lovers as the inevitable husband or wife arrives.

The "psychology of farce," as Eric Bentley calls it, is that special opportunity for the fulfillment of our un-

Figure 8-7. Farce's familiar situation. The hero successfully seduces the wife only to have their affair almost discovered by her husband who, by chance, is meeting his mistress at the same hotel. Louis Jourdan is the lover and Patricia Elliott the wife in the Circle-in-the-Square's 1978 production in New York of Georges Feydeau's 13 Rue de L'Amour. (Photo by Martha Swope.)

mentionable wishes without taking responsibility for our actions or suffering the guilt.[3] Farce as a dramatic form recklessly abandons us in a fantasy world of violence (without harm), adultery (without consequences), brutality (without reprisal), and aggression (without risk). We enjoy farce in the films of Charlie Chaplin, W. C. Fields, the Marx Brothers, Laurel and Hardy, Abbott and Costello, and Peter Sellers; in the Monty Python television series; and in the plays of Georges Feydeau and Neil Simon. Farce has also been part of some of the world's great comedies, including those of Shakespeare, Moliere, and Chekhov.

EPIC THEATRE

Bertolt Brecht, the German director and playwright, has probably had more influence on our postwar theatre than any other theatrical artist. Brecht reacted against western traditions of the **well-made play** and the **proscenium** theatre. Over a lifetime, he adapted methods from Erwin Piscator, Chinese opera, Noh drama, chronicle history plays, English music-hall routines, and films to create "epic" theatre.

Episodic and Narrative Theatre

When Brecht spoke of *epic* theatre, he was thinking of drama as *episodic* and *narrative:* as a sequence of incidents or events narrated without artificial restrictions as to time, place, or formal plot, with a structure more like that of a narrative poem than of a well-made play.

Since Brecht wanted to represent historical process in the theatre and have it judged critically by audiences, he rejected many theatrical traditions. First, he thought of the stage as a platform on which political and social issues could be debated. And he rejected the idea that a play should be "well made," reminding us that history does not end but moves on from episode to episode. Why should plays do otherwise? His epic play is, therefore, *historical, narrative,* and *episodic.* It treats humans as social beings in their economic, social, and political milieus.

Brecht's characters are both individuals and collective beings. This type of characterization dates back to the morality plays of the late middle ages, where "Everyman" is both a recognizable individual and a representative of all human beings. In keeping with the idea that the theatre is a platform to discuss political and social issues, Brecht's theatrical language is direct and discursive.

Epic Theatre as Eyewitness Account

Brecht tells us his theatre is similar to an eyewitness account of a traffic accident. This follows the idea that epic theatre is narrative as distinct from imitative. Brecht writes:

It is comparatively easy to set up a basic model for epic theatre. For practical experiments I usually picked as my example of completely simple, "natural" epic theatre an incident such as can be seen at any street corner; an eyewitness demonstrating to a collection of people how a traffic accident took place. The bystanders may not have observed what happened, or they may simply not agree with him, may "see things a different way": the point is that the demonstrator acts the behavior of driver or victim or both in such a way that the bystanders are able to form an opinion about the accident.[4]

This "eyewitness" account of past events, sometimes called *historification* to emphasize that the play's events occurred in the past, requires (1) the chronicle history play's structure, (2) theatre and film's technology, and (3) the actor's presence.

Today, the term *epic theatre* is synonymous with the plays of Bertolt Brecht: historical subject, episodic struc-

Figure 8-8. Bertolt Brecht. (Photo courtesy of the German Information Center, New York.)

Bertolt Brecht (1898–1956) was born in Augsburg, Germany, where he spent his early years. In 1918, while studying medicine at Munich University, he was called up for military service as a medical orderly. He began writing poems about the horrors of war and his first play, *Baal* (1918), dates from this period. After World War I, Brecht drifted as a student into the Bohemian world of theatre and literature, singing his poetry in Munich taverns and coffeehouses. By 1921, Brecht had seriously entered the theatre world as a reviewer, **dramaturg,** and playwright. During the 1920s in Berlin, Brecht became a Marxist, wrote plays, and solidified his theories of epic theatre. *The Threepenny Opera* (1928)— produced in collaboration with the composer Kurt Weill—was an overnight success and made both Brecht and Weill famous. With the rise of the Nazi movement, many German artists and intellectuals fled Germany. Brecht took his family and fled in 1933, first to Scandinavia and then to America, where he lived until 1947. In October of 1947, Brecht was subpoenaed to appear before the House Committee on Un-American Activities to testify on the "Communist infiltration" of the motion-picture industry. He left the United States the day following his testimony. He settled in East Berlin, where he founded the Berliner Ensemble. This great theatre company continues to perform his works at the Theater am Schiffbauerdamm, where he first produced *The Threepenny Opera.* Brecht's greatest plays date from his years of exile (1933–1948): *The Good Woman of Setzuan, Mother Courage and Her Children, Galileo,* and *The Caucasian Chalk Circle.*

Figure 8-9. Brecht's theatre. Brecht began his international career in the Theater am Schiffbauerdamm (now in East Berlin) with the 1928 production of The Threepenny Opera. *He returned to this theatre in 1954 with his new company, the Berliner Ensemble, where he produced* The Caucasian Chalk Circle. *The Berliner Ensemble still produces here. (Photo courtesy of The Berliner Ensemble.)*

ture, projected scenery and scene titles, music (largely created by Kurt Weill and Paul Dessau), and an acting style that "shows" the character rather than "becomes" the character. These devices are also part of Brecht's efforts to distance or alienate the audience emotionally from what is happening on stage.

The Alienation Effect

Brecht called this jarring of the audience out of its sympathetic feelings for what is happening on stage his alienation effect (A-effect or *Verfremdungseffekt*). He wanted to break down the audience's "willing suspension of disbelief," to force them to look at everything in a fresh light and to think. Brecht wanted audiences to absorb his social criticism and to carry their new insights out of the theatre into their own lives.

Figure 8-10. Brecht's table, published in 1930, shows the difference between dramatic theatre (for example, Ghosts*) and epic theatre. (From* Brecht on Theatre, *courtesy Hill and Wang.)*

From Brecht's
The Modern Theatre Is the Epic Theatre

Dramatic Theatre	*Epic Theatre*
Plot	Narrative
Implicates the spectator in a stage situation	Turns the spectator into an observer, but
Wears down his capacity for action	Arouses his capacity for action
Provides him with sensations	Forces him to take decisions
Experience	Picture of the world
The spectator is involved in something	He is made to face something
Suggestion	Argument
Instinctive feelings are preserved	Brought to the point of recognition
The spectator is in the thick of it, shares the experience	The spectator stands outside, studies
The human being is taken for granted	The human being is the object of the inquiry
He is unalterable	He is alterable and able to alter
Eyes on the finish	Eyes on the course
One scene makes another	Each scene for itself
Growth	Montage
Linear development	In curves
Evolutionary determinism	Jumps
Man as a fixed point	Man as a process
Thought determines being	Social being determines thought
Feeling	Reason

Figure 8-11. The chalk circle test. In the test of the chalk circle, Brecht wants the audience to reflect upon differences of social class between the governor's wife (left) and Grusha (right), and to learn from Azdak's reversal of the chalk circle. He gives the child to Grusha because she will not engage in the tug-of-war for Michael for fear of harming him. Brecht lets the audience conclude that the disputed valley will also be awarded to. the farmers who can make it most productive. (Photo courtesy of The Berliner Ensemble.)

ABSURDIST THEATRE

In 1961 Martin Esslin, an English critic, wrote a book called *The Theatre of the Absurd* about trends in the postwar theatre. He used the label to describe new theatrical ways of looking at existence.

The Medium Is the Message

In absurdist theatre the play takes its subject and form from a basic situation showing life's deadness, senselessness, and uncertainty. The absurdist writer does not tell a story or discuss social problems. Instead, the writer *presents* in a concrete stage image, such as two tramps waiting for a person who never shows up, *a sense of being* in an absurd universe.

The Absurd

Absurdist playwrights begin with the premise that our world is *absurd*. Albert Camus (1913–1960)—a French philosopher, novelist, and playwright—diagnosed the human condition as absurd in *The Myth of Sisyphus*.

A world that can be explained even with bad reasons is a familiar world. But, on the other hand, in a universe suddenly divested of illusions and lights, man feels an alien, a stranger. His exile is without remedy since he is deprived of the memory of a lost home or the hope of a promised land. This divorce between man and his life, the actor and his setting, is properly the feeling of absurdity.[5]

Eugene Ionesco defined *absurd* as "anything without a goal . . . when man is cut off from his religious or metaphysical roots, he is lost; all his struggles become senseless, futile and oppressive."[6]

The common factors in absurdist plays are: no recognizable plots; characters who are almost mechanical puppets; dreams and nightmares replacing social statement; and dialogue becoming incoherent babblings. Absurd writers *present,* without comment or moral judgment, situations showing life's senselessness and irrationality. The meaning of Ionesco's plays *is* simply what happens on stage. The old man and old woman in *The Chairs* (1952) gradually fill the stage with an increasing number

Figure 8-12. Eugene Ionesco. (Photo courtesy of the French Cultural Services.)

Eugene Ionesco (b. 1912) is a Rumanian-born school teacher and refugee from Nazism who lives in France. Twenty-five years ago he puzzled and outraged audiences with plays about bald sopranos, octogenarian suicides, homicidal professors, and human rhinoceroses as metaphors for the world's absurdity. Today, *The Bald Soprano, The Chairs, The Lesson,* and *Rhinoceros* are modern classics. Since *The Bald Soprano* was first produced in Paris at the Théâtre de Noctambules in 1950, Ionesco has written over thirty plays in addition to journals, essays, and children's stories. Ionesco says that his theatre expresses the malaise of contemporary life, language's failure to bring people closer together, the strangeness of existence, and a parodic reflection of the world. Breaking with the theatre of psychological realism, Ionesco pioneered a form of theatre closer to our dreams and nightmares.

of empty chairs. They address absent people in the chairs. At the play's end the two old people leave the message of their life's meaning to be delivered by an orator, and jump to their deaths out of the windows. The orator addresses the empty chairs, but he is a deaf mute and cannot make a coherent statement. The subject of Ionesco's play is the chairs themselves—the emptiness and unreality of the world. The conversation about Bobby Watson in *The Bald Soprano* has a similar impact and meaning.

Figure 8-13. Ionesco's absurd world. The "Bobby Watson" speech from Ionesco's The Bald Soprano *(1950) presents aural and visual images showing the banality of middle-class suburban life. Mr. and Mrs. Smith, seated in their middle-class English living room discussing their middle-class English dinner, engage in conversation about Bobby Watson. (Courtesy Grove Press.)*

[*Another moment of silence. The clock strikes seven times. Silence. The clock strikes three times. Silence. The clock doesn't strike.*]

MR. SMITH [*still reading his paper*]: Tsk, it says here that Bobby Watson died.

MRS. SMITH: My God, the poor man! When did he die?

MR. SMITH: Why do you pretend to be astonished? You know very well that he's been dead these past two years. Surely you remember that we attended his funeral a year and a half ago.

MRS. SMITH: Oh yes, of course I do remember. I remembered it right away, but I don't understand why you yourself were so surprised to see it in the paper.

MR. SMITH: It wasn't in the paper. It's been three years since his death was announced. I remembered it through an association of ideas.

MRS. SMITH: What a pity! He was so well preserved.

MR. SMITH: He was the handsomest corpse in Great Britain. He didn't look his age. Poor Bobby, he'd been dead for four years and he was still warm. A veritable living corpse. And how cheerful he was!

MRS. SMITH: Poor Bobby.

MR. SMITH: Which poor Bobby do you mean?

MRS. SMITH: It is his wife that I mean. She is called Bobby too, Bobby Watson. Since they both had the same name, you could never tell one from the other when you saw them together. It was only after his death that you could really tell which was which. And there are still people today who confuse

	her with the deceased and offer their condolences to him. Do you know her?
MR. SMITH:	I only met her once, by chance, at Bobby's burial.
MRS. SMITH:	I've never seen her. Is she pretty?
MR. SMITH:	She has regular features and yet one cannot say that she is pretty. She is too big and stout. Her features are not regular but still one can say that she is very pretty. She is a little too small and too thin. She's a voice teacher.

[*The clock strikes five times. A long silence.*]

MRS. SMITH:	And when do they plan to be married, those two?
MR. SMITH:	Next spring, at the latest.
MRS. SMITH:	We shall have to go to their wedding, I suppose.
MR. SMITH:	We shall have to give them a wedding present. I wonder what?
MRS. SMITH:	Why don't we give them one of the seven silver salvers that were given us for our wedding and which have never been of any use to us? [*Silence.*]
MRS. SMITH:	How sad for her to be left a widow so young.
MR. SMITH:	Fortunately, they had no children.
MRS. SMITH:	That was all they needed! Children! Poor woman, how could she have managed!
MR. SMITH:	She's still young. She might very well remarry. She looks so well in mourning.
MRS. SMITH:	But who would take care of the children? You know very well that they have a boy and a girl. What are their names?
MR. SMITH:	Bobby and Bobby like their parents. Bobby Watson's uncle, old Bobby Watson, is a rich man and very fond of the boy. He might very well pay for Bobby's education.
MRS. SMITH:	That would be proper. And Bobby Watson's aunt, old Bobby Watson, might very well, in her turn, pay for the education of Bobby Watson, Bobby Watson's daughter. That way Bobby, Bobby Watson's mother, could remarry. Has she anyone in mind?

(continued)

Figure 8-14. Ionesco's absurd theatre. The maid dominates the scene with the Smiths, the Martins, and the fire chief. In The Bald Soprano, *Ionesco presents the banality and purposelessness of his characters' lives in an effort to show us the world's absurdity. The photo is from the original Paris production at Théâtre des Noctambules, 1950, directed by Nicholas Bataille. (Photo courtesy of French Cultural Services of the French Embassy, New York.)*

MR. SMITH:	Yes, a cousin of Bobby Watson's.
MRS. SMITH:	Who? Bobby Watson?
MR. SMITH:	Which Bobby Watson do you mean?
MRS. SMITH:	Why, Bobby Watson, the son of old Bobby Watson, the late Bobby Watson's other uncle.
MR. SMITH:	No, it's not that one, it's someone else. It's Bobby Watson, the son of old Bobby Watson, the late Bobby Watson's aunt.
MRS. SMITH:	Are you referring to Bobby Watson the commercial traveler?
MR. SMITH:	All the Bobby Watsons are commercial travelers.
MRS. SMITH:	What a difficult trade! However, they do well at it.
MR. SMITH:	Yes, when there's no competition.
MRS. SMITH:	And when is there no competition?
MR. SMITH:	On Tuesdays, Thursdays, and Tuesdays.
MRS. SMITH:	Ah! Three days a week? And what does Bobby Watson do on those days?
MR. SMITH:	He rests, he sleeps.
MRS. SMITH:	But why doesn't he work those three days if there's no competition?
MR. SMITH:	I don't know everything. I can't answer all your idiotic questions! . . .

SUMMARY

Drama's forms are the organization of the playwright's vision and statement about the world. Dramatic form permits us to see *how* the playwright views the world and human behavior. Tragedy, comedy, tragicomedy, melodrama, farce, epic, and absurdist drama are means used in the theatre to show us the world's form and substance. Dramatic form is conveyed to us in the theatre through many visual and aural means. One of them is language, the subject of the next chapter.

QUESTIONS FOR STUDY

1. Tragedy is the name of a dramatic form. Can you name six others?

2. What terms do we use to describe a playwright's vision of his or her world?

3. What was Aristotle's understanding of tragedy?

4. How does the hero of modern tragedy differ from Oedipus or Hamlet?

5. What are comedy's subjects?

6. How does tragicomedy combine elements of both comedy and tragedy?

7. What is the origin of the word *melodrama*?

8. What different kinds of melodrama are found today on television?

9. How does farce fulfill our darkest wishes?

10. Can you describe the farce situation in a recent play, film, or TV series that you have seen?

11. What is *epic theatre*?

12. What is meant by Brecht's "alienation effect"?

13. In what ways does *The Caucasian Chalk Circle* demonstrate Brecht's concept of epic theatre?

14. How does the playwright Eugene Ionesco define *absurd*?

15. How does Ionesco present life's absurd quality in *The Bald Soprano* without debating or discussing it?

NOTES

[1]Peter Brook, *The Empty Space* (New York: Avon Publishers, 1968), p. 15.

[2]Lane Cooper, *Aristotle on the Art of Poetry* (Ithaca, New York: Cornell University Press, 1947), p. 17.

[3]Eric Bentley, "The Psychology of Farce," in *Let's Get A Divorce! and Other Plays* (New York: Hill and Wang, 1958), pp. vii–xx.

[4]John Willett, *Brecht On Theatre: The Development of an Aesthetic* (New York: Hill and Wang, 1964), p. 121.

[5]Albert Camus, *The Myth of Sisyphus and Other Essays* (New York: Alfred A. Knopf, 1955), p. 5.

[6]Eugene Ionesco, *Notes and Counter Notes: Writings on the Theatre,* translated by Donald Watson (New York: Grove Press, 1964), p. 257.

9

Theatre Language

Like other stage elements, theatre's language is special and complex. It organizes our perceptions of what is taking place before us and communicates meaning and activity to us in many ways—verbal and nonverbal. Theatre's language is a way of seeing that engages our eyes, ears, and minds.

. . . Theatre is more than words: drama is a story that is lived and relived with each performance, and we can watch it live. The theatre appeals as much to the eye as to the ear.

Eugene Ionesco, *Notes and Counter-Notes: Writings on the Theatre*

In theatre we see and hear a story being lived before us with each performance. Playwrights, directors, designers, and actors use a special *language* to organize our perceptions of it, one that is both *visual* and *aural*.

Language in the theatre is both like and unlike the way people talk in real life. First, it is the playwright's *means* for expressing what characters experience, for developing plot and action, and for the audience's experience of the theatrical event. Unlike conversation in real life, actors speak highly selective words and express themselves in highly selective bodily gestures. Hamlet's soliloquies are some of the most beautiful verse written in English for the theatre. We hear his feelings and thoughts expressed in blank verse, revealing what he actually experiences—what he feels and thinks. This unusual and eloquent language is acceptable to us because it has its own reality, expressing a world other than our own.

Let us say, then, that theatre language is the language of the characters and of the stage world and that it expresses the life of the play. Language spoken by actors as characters reveals the consciousness of the characters; it makes their decisions to act dramatically meaningful. Therefore, it is expressive of ideas, feelings, gestures, and actions. Words in the theatre are also enhanced by nonverbal language; for example, gestures, sounds, and light express moods, intentions, and meanings. Bertolt Brecht argued that to be effective stage language carried gesture in its rhythm and intention, leading the actor into attitudes and movements. "If thine eye offend thee, pluck it out" was for him the best theatrical use of those eight words in combination. Why was this? For Brecht, the concrete image ("thine eye") and the actor's intended gesture ("pluck it out") are conveyed in the careful arrangement of the words to stress attitudes and assumptions.

Others have also remarked that one characteristic of theatre language is that words have their source in gesture. Therefore, theatre language expresses not only the characters' thoughts, attitudes, and intentions, but also the *presence* of human beings in a living world. For this reason, the diagram on the next page includes along with words many other facets of theatre language. It has been argued

Figure 9-1. Theatre language, like our ways of communicating in real life, has both verbal and nonverbal characteristics. Language for the theatre is carefully selected by the playwright, actors, director, and designers. For this reason, it can be divided into the many different ways that meaning is communicated to an audience. The diagram lists sixteen ways of communicating the characters' experience, the plot and action, and the stage's living reality.

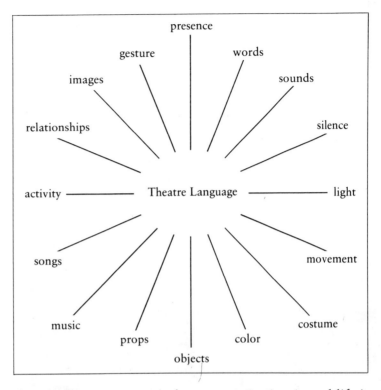

that the language we use for communication in real life is also multifaceted and theatrical: Our clothes are costumes, we speak words and make gestures, we carry props (books or smoking pipes), we wear makeup, and we are affected by the environment's sounds and silences. Although this is true, there is an important difference between language in the theatre and in life. In the theatre, language (both verbal and nonverbal) is selected and controlled. It is carefully patterned and orchestrated by playwright, actor, director, and designer to express the consciousness and presence of the characters in meaningful actions, which can be repeated night after night.

Let us examine in this chapter the verbal and nonverbal characteristics of theatre language.

VERBAL AND NONVERBAL

Language in the theatre, both verbal and nonverbal, influences the way we hear and see a play. On the page of a script, words are signs and symbols with the potential for making something happen in the theatre. When spoken by an actor, they communicate to other actors and to the audience. And besides words, other kinds of signals make up the theatre's language: sound, light, shape, movement, silence, inactivity, gesture, color, music, song, objects, costumes, props, and images.

In communication theory, a *sign* has a direct physical relationship to the thing it represents—to its referent. Thunder is a sign of rain: It has a real physical connection with changes in the atmosphere. *Symbols* differ from signs in that they have an arbitrary connection to their referents. The American flag, for example, is a symbol of our country, and many people associate everything good in America with the flag that represents it. But during the Vietnam War, some people associated the flag with everything

Figure 9-2. Actors with the American flag in Hair *(1967), directed by Tom O'Horgan, New York, make a visual statement about the attitudes of counterculture groups in the 1960s toward the establishment. In this rock-musical, songs reinforce the visual statement made by the actors, scenery, lighting, and properties. (Photo by Martha Swope.)*

wrong with America. When they wore motorcycle helmets or clothing painted with the flag, they revised its meaning. This was possible because its meaning was arbitrary—it was a symbol, not a sign.

In the theatre both verbal and nonverbal symbols and signs are used to enhance our perception of the actors' living presence. In Anton Chekhov's *The Cherry Orchard* (1904), the orchard (usually located offstage) is a verbal symbol variously interpreted as the passing of the old way of life or of the coming of a new social order. Characters refer to the orchard as a family treasure, a local tradition, a beautiful object, or the means of saving the estate from auction. The orchard is symbolic of the ways Chekhov's characters deal with or fail to deal with life's demands. In addition to this verbal symbol, the sound of the ax cutting down the trees at the play's end is a nonverbal sign, communicating the physical removal of the trees. The sound of the ax is a sign of the destruction of the family's treasure, and, in a larger sense, a symbol of the end of a social order.

The Cherry Orchard is a fine example of how verbal symbol and aural sign reinforce one another in communicating to us the play's meaning.

Anton Pavlovich Chekhov (1860–1904) was born in southern Russia and studied medicine at Moscow University. During his student years he wrote short stories to earn money. He began his play-writing career in the 1880s with one-act farces, *The Marriage Proposal* and *The Bear. Ivanov* (1887) was his first full-length play to be produced.

Chekhov redefined stage realism during the years of his association with the Moscow Art Theatre (1898–1904). The meaning of his plays is not in direct, purposive action, but in the truth of the representation of a certain kind of rural Russian life, which he knew first hand. Stanislavsky's style of interpreting the inner truth of Chekhov's characters and the mood of his plays resulted in one of the great theatrical collaborations.

During his last years Chekhov lived in Yalta, where he had gone for his health, and made occasional trips to Moscow to participate in the productions. He died of tuberculosis in a German spa in 1904, soon after the production of *The Cherry Orchard*, and was buried in Moscow.

During his short life Chekhov wrote four masterpieces of modern stage realism: *The Sea Gull, Uncle Vanya, The Three Sisters, The Cherry Orchard.*

The Cherry Orchard, Chekhov's last play, was produced at the Moscow Art Theatre in 1904.

After some years abroad the widowed Madame Ranevsky returns to her Russian estate to find that it has been heavily mortgaged to pay her debts, and that it is to be auctioned. Generous and irresponsible, she seems incapable of recognizing her financial situation. A halfhearted attempt is made to collect money owed them by a neighboring landowner, but he is also in financial straits. Gaev, Madame Ranevsky's brother, makes some suggestions, but his chief hope lies in an uncertain legacy from a relative, or a rich marriage for Anya, Madame Ranevsky's young daughter. The only realistic proposal comes from Lopahin, a merchant whose father was once a serf of the Ranevsky family. He suggests cutting down the famous cherry orchard and dividing the land into plots for summer cottages. The family rejects the idea of destroying such beauty and tradition.

With no specific plan in mind for saving the estate, the family drifts aimlessly toward the day set for the auction. On the evening of the sale, Madame Ranevsky gives a party she cannot afford. In the middle of the festivities, Lopahin arrives; when questioned he reveals that he has bought the estate and intends to carry out his plan for cutting down the orchard.

With the estate and orchard now sold, the family prepares to leave. Forgotten in the confusion is the old and ailing Firs, the devoted family servant. As the sound of the ax rings from the orchard, he lies down to rest and is soon motionless in the empty house.

EXAMPLES OF THEATRE LANGUAGE

To understand communication in the theatre, we must ask basic questions about theatre language: What do we hear? What do we see? What is taking shape before us? What growing image creates the life of the play? When the various elements of theatre language are really working together, however, we do not ask these questions, for there is no time; we experience sensation without particularly analyzing the experience.

We are so used to equating language with words (and communication with words) that it is difficult to shift ground in the theatre where the word is what Brook called "a small visible portion of a gigantic unseen formation."[1] Let us consider several examples from familiar plays of theatre language's variety and immediacy.

Hamlet

The Shakespearean **soliloquy** is a means of taking the audience into the character's mind to see and hear its contents. In Hamlet's "How all occasions do inform against me," he begins with concern for his delayed revenge, then meditates on man's nature, and on the "thing" to be done. The precision of Hamlet's argument with himself reveals the brilliance of a mind that perceives the cause, proof, and means of revenge. The speech's length betrays the habit of mind that has delayed revenge against Claudius, filling time and space with words rather than actions. Measuring himself against his kinsman Fortinbras, the man of action, Hamlet finds the example by which to act.

We must know the meaning of Hamlet's words, and the emotions, consciousness, and situation articulated in those words. It is important that this speech is delivered as a soliloquy; for Hamlet is indeed alone in the charge from his father's ghost and in the eventual killing of Claudius.

Figure 9-3. Hamlet's soliloquy. The soliloquy is a stage convention for expressing a character's inner thoughts and feelings. As the actor speaks, we hear the way the character's mind works and understand those hidden thoughts that result in action.

HAMLET: How all occasions do inform against me,
And spur my dull revenge! What is a man,
If his chief good and market of his time
Be but to sleep and feed? A beast, no more.
Sure he that made us with such large discourse,
Looking before and after, gave us not
That capability and godlike reason
To fust in us unused. Now, whether it be
Bestial oblivion, or some craven scruple
Of thinking too precisely on the event,
A thought which, quartered, hath but one part wisdom
And ever three parts coward—I do not know
Why yet I live to say, "This thing's to do,"
Sith I have cause, and will, and strength, and means
To do't. Examples gross as earth exhort me.
Witness this army of such mass and charge,
Led by a delicate and tender prince,
Whose spirit, with divine ambition puffed,
Makes mouths at the invisible event,
Exposing what is mortal and unsure

(continued)

To all that fortune, death, and danger dare,
Even for an eggshell. Rightly to be great
Is not to stir without great argument,
But greatly to find quarrel in a straw
When honor's at the stake. How stand I then,
That have a father killed, a mother stained
Excitements of my reason and my blood,
And let all sleep, while to my shame I see
The imminent death of twenty thousand men
That for a fantasy and trick of fame
Go to their graves like beds, fight for a plot
Whereon the numbers cannot try the cause,
Which is not tomb enough and continent
To hide the slain? O, from this time forth,
My thoughts be bloody, or be nothing worth!
(*Hamlet*, IV, iv, 32–66)

Figure 9-4. The actor's language. Hamlet's costume in the final two acts is that of a man of action. From the audience's viewpoint he is visibly dressed for action. The actor's dialogue, costume, gestures, and movements complement the character's determination to rid Denmark of the corrupt king. Albert Finney plays Hamlet in the 1976 production at London's National Theatre. (Photo by Anthony Crickmay.)

The costume Hamlet wears is that of a man of action. He is no longer dressed in the "solemn black" of mourning, nor in the disheveled dress of his "antic disposition." Stage tradition has him visibly dressed for action.

The speech moves in thirty-five lines from inactivity to activity, concluding with: "O, from this time forth,/My thoughts be bloody, or be nothing worth!" Hamlet, the hitherto *invisible* man of action, takes shape before our eyes and ears. The language of Hamlet's speech includes costume, space, physical presence, words, and gestures.

Ghosts

The language of the nineteenth-century play is influenced by a theatre technology unknown in Shakespeare's day, and reflects a concern for reproducing speech appropriate to the characters' socioeconomic background and psychological makeup. Ibsen introduces nonverbal signs and symbols in stage directions that are like descriptive passages in realistic novels.

The final scene of *Ghosts* begins with stage directions that indicate that Mrs. Alving puts out the table lamp as the sun rises. She is alone with her son, Oswald, who is talking about the sun. In Ibsen's play the *sun* is a symbol for the *truth*—for the hidden secrets of the past and the fading light of Oswald's brain, which is being consumed by the disease inherited from his father.

Oswald is seated in a chair facing the audience, and we "see" the change that comes over him. As Oswald slumps into the immobile state of the catatonically ill, Mrs. Alving's "truth" *is made visible*. She has not eradicated the ghosts of the past, and she is faced with a terrible choice in the present: to give Oswald drugs that will kill him, or to permit him to live. Ibsen's language reflects Mrs. Alving's horror over the truth and her indecision. Using monosyllables Ibsen indicates the choice Mrs. Alving will make. Five "no's," indicating that she can't give Oswald the drug, are placed against the one "yes." That repressive nineteenth-century society that has dictated Mrs. Alving's principal life decisions becomes visible in her frantic inability to speak or to act.

Light, gesture, movement, physical relationships—in addition to the spoken word—are important to the play's meaning. The background lighting effect ("the sun rises") reinforces the truth of Mrs. Alving's tragic dilemma: The visual design is repeated in Oswald's words "the sun." Truth and light have come too late for them. In Ibsen's play, the prose dialogue, supported by nonverbal scenic effects, reveals character and furthers plot.

Figure 9-5. Final scene from Ghosts. By using stage directions, playwright Henrik Ibsen relates the characters' words to their bodily gestures and the stage lighting. His concern is to make visible the symbolic truth of the light (the sunrise illuminating the situation) and the darkness (Oswald's disease). Ibsen's symbols are found both in dialogue and stage directions. (Courtesy New American Library.)

OSVALD: . . . And now let's live together as long as we can. Thank you, Mother.

(He settles down in the armchair that MRS. ALVING *had moved over to the sofa. The day is breaking; the lamp still burns on the table.)*

MRS. ALVING: Now do you feel all right?

OSVALD: Yes.

MRS. ALVING *(bending over him)*: What a fearful nightmare this has been for you, Osvald—but it was all a dream. Too much excitement—it hasn't been good for you. But now you can have your rest, at home with your mother near, my own, my dearest boy. Anything you want you can have, just like when you were a little child. There now, the pain is over. You see how quickly it went. Oh, I knew it would—And look, Osvald, what a lovely day we'll have. Bright sunlight. Now you really can see your home.

(She goes to the table and puts out the lamp. Sunrise. The glaciers and peaks in the background shine in the brilliant light of morning. With his back toward the distant view, OSVALD *sits motionless in the armchair.)*

OSVALD *(abruptly)*: Mother, give me the sun.

MRS. ALVING *(by the table, looks at him, startled)*: What did you say?

OSVALD *(repeats in a dull monotone)*: The sun. The sun.

MRS. ALVING *(moves over to him)*: Osvald, what's the matter?

*(*OSVALD *appears to crumple inwardly in the chair; all his muscles loosen; the expression leaves his face; and his eyes stare blankly.)*

*Figure 9-6.   In a final scene of
Ghosts, Oswald tells his mother
about his mysterious disease,
and she reveals to him its cause:
the kind of corrupt life his
father really led. Oswald
becomes the living embodiment
of the play's tragedy: that the
forces of the past are at work in
the present, influencing and
destroying the living. The photo
shows the Stratford, Ontario,
Shakespeare Festival Theatre
production (1977) with (left to
right) Margaret Tyzack,
Nicholas Pennell, and Marti
Maraden. (Photo by Robert C.
Ragsdale.)*

MRS. ALVING *(shaking with fear)*: What is it? *(in a shriek)*
Osvald! What's wrong! *(drops to her knees
beside him and shakes him)* Osvald!
Osvald! Look at me! Don't you know me?

OSVALD *(in the same monotone)*: The sun—the sun.

MRS. ALVING *(springs to her feet in anguish, tears at her
hair with both hands and screams)*: I can't
bear this! *(whispers as if paralyzed by
fright)* I can't bear it! Never! *(suddenly)*
Where did he put them? *(Her hand skims
across his chest.)* Here! *(She shrinks back
several steps and shrieks.)* No, no, no!—
Yes!—No, no! *(She stands a few steps
away from him, her fingers thrust into her
hair, staring at him in speechless horror.)*

OSVALD *(sitting motionless, as before)*: The sun—the sun.

The Cherry Orchard

Chekhov ends *The Cherry Orchard* with language that also combines verbal and nonverbal effects: sounds with silence, words with noise. Firs is the elderly valet left behind by the family in their hurried departure from the estate that has been sold at auction. His last speech is placed between stage directions suggesting offstage sounds of departure, of a breaking string, and of the stroke of an ax.

The *pauses* in Firs's speech indicate a coming to an end of a life and also a way of life. The fact that he is alone, locked in the house, and motionless tells us more vividly that "life has passed him by" than his saying it.

In Chekhov's plays, what people do—their gestures—is frequently more important than what they say. Like gesture, the sound of the breaking string juxtaposed with the sound of the ax is more important than the character's words. Even the order of sound effects is important.

Figure 9-7. The final scene of The Cherry Orchard. *In the modern theatre, stage directions have become important means by which the playwright communicates his imaginative world to the director, actors, and designers. Chekhov describes the stage's appearance; the various sounds; Firs's costume, manner, and words; and the final moments of the play. (Courtesy Oxford University Press.)*

(*The stage is empty. There is the sound of the doors being locked up, then of the carriages driving away. There is silence. In the stillness there is the dull stroke of an ax in a tree, clanging with a mournful lonely sound. Footsteps are heard.* FIRS *appears in the doorway on the right. He is dressed as always—in a pea-jacket and white waistcoat with slippers on his feet. He is ill.*)

FIRS (*goes up to the doors, and tries the handles*): Locked! They have gone . . . (*sits down on sofa*). They have forgotten me. . . . Never mind . . . I'll sit here a bit . . . I'll be bound Leonid Andreyevitch hasn't put his fur coat on and has gone off in his thin overcoat (*sighs anxiously*). I didn't see after him. . . . These young people . . . (*mutters something that can't be distinguished*). Life has slipped by as though I hadn't lived. (*lies down*) I'll lie down a bit. . . . There's no strength in you, nothing left you—all gone! Ech! I'm good for nothing (*lies motionless*).

(*A sound is heard that seems to come from the sky, like a breaking harp-string, dying away mournfully. All is still again, and there is heard nothing but the strokes of the ax far away in the orchard.*)

Curtain

Figure 9-8. *Chekhov's ending. At* The Cherry Orchard's *end, Firs, the old valet, lies down alone—the final symbol of the passing of a way of life. This visual image of the dying man is reinforced by the sound of a breaking string. Finally, the sounds of ax strokes suggest the arrival of a new way of doing things—a more vital force is taking over from the old. Sound and visual images, more than dialogue, communicate meaning in many modern plays. This scene was staged by director Andrei Serban in the 1977 New York Shakespeare Festival production at the Vivian Beaumont Theatre, Lincoln Center, New York City. (Photo by George E. Joseph.)*

The breaking string's mournful sound, symbolic of the release of tensions and the passing of a way of life, subsides into silence *before* the ax stroke, the sound of the aggressive new order, intrudes on the scene. At the end of *The Cherry Orchard,* the audience hears and sees a world in transition.

The Caucasian Chalk Circle

Brecht adds music, songs, placards, film projections, and *gest* to what we have been learning about theatre language. Brecht's concept of gest or gestic language is a matter of the actor's overall attitude to what is going on around him and what he is asked to do on stage. Brecht insisted that words follow the gest of the person speaking.

Brecht's definition of gest: "Gest" is not supposed to mean gesticulation: it is not a matter of explanatory or emphatic movements of the hands, but of overall attitudes. A language is gestic when it is grounded in a gest and conveys particular attitudes adopted by the speaker towards other men. The sentence "pluck

Figure 9-9. Brecht's gestic language. The circle drawn in white chalk on the stage floor signifies a test of true motherliness and rightful ownership based upon mutual interests and well-being. The governor's wife (left) and Grusha (right) pull at the child as Judge Azdak looks on in the 1965 production of The Caucasian Chalk Circle *at The Guthrie Theater. Grusha (Zoe Caldwell) releases the child before harming him. (Photo courtesy of The Guthrie Theater.)*

the eye that offends thee out" is less effective from the gestic point of view than "if thine eye offend thee, pluck it out." The latter starts by presenting the eye, and the first clause has the definite gest of making an assumption; the main clause then comes as a surprise, a piece of advice, and a relief.[2]

The characters' gestic language becomes visible in the test of the chalk circle. The materialistic attitudes of the lawyers and the governor's wife toward the child are contrasted with Grusha's humanitarian feelings. Grusha refuses to tug at the child while the governor's wife pulls the child twice out of the circle. The wife's attitudes, words, and gestures betray the fact that her access to wealth and power depends upon the return of the child to her. We see that she is selfish and "grasping."

Brecht's working notes call for musicians to be included on stage and for background scenery to be indicated by projections. A narrator interrupts the play's action to sing songs that pinpoint social attitudes and wrongs. A song is sung to reveal what Grusha *thinks* but does not say. As the narrator "sings" Grusha's thoughts, Brecht allows us to understand, without sentiment, Grusha's selfless concern for the child's humanity. We understand also why Brecht's judge renders the verdict in her favor.

Brecht's theatre language uses traditional dialogue and song in addition to modern theatre technology (placards, film projections, stage floor turntable) to comment upon social conditions and attitudes.

Figure 9-10. The language of song. Brecht used music and song as well as dialogue to express characters' thoughts and feelings. The narrator in The Caucasian Chalk Circle *(scene vi) sings the girl's thoughts as a means of expressing, without becoming sentimental, Grusha's love for the child. (Courtesy Random House.)*

THE SINGER: Hear now what the angry woman
      thought and did not say: *(Sings)*
If he walked in golden shoes
Cold his heart would be and stony.
Humble folk he would abuse
He wouldn't know me.

Oh, it's hard to be hard-hearted
All day long from morn to night.
To be mean and high and mighty
Is a hard and cruel plight.

Let him be afraid of hunger
Not of the hungry man's spite
Let him be afraid of darkness
But not fear the light.

NEW TRENDS

Antonin Artaud, one prophet of our new theatre, militated against traditional dialogue that furthers plot and reveals character. He favored inducing in audiences a shock reaction and a visceral response. Followers of Artaud have taken theatre language in two directions, toward *violent images* and toward *physicalization*.

Antonin Artaud (1896–1948) was a French poet-actor-play-wright-essayist. During the 1920s in Paris, Artaud wrote plays, essays, poems, filmscripts; he acted, produced, and directed. He established one theatre company that failed, the Alfred Jarry Theatre, and conceived of the Theatre of Cruelty. In 1938, Artaud published *The Theatre and Its Double,* a collection of lectures and articles on theatre. The most powerful essay is "The Theatre and the Plague" in which Artaud draws parallels between theatrical action and a plague as purifying events. Ill health drew him to a dependency on drugs. Confined to many institutions, the most famous being Rodez, Artaud was released five years before his death in 1948.

Even though Artaud's theatrical successes were few, it is almost impossible to discuss our new theatre without mentioning his theories. He called for theatre to purge the audience's feelings of hatred,

violence, and cruelty by using nonverbal sounds, lighting effects, unusual theatre spaces, violent movements. Artaud wanted to assault the audience's senses, to cleanse it morally and spiritually, for the improvement of humankind.

Figure 9-11.   Antonin Artaud (right) playing the part of a young monk who defended Joan of Arc in Carl Dreyer's 1928 film, The Passion of Joan of Arc. *(Photo from The Museum of Modern Art/Film Stills Archives.)*

Violent Images in Marat/Sade

The first direction confronts the audience with violent images and sounds that communicate viscerally rather than intellectually.

Peter Brook's 1965 production of *Marat/Sade* for the Royal Shakespeare Company played up the grimness of Peter Weiss's play. A quartet of inmates wearing colored sacks sing sardonic songs while the action described by the songs is mimed by other inmates. Some inmates wear shapeless white tunics and strait jackets to contrast with the formal nineteenth-century costumes of de Sade, the asylum director, and his family. The verbal debate between Jean-Paul Marat and the Marquis de Sade is repeatedly

Figure 9-12. Marat in his bath. Jean-Paul Marat, the social reformer, played by English actor Ian Richardson, debates the importance of violent revolution while asylum inmate Simonne Evrard (actress Susan Williamson) attends to his skin disease. (Photo reproduced by permission of the Governors of the Royal Shakespeare Theatre, Stratford-upon-Avon, England.)

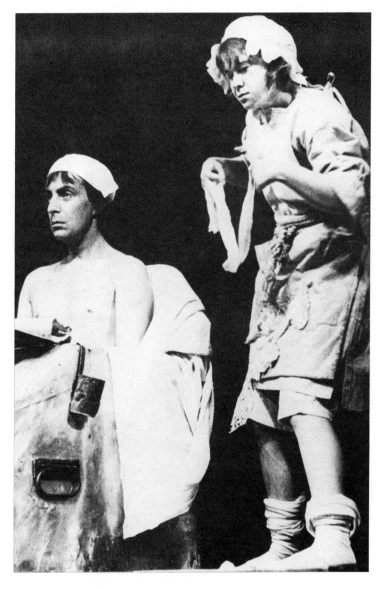

interrupted by the lunatics acting out Marat's story and their own passions. In the mass guillotining sequence, inmates make metallic rasping noises and pour buckets of paint—blood—down drains, while other inmates jump into a pit in the center of the stage so that their heads are piled above stage level, next to the guillotine.

Marat/Sade uses shock to make its point. Marat, the political idealist committed to violent social reform (he is played by a naked asylum inmate seated in a bathtub), and the Marquis de Sade, the skeptic committed to anarchic individualism, debate the value of revolution during one of de Sade's theatrical productions. For de Sade, man, not the political or economic system, is the root of all social evil. He argues, therefore, that revolution is futile and merely perpetuates violence. To make his point that the guillotine—the Revolution's tool—made dying wholesale and meaningless, de Sade describes the four-hour execution of Damiens, King Louis XV's would-be assassin. Damiens's death, for de Sade, is an example of significant individual suffering lost in the impersonal mass deaths of the guillotine.

Figure 9-13. Language's violent effects. Peter Weiss's concrete verbal images of torture and death express de Sade's attitudes toward human corruption and unreason. The actor playing de Sade can also express, by luxuriating in the vowel sounds, how the witnesses to the execution luxuriated in the spectacle of Damiens's death. By doing so, the actor's word-sounds have a visceral effect on the audience. (Courtesy Atheneum.)

DE SADE (to Marat):

Let me remind you of the execution of Damiens
after his unsuccessful attempt to assassinate
Louis the Fifteenth (now deceased)
Remember how Damiens died
How gentle the guillotine is
compared with his torture
It lasted four hours while the crowd goggled
and Casanova at an upper window
felt under the skirts of the ladies watching
   [*pointing in the direction of the tribunal
   where* COULMIER *sits*]
His chest arms thighs and calves were slit open
Molten lead was poured into each slit
boiling oil they poured over him burning tar
   wax sulphur
They burnt off his hands
tied ropes to his arms and legs
harnessed four horses to him and geed them up
They pulled at him for an hour but they'd
   never done it before
and he wouldn't come apart
until they sawed through his shoulders and hips

So he lost the first arm then the second
and he watched what they did to him and
    then turned to us
and shouted so everyone could understand
And when they tore off the first leg and then
    the second leg
he still lived though his voice was getting weak
and at the end he hung there a bloody torso
    with a nodding head
just groaning and staring at the crucifix
which the father confessor was holding up to him
    [*In the background a half-murmured litany*
        is heard.]
That
was a festival with which
today's festivals can't compete
Even our inquisition gives us no pleasure
nowadays
Although we've only just started
there's no passion in our post-revolutionary
    murders
Now they are all official
We condemn to death without emotion
and there's no singular personal death to be
    had
only an anonymous cheapened death
which we could dole out to entire nations
on a mathematical basis
until the time comes
for all life
to be extinguished

Words are only one aspect of the visceral impact of Weiss's language. The verbal images that describe Damiens's violent death are reinforced by the starkness of the white bathhouse where the performance of de Sade's play takes place. The onstage sexual and physical violence of the inmates—Charlotte Corday stabs Marat to death in his bathtub and the inmates revolt against their keepers—blends image and gesture, words and actions, into a total theatrical effect.

Joseph Chaikin (b. 1935), American actor and director, founded The Open Theatre in New York City in 1963 after working with The Living Theatre for three years. Among works that he has directed or codirected for The Open Theatre are *America Hurrah!*, *Viet Rock*, *The Serpent*, *Terminal*, and *The Mutation Show*. In 1972 he published *The Presence of the Actor*, notes on his work with The Open Theatre.

From 1963 to 1973 The Open Theatre was a leading experimental company, engaging actors and playwrights in a group effort to explore questions about acting, audience, and performance. It was a "poor theatre," putting aside all such nonessentials as costume, makeup, scenery, and properties. The emphasis was on the actor, as well as contemporary political and social problems. After ten years the group disbanded, largely to avoid becoming an "institution."

Physicalization and The Open Theatre

In the late 1960s and early 1970s, theatre language took on other characteristics in the American theatre. In many workshops and productions by groups, such as The Living Theatre and The Open Theatre, ordinary stage dialogue is replaced by two basic kinds of physical work: *exercises in sound-and-movement* and *character transformation*. The work of The Open Theatre, Joseph Chaikin's group, involves actors, directors, playwrights, and sometimes audiences to develop theatre pieces using physicalization to convey situation, relationships, character, sound, and action.

The Open Theatre   Under Chaikin's leadership, The Open Theatre evolved a "physical" theatre language: sound, movement, improvised situations, words, transformations. The group members' backgrounds, interests, training, and life-styles were put to use in workshop performances. Writers participated in the workshops before writing anything down—their scripts were related to the group's improvisations from which they selected the most effective work within a social or political context. The scripts were usually performed by the same actors who had been in the workshops. Jean-Claude van Itallie, author of *America Hurrah!* and *The Serpent*, wrote most consistently with The Open Theatre during those years. In a special 1977 issue of *The Drama Review* on playwriting, van Itallie talked about writing for the theatre as the expression of a new way of seeing. He said:

A play is the expression of a new way of seeing, not only because you've decided to see things in a new way, but because you are seeing something clearly, being who you are right then. There's a discrepancy between your point of view and the way that, say, the audience is accustomed to seeing. It's called "new" more by them than by you. You have to find the language with which to express the particular vision you have of ordinary reality. It may seem to you to be absolute common sense and obvious, but often the more obvious it seems to you, the more "new" it will seem to the world.[3]

Chaikin developed two performance techniques that later came to be known as "Open Theatre techniques": "sound-and-movement," in which the actor developed physical movements and sounds to communicate emotions through visual and aural language, and character "transformation," in which the actor switched from one identity to another without establishing motivation or a realistic transition. "Image plays" were the results of these techniques. Each play presented an image or series of images coordinated by a central theme or idea. The literal meanings of spoken words were of relatively minor importance. Communication with the audience depended upon the effectiveness of the actor's sound-and-movement patterns and the transformational roles.

Chaikin's basic strategy was *to make things visible in action.* His questions, subjects, and ideas were not talked through but acted out by the group—physicalized. Chaikin writes in his notebook:

We have been taught in acting school how singular are the emotions of a character—the simple, unilateral expression of sadness or happiness. Yet life is not like that. That's not what things seem to be, nor what I seem to be. Experience is richer, more complex, less ordered, more mysterious. . . . We have to try to express the complexity of things as we see them now . . . not simply to analyze, criticize and to sweep under the rug. We can do that by seeking ways to make things visible in action.[4]

America Hurrah!   In *Interview,* one of three short plays produced as *America Hurrah!* (Pocket Theatre, New York City, 1966), Chaikin's group with playwright van Itallie recreated the mechanical behavior, isolation, and depersonalization of urban America. *Interview* begins and ends with automatic questions: What's your name? What job do you want? What experience have you had? How many years' experience? Age? Dependents? Social Security Number?, and so on. A typical interview begins and ends the play. In the middle are short scenes revealing the sounds and rhythms of people's lives: a telephone switchboard operator, cocktail party loner, analyst's patient.

Figure 9-14.   Jean-Claude van Itallie, playwright. (Photo courtesy of International Creative Management, New York.)

Jean-Claude van Itallie (b. 1936 in Brussels, Belgium), educated at Harvard University, has written largely for New York avant-garde theatres such as The Open Theatre. He is best known for *America Hurrah!* (1966), *The Serpent* (1968), and the English version of Chekhov's *The Cherry Orchard* performed by the New York Shakespeare Festival (1976) and directed by Andrei Serban.

Figure 9-15. The language of transformations in Interview. *Playwright Jean-Claude van Itallie writes into the stage directions the various characters that the actors become (Third Interviewer, Telephone Operator, and so on). He also describes the sounds-and-movements that the actors must improvise to resemble telephone circuits and their sounds. (Courtesy Coward, McCann & Geoghegan.)*

(The actress who played the Third Interviewer slips out of the subway as though it were her stop and sits on a box, stage right, as a Telephone Operator. The other actors form a telephone circuit by holding hands in two concentric circles around the boxes, stage left; they change the hissing sound of the subway into the whistling of telephone circuits.)

TELEPHONE OPERATOR: Just one moment I will connect you with Information.

(The Telephone Operator alternates her official voice with her ordinary voice; she uses the latter when she talks to her friend Roberta, another operator whom she reaches by flipping a switch. When she is talking to Roberta, the whistling of the telephone circuits changes into a different rhythm and the arms of the actors, which are forming the circuit, move into a different position.)

TELEPHONE OPERATOR: Just one moment and I will connect you with Information. Ow! Listen, Roberta, I said, I've got this terrible cramp. Hang up and dial again, please; we find nothing wrong with that number at all. You know what I ate, I said to her, you were there. Baked macaroni, Wednesday special, maple-nut fudge, I said. I'm sorry but the number you have reached is not—I can feel it gnawing at me at the bottom of my belly, I told her. Do you think it's serious, Roberta? Appendicitis? I asked. Thank you for giving us the area code but the number you have reached is not in this area. Roberta, I asked her, do you think I have cancer? One moment, please, I'm sorry the number you have reached—ow! Well, if it's lunch, Roberta, I said to her, you know what they can do with it tomorrow. Ow! One moment, please, I said. Ow, I said, Roberta, I said, it really hurts.

(The Telephone Operator falls off her seat in pain. The whistling of the telephone circuit becomes a siren. Three actors carry the Telephone Operator over to the boxes, stage left, which now serve as an operating table. Three

actors imitate the Telephone Operator's breathing pattern while four actors behind her make stylized sounds and movements as surgeons and nurses in the midst of an operation. The Telephone Operator's breathing accelerates, then stops. After a moment the actors begin spreading over the stage and making the muted sounds of a cocktail party: music, laughter, talk. The actors find a position and remain there, playing various aspects of a party in slow motion and muted tones. They completely ignore the First Interviewer who, as a Girl At The Party, goes from person to person as if she were in a garden of living statues.)

Figure 9-16. Mechanical behavior. Interview *was produced as part of* America Hurrah! *(New York, 1966) on a bare stage with gray lighting. Wearing nondescript clothing, the actors worked in a depersonalized space with modules (a set of boxes) as furniture and props. The sparseness and colorlessness of the stage reinforce the playwright's statement about the quality of urban American life. (Photo courtesy of International Creative Management, New York.)*

Interview's essential language, like that of most Open Theatre pieces, is:

Physicalization—actors mime the action of electronic circuitry.

Basic scene ideas and images—job interview, psychiatrist's couch.

Transformations—the interviewer becomes a telephone operator who becomes a party loner.

Sounds (by humans rather than a sound system)—actors make the sounds of ambulance sirens, subway noises, hum of telephone circuits.

Visual and aural images—of social behavior in the America of the 1960s.

Masks—to capture expressionless and plastic lives.

Words and phrases—brief sounds and movements repeated a number of times to label social types.

Interview is an example of theatre language that makes a whole way of life visible through actors' physical and vocal techniques.

SUMMARY

Language in the theatre is a way of seeing. It is not merely the spoken word, although we tend to equate theatre language with words and words with the playwright's message or meaning. But theatre is not a philosophical treatise or critical essay. It is a means of participating in a *universal way of seeing.*

As in life, in the theatre we are subject to sounds, images, and people. All contribute to the universal illusion that life is taking place before us. These images may be familiar, strange, or fantastic. Oedipus's bleeding eyes, Oswald's likeness to his father, Marat's skin disease are visible images of certain kinds of experiences.

One critic says: "Theatre is the art of the self-evident, of what everybody knows—the place where *things mean what they sound and look like they mean.*"⁵ Chekhov's meaning at the end of *The Cherry Orchard is* the sound of the breaking string, for a way of life is dying.

Chekhov shows us that theatre does not communicate images and aliveness through words alone. As Ionesco says, *"Words are only one member of theatre's shock troops."*⁶

QUESTIONS FOR STUDY

1. Study the diagram on page 201. What aspects of theatre language communicate meaning to us?

2. What is a *sign*? Why is a sign important in the theatre?

3. What is the function of a *soliloquy*?

4. Read the section from *Ghosts* on page 208 and comment upon Ibsen's use of lighting, movement, properties, and sentence structure. What are the characteristics of Ibsen's realistic language?

5. What nonverbal language does Chekhov use in the final stage direction of *The Cherry Orchard*?

6. What is an example of Brecht's *gestic* language?

7. What are two recent trends in language for the new theatre?

8. How does Peter Weiss achieve a visceral impact with language in *Marat/Sade*?

9. Study the excerpt from *Interview* on page 220. How does the language of *Interview* communicate to us the mechanical quality of modern American life?

10. What do the following terms mean: *physicalization, sound and movement* exercises, *character transformation*?

The New York Shakespeare Festival Theatre
opened a new production of Chekhov's play on February
17, 1977, at the Vivian Beaumont Theatre, Lincoln
Center. It was directed by Andrei Serban and designed
by Santo Loquasto. A disciple of Peter Brook, Serban
builds a production from movement, myths, and sounds.
For this reason his work is sometimes called "theatre of
ritual." It involves the use of carefully posed sculptural
groups, choreographic masses of people and a specific
acting style.

Figure 9-17a (right). The period costume worn by Irene
Worth as Madame Ranevsky is one of the carefully
selected realistic details that suggest the diminishing way
of life that Chekhov's play deals with.

Figure 9-17b (below). Designer Loquasto's basically
white setting and draped furniture create a sculptural
effect as Irene Worth (as Madame Ranevsky, center)
rejoices over the cherry trees in full blossom.

Figure 9-17c.   The orchestra plays in the anteroom while the family waits to hear news of the orchard's sale. Irene Worth (seated right) as Madame Ranevsky is dressed in black in anticipation of the loss of the estate.

Figure 9-17d. Serban's production makes a statement about the death of a civilization. In this photo the setting sun, decaying bench, and tombstones visually reinforce the play's interpretation as the dying of a way of life. But the telegraph poles in the background suggest that the future has already made inroads on the past. Working as a creative director, Serban also adds visually to Chekhov's ending. After the dying Firs lies down (see Figure 9-8), a young girl rushes in at the back of the stage carrying flowers, and a symbolic picture of the new, industrialized Russia lights up dimly in the background. (Photos by George E. Joseph.)

NOTES

[1]Peter Brook, *The Empty Space* (New York: Atheneum, 1968), p. 12.

[2]Bertolt Brecht, "On Gestic Music" in *Brecht on Theatre: The Development of an Aesthetic,* translated by John Willett (New York: Hill and Wang, 1964), p. 104.

[3]Jean-Claude Van Itallie, "A Reinvention of Form," *The Drama Review* (Playwrights and Playwriting Issue), 21, No. 4 (December 1977), 66–74.

[4]Robert Pasolli, *A Book on the Open Theatre* (New York: Bobbs-Merrill, 1970), pp. 11–12.

[5]David Cole, *The Theatrical Event: A Mythos, A Vocabulary, A Perspective* (Middletown, Conn.: Wesleyan University Press, 1975), p. 141.

[6]Eugene Ionesco, *Notes and Counter-Notes: Writings on the Theatre,* translated by Donald Watson (New York: Grove Press, 1964), p. 23.

10

Visualizing the Script

As readers we must "see" the script as theatre in our mind's eye and ear. It takes a special skill to bring characters, settings, words, and events to life as we read the printed page.

The reader of a play must be ready to see and hear in his mind's eye and in his mind's ear.
J. L. Styan, *The Dramatic Experience*

When Anton Chekhov, the great Russian playwright, was asked about the meaning of life, he replied that a carrot is a carrot and nothing else is known. In life, unless the circumstances are extreme and arresting, we ordinarily do not ask ourselves what a certain event or accident *means.* We simply respond to and flow with our experiences. But when see or read a play, we frequently do the reverse. We ask *what it means,* forgetting that theatre is theatre and not philosophy, religion, psychology, or history, although it may include some of each.

> You ask: what is life? It is the same as asking what is a carrot. A carrot is a carrot, and that's all that's known.
>
> Anton Chekhov, *Letters*

Like Chekhov's carrot, however, the theatre does not mean, but *is.* Theatre exists apart from anything else, with its own forms and unique qualities. As we read the script of a play, although we are dealing with words on a printed page, we must go beyond asking what they mean. We must "see" them in our mind's eye and ear as theatre. We must *hear* the words spoken by the actors; *observe* the event's shape and dynamics; and *see* the visual elements of scenery, lighting, sound, costume, properties.

What follows is a discussion of six tools for seeing and hearing the script as theatre.

A MODEL

How do we use our imaginations to see and hear a script enacted on stage? It helps to think of the script as *a paper blueprint* comprised of words and signs setting forth the performance's emotional, intellectual, and graphic values. These values can be divided into six components: imagined human activity, space, character, purpose (or concept), organization, and performance style.

Human Activity   Imaginative material (composed of human behavior) for actors to work with as individuals and in groups

Space   Specifications as to the nature of the performance space

Character   A basis in language, gesture, sound, and movement for communicating patterns of relationships among actors as characters in action

Purpose   The purpose or concept behind the action

Organization   The sequence or shape of incidents that makes the concept visible

Performance Style   The visual projection of the play's inner nature[1]

Let us examine these six components as they appear in *Agamemnon, Othello, The Cherry Orchard,* and *A Streetcar Named Desire.*

HUMAN ACTIVITY

What is the imaginative material? A play is fabricated out of imagined activities engaging two or more human beings in conflict leading to crisis and change. The script's imaginative material, therefore, has a completeness and unity that life does not have. For one thing, it has a beginning and an end. In addition, the material shows physical and psychological behavior that the actor brings to life —makes *visible*—in words and actions. Iago's plotting, Othello's jealousy, and Blanche DuBois's emotional vulnerability can be seen and heard.

Each play's imaginative material is different. In *Agamemnon,* Aeschylus gives actors the part of the tragic story of the House of Atreus dealing with the lives of Clytemnestra, Agamemnon, and Cassandra. In the trilogy's three parts, Aeschylus explores the passions, politics, and fates of individuals, as well as the emergence of an enlightened Hellenistic civilization out of a barbaric society. In the first play, we are concerned with the *how* and the *why* of Agamemnon's death at the hands of Clytemnestra and her lover. We see Clytemnestra's false devotion, Agamemnon's triumphant return, Cassandra's beauty, and the results of the queen's death plot.

Figure 10-1. Tennessee Williams. (Photo courtesy of International Creative Management, New York.)

Tennessee Williams (b. 1911), the American playwright, was born Thomas Lanier Williams in Columbus, Mississippi, son of a traveling salesman and Episcopalian minister's daughter. The family moved to St. Louis in 1918. He was educated at Missouri University, Washington University in St. Louis, and later Iowa University, where he received his B.A. degree.

In 1939, *Story* magazine published his short story, "A Field of Blue Chicken," the first work to appear under his nickname "Tennessee," which was given to him because of his Southern accent. That same year he compiled four one-act plays under the title *American Blues,* and won a prize in the Group Theatre's American play contest. This aroused the interest of New York agent Audrey Wood, who asked to represent him. In 1944, *The Glass Menagerie* marked Williams's first major success and established him as an important American play-wright. It was followed by his major plays: *A Streetcar Named Desire* (1947), *The Rose Tattoo* (1951), *Cat on a Hot Tin Roof* (1955), *Sweet Bird of Youth* (1959), and *The Night of the Iguana* (1961). Although his recent plays have failed to please critics, he continues to write and be produced in New York and London.

Shakespeare's *Othello* is the tragic story of the Moor of Venice, his marriage to Desdemona, and the calumny of Iago that results in their deaths. The Ranevskys in Chekhov's *The Cherry Orchard* return to Russia from France to save the family estate from bankruptcy sale. The play's action recreates a life-style of routine and com-monplace concerns about money, love, happiness, success, and failure. In Tennessee Williams's *A Streetcar Named Desire,* Blanche DuBois comes from Laurel, Mississippi, to Stanley Kowalski's home in New Orleans to clash tragi-cally with his personality and life-style.

SPACE

How is space defined in the script? In the beginning of a play's script, the playwright builds in the mind's eye a three-dimensional space within which actors move about and interact as characters. When we read, we need to ask ourselves certain questions: What does the space look like? What are the setting's configuration, color, details? How is the space filled by the characters? What are the visual clues about manners, style, thoughts, and attitudes? It is important to visualize how the playwright uses the space, since this use sets the action and defines the characters' lives.

Opening speeches and stage directions give detailed information about how the playwright has imagined the stage space, including geography, time of day, weather, dress, mood, and general impressions of place.

Agamemnon

At the beginning of *Agamemnon,* the watchman's speech establishes a mood of fearful weariness. He stands atop Agamemnon's palace telling us of his personal agony. For years he has been on duty waiting to glimpse beacon lights signaling the Trojan War's end and the Greek army's homecoming. It is night again and the watchman is afraid that he will fall asleep and miss the signal. He suffers from the cold weather, his longing for his wife, and anxiety about the king's homecoming.

Aeschylus establishes the watchman's personal dilemma before introducing the political situation or the principal characters. We see the lowly watchman isolated in his dilemma, even located in a remote place to emphasize this isolation. Only with the chorus's entrance does the focus broaden to include the entire society.

The use of space in the beginning is characteristic of the entire play: Aeschylus focuses upon the individual tragedies of Agamemnon, Cassandra, and Clytemnestra as a way of representing the global tragedy of the Greek and Trojan states. The play takes place before Agamemnon's palace, but the palace is the site of political, military, and domestic authority.

Othello

The play begins at night on a street in Venice with a quietly intense conversation between two friends—Iago and Roderigo. Iago is disturbed at being passed over for promotion. As he thinks about his treatment, his emotions turn to hatred of Othello in particular and Venetian society in general. The scene ends when the spontaneous clamor created by Iago and Roderigo rouses Brabantio to discover his daughter's elopement. Thereafter the play sweeps across the society for which the Island of Cyprus becomes a microcosm, or little world.

The disturbance created by Iago and Roderigo in the beginning impels the play's action forward. Shakespeare shows us the way Iago uses people "to serve his turn" upon Othello while remaining concealed—here it is by night. In the darkness Brabantio recognizes Roderigo's voice because he has been a former suitor to Desdemona. The other voice, Iago's, remains undetected, and for four acts it remains undetected as it plots the destruction of all around.

All *clues* for movement, time, place, motive, and behavior are in Shakespeare's verse. There were no stage directions until after his era. So we must read carefully what the characters say and watch what they do. In their speech and actions they define their environment, feelings, and behavior. *Othello* illustrates how the malicious behavior that cannot be detected at first by other characters affects their lives. For example, Brabantio, Othello, Desdemona, and Cassio are all worked upon by an "unseen" Iago. It is appropriate, therefore, that much of the play takes place in darkness and ends with Desdemona's and Othello's lives being put out like candles. The dark street in Venice establishes the play's scene, atmosphere, and conflicts.

The Cherry Orchard

In scripts written at the beginning of our century, playwrights gave special attention to details of setting, lighting, costume, properties, and the characters' physical looks—age, sex, coloring, class. These details were usually set down in descriptive stage directions at the beginning of each act.

Chekhov begins *The Cherry Orchard* with a description:

A room which is still known as 'the nursery'. One of the doors leads to ANYA's room. Dawn is breaking and the sun will soon be up. It is May. The cherry trees are in bloom, but it is cold and frosty in the orchard. The windows of the room are shut.

Enter DUNYASHA carrying a candle, and LOPAKHIN with a book in his hand.

Time of day, month, dawn light, weather, the presence of the flowering cherry trees, silence followed by footsteps, and the closed-in room are all established. The properties (the candle and the book) tell us visually that Dunyasha and Lopahin have been up all night. The room's physical details reveal this before the two characters speak, and establish that they have been waiting all night for the train to arrive. Only after establishing the facts of time, place, and event does Chekhov reveal who Dunyasha and Lopahin are and for whom they are waiting. This information prepares for the entrance of Madame Ranevsky and her entourage. The problem of the cherry orchard (and the estate) is not mentioned, but the trees, like the financial problem, are always apparent in the play's background (see Figure 10-9).

A Streetcar Named Desire

The opening stage direction is a page in length. It must be read carefully for clues about mood, style, environment, and attitudes. In this description, Williams evokes atmosphere and graphic details of place, time, light, and sound: New Orleans, Elysian Fields Avenue, a May twilight, blue sky, barroom piano music. Stanley and Mitch are described for age, dress, and movement: They are twenty-eight or thirty years old and wear blue denim work clothes. Stanley's first gesture is to throw a package of meat up to his wife, Stella. He is the breadwinner bringing his prize home to his wife. Blanche, Stella's sister—dressed for a garden party in white suit, hat, gloves—comes unexpectedly into this setting. Williams describes her appearance:

She is about five years older than Stella. Her delicate beauty must avoid a strong light. There is something about her uncertain manner, as well as her white clothes, that suggest a moth.

Figure 10-2. Stage directions from A Streetcar Named Desire. *(Courtesy New Directions.)*

SCENE ONE

The exterior of a two-story corner building on a street in New Orleans which is named Elysian Fields and runs between the L & N tracks and the river. The section is poor but, unlike corresponding sections in other American cities, it has a raffish charm. The houses are mostly white frame, weathered grey, with rickety outside stairs and galleries and quaintly ornamented gables. This building contains two flats, upstairs and down. Faded white stairs ascend to the entrances of both.

It is first dark of an evening early in May. The sky that shows around the dim white building is a peculiarly tender blue, almost a turquoise, which invests the scene with a kind of lyricism and gracefully attenuates the atmosphere of decay. You can almost feel the warm breath of the brown river beyond the river warehouses with their faint redolences of bananas and coffee. A corresponding air is evoked by the music of Negro entertainers at a barroom around the corner. In this part of New Orleans you are practically always just around the corner, or a few doors down the street, from a tinny piano being played with the infatuated fluency of brown fingers. This "Blue Piano" expresses the spirit of the life which goes on here.

Two women, one white and one colored, are taking the air on the steps of the building. The white woman is Eunice, who occupies the upstairs flat; the colored woman a neighbor, for New Orleans is a cosmopolitan city where there is a relatively warm and easy intermingling of races in the old part of town.

Above the music of the "Blue Piano" the voices of people on the street can be heard overlapping.

[Two men come around the corner, Stanley Kowalski and Mitch. They are about twenty-eight or thirty years old, roughly dressed in blue denim work clothes. Stanley carries his bowling jacket and a red-stained package from a butcher's. They stop at the foot of the steps.]

Jo Mielziner, scene designer for the 1947 Broadway production, visualized a single setting with several levels that showed all rooms of the apartment simultaneously. The furniture and details of the set (the naked lightbulb, for example) are clues to the Kowalski life-style that destroys Blanche's fragile truce with reality. She has nowhere

Figure 10-3. Setting for A Streetcar Named Desire *(1947). Stanley Kowalski's friends play poker while Blanche DuBois is taken away to an asylum. The foreground of the photo shows the realistic details of Jo Mielziner's setting: bed, tables, and chairs. Stanley comforts Stella on a stairway while Blanche is led away by a doctor and nurse in an upstage area that seems far removed from the poker game. (Photo Vandamm Collection, New York Public Library at Lincoln Center.)*

to go—this is her last refuge—and when this environment becomes threatening she retreats into a fantasy world devoid of mental cruelty, rape, and death. Yet the quality of the stage lighting and the open walls of Mielziner's setting suggest this very fantasy world with its atmosphere of unreality.

CHARACTER

Dramatic action is like a set of building blocks creating a human scaffolding of physical and psychological relationships. In drama, characters are defined by their physical characteristics, their socioeconomic status, their

psychological makeup, and their moral or ethical choices. And characters are made visible through what the playwright says about them in stage directions and what others say about them.

As readers we must use our imaginations to hear and see characters as the actors would represent them in performance: the words spoken, the stresses, nuances, and attitudes of the speakers; their costumes, movements and inactivity, silences, visual strengths, psychological masks, and so on.

Agamemnon

Because the audience knew the story of Agamemnon and Clytemnestra, Aeschylus could develop the action indirectly. Clytemnestra does not explicitly tell us that she intends to kill Agamemnon and Cassandra. Her key speech is a lie and the audience knows it. Tension is aroused by the lie that she speaks, her awareness of her calumny, and the audience's knowledge of her plans.

> CLYTEMNESTRA: . . . take this message to the king: Come, and with speed, back to the city that longs for him, and may he find a wife within his house as true as on the day he left her, watchdog of the house gentle to him alone, fierce to his enemies, and such a woman in all her ways as this, who has not broken the seal upon her in the length of days. With no man else have I known delight, nor any shame of evil speech, more than I know how to temper bronze.

Clytemnestra welcomes Agamemnon with apparent joy. As she spreads the crimson carpet for Agamemnon to walk to his death upon, the *color,* more than words, serves as a reminder to the audience of his imminent danger. Tension is increased as Agamemnon hesitates before stepping on the carpet—to walk on it would be a godlike gesture on his part. Yielding finally to his wife's arguments and to his own sense of pride, he removes his sandals and walks upon the rich carpet. We must try to see in our mind's eye Agamemnon's bare feet, for he speaks of

Figure 10-4. Agamemnon prepares to walk on the carpet. The audience instantly perceives what we have to visualize for ourselves as we read a script. Having removed his sandals, Agamemnon (played by Jamil Zakkai) is prepared to walk to his death on the carpet in the 1977 New York Shakespeare Festival production at the Vivian Beaumont Theatre in Lincoln Center. The costume is by Santo Loquasto. (Photo by George E. Joseph.)

his feet crushing "purple" as he passes within the hall. They evoke an image of the naked king in his bath, pinioned in a net and stabbed to death by his wife and her lover, Aegisthus.

After she murders the king, Clytemnestra stands before the palace doors and discloses the bodies of Agamemnon and Cassandra, the Trojan princess brought back with

Figure 10-5. Desdemona's death. Othello puts out the candles (on the left) and then "puts out" Desdemona's life. The reader has to follow this sequence of action through the lines and images of the text, but the audience can see the actor perform the one act before the other. On stage, gesture makes language instantly meaningful. James Earl Jones is Othello in the 1964 New York Shakespeare Festival Theatre production, Delacorte Theatre. (Photo by George E. Joseph.)

him from Troy as slave and mistress. The queen now speaks freely of the deed, which the audience knows will continue the unbroken chain of barbaric justice: an eye for an eye. But she does not know this, and for her the moral and ethical choices are clear. Her relationship to the watchman, chorus, and others is that of avenger seeking the death of her husband for crimes he has committed long ago.

Othello

The character relationships in *Othello* are one thing on the surface and another underneath, but they are always clear to the audience. Unlike Aeschylus, Shakespeare has his characters tell us directly, in dialogue and soliloquies, what they are planning and feeling.

Shakespeare's play illustrates tragic social and psychological relationships. Othello and Iago begin as commander and ensign, but end as slave and master—Iago completely manipulates Othello's view of reality. The critical relationship between Othello and Desdemona also changes, as Iago's plot to destroy Othello proves more and more effective. Iago works upon Othello by using his strangeness to Venetian society, his unfamiliarity with Venetian women, and his sensitivity to his position as an alien in a strange society, and transforms him from a noble soldier into an inhuman monster.

The Cherry Orchard

We ordinarily assume that words spoken by characters clarify relationships, define what is happening between characters, amplify emotions, and provide information. This is usually true. But Chekhov teaches us most forcefully in his plays that characters also use language not to reveal their intentions but to *conceal* them. This is despite the fact that the playwright's intention is to make human behavior visible to an audience. In Chekhov's plays, behavior is frequently visible in the wide gap between *what is being said* and *what is being done*. The reader must listen beneath the surface of Chekhov's dialogue—and the dialogue of many modern plays—to hear and see the characters' unspoken feelings and needs.

How do we read Chekhov's silences and pauses? First, we must know where the silences come in the script, gauge their length, and imagine their effect. Playwrights indicate silences and pauses in stage directions by writing a phrase like "after a pause" or "hesitating." But a more difficult kind of stage silence is that disguised by a torrent of words, when characters fill the stage with word-sounds in order to hide feelings. Harold Pinter, a modern British playwright, described this use of sound and words:

There are two silences. One when no word is spoken. The other when perhaps a torrent of language is being employed. This speech is speaking of a language locked beneath it. That is its continual reference. The speech we hear is an indication of that we don't hear. It is a necessary avoidance, a violent, sly, anguished or mocking smokescreen which keeps the other in its place. When true silence falls we are still left with echo but are nearer nakedness. One way of looking at speech is to say it is a constant stratagem to cover nakedness.[2]

Harold Pinter (b. 1930), British playwright, director and actor, was born in London. Before becoming a playwright, Pinter worked as a professional actor. In 1957, he wrote *The Room, The Dumb Waiter,* and *The Birthday Party. The Caretaker* followed in 1959. *The Homecoming* (1965) was produced in London by the Royal Shakespeare Company and later seen on Broadway, as were *Old Times* (1970) and *No Man's Land* (1975). Pinter has also written screenplays: *The Servant, The Quiller Memorandum, The Pumpkin Eater, Accident,* and *The Go-Between.* He is known for plays about dislocated working-class people struggling for power. For Pinter, language, with its *non sequiturs*, pauses, and silences, is a source of power and menace. Today. the "Pinter pause" has almost become a theatrical cliché.

Chekhov uses both pauses and torrents of words to get at the truth of human behavior. In the final act of *The Cherry Orchard*, the family is moving out of the house, which has been bought by the businessman Lopahin. Madame Ranevsky arranges for her adopted daughter, Varya, and Lopahin to have a few moments alone together. Apparently he wants to marry the girl, but he has never asked her. Alone with Madame Ranevsky, he says: "Let's get it over and done with. I don't feel I'll ever propose to her without you here." The scene progresses in this way:

VARYA [*spends a long time examining the luggage*]: That's funny, I can't find it anywhere.

LOPAKHIN: What are you looking for?

VARYA: I packed it myself and I still can't remember. [*Pause.*]

LOPAKHIN: Where are you going now, Varya?

VARYA: Me? To the Ragulins'. I've arranged to look after their place, a sort of housekeeper's job.

LOPAKHIN: That's in Yashnevo, isn't it? It must be fifty odd miles from here. [*Pause.*] So life has ended in this house.

VARYA [*examining the luggage*]: Oh, where can it be? Or could I have put it in the trunk? Yes, life has gone out of this house. And it will never come back.

LOPAKHIN: Well, I'm just off to Kharkov. By the next train. I have plenty to do there. And I'm leaving Yepikhodov in charge here, I've taken him on.

VARYA: Oh, have you?

LOPAKHIN: This time last year we already had snow, remember? But now it's calm and sunny. It's a bit cold though. Three degrees of frost, I should say.

VARYA: I haven't looked. [*Pause.*] Besides, our thermometer's broken. [*Pause.*]

[*A voice at the outer door:* 'Mr. Lopakhin!']

LOPAKHIN [*as if he had long been expecting this summons*]: I'm just coming. [*Goes out quickly.*]

[VARYA *sits on the floor with her head on a bundle of clothes, quietly sobbing. The door opens and* MRS. RANEVSKY *comes in cautiously.*]

MRS. RANEVSKY: Well? [*Pause.*] We'd better go.

(Act IV)

Varya knows why she has been summoned, but as an excuse for her entrance she pretends to be looking for something. Alone, she and Lopahin talk about the lost object, their travel plans, household arrangements, the train, weather, and the broken thermometer. Chekhov uses "a pause" and dashes to show the conversation gaps. After each silence, they take up another topic without ever getting to the true subject: love and marriage. Neither can speak about true feelings; they substitute small talk to cover them.

The rhythm of the pauses contributes to the effectiveness of this type of stage speech. The two pauses in Varya's last speech allow opportunities for Lopahin to propose to her, but he cannot do so, and he responds to the unexpected summons as a reprieve. Varya collapses and her posture answers Madame Ranevsky's question about the outcome of the scene. Words are unnecessary, because the girl's appearance projects what happened between her and Lopahin.

Character relationships are illustrated by what characters say and do, and also by what they don't say or do. The omissions are often more difficult for the reader to detect, but the playwright builds in signals: pauses, silences, and word torrents.

A Streetcar Named Desire

In Williams's play the relationships between Blanche, Stanley, and Mitch are based on "the law of the jungle": The weaker, in this case Blanche and Mitch, are physically and psychologically violated by Stanley, the stronger. Stanley's need to dominate and control his world destroys Mitch's happiness and Blanche's ability to cope with reality.

The character relationships in this play are illustrated in a seesaw manner. We see Stanley, Stella, and Mitch as a compatible threesome, the sort who go bowling together. Blanche arrives on the scene and tries to alienate Stella's affections from Stanley. She engages Mitch's affections and he asks her to marry him. Sensing his loss of affection and authority, Stanley retaliates physically and psychologically. He fights to preserve his home just as Blanche works to create a refuge for herself. Stanley finally destroys Blanche's relationship with Mitch by revealing her past sexual escapades; then he rapes her. At the play's end, Stanley has reestablished control of his own world—his wife and friend—while Blanche has relinquished her tenuous hold on a world she could not cope with. She is taken away to a mental institution, where she will depend on "the kindness of strangers" to see her through.

PURPOSE

What is the purpose or concept behind the action? As readers, we must visualize what the characters do, where they do it, and with whom. We must also consider *why* characters do what they do, for a play represents persons in effective, complete, and meaningful action. In order to be complete and meaningful—that is, to illustrate the why of experience—dramatic action is shaped or arranged with some purpose in mind. It is not a random collection of unrelated events, although in plays like Chekhov's, action may appear to be random. The purpose of the action and the playwright's underlying concept are usually not entirely clear until the end of the play. However, there are five clues to it: title, climax, resolution, metaphor, and theme.

Agamemnon

Aeschylus names the play after a king whose death is an incident in an unending chain of violence brought about by a barbaric system of justice. The principal emphasis here is on *theme*. Each choral ode alludes to the chain of violent deeds connected with the House of Atreus, and each episode builds toward the king's death. The two other plays in the trilogy complete the story of the House of Atreus and of the evolution of an Athenian judicial system. In *The Libation Bearers,* the son Orestes avenges his father's death by killing his mother and her lover. And in *The*

Eumenides, Athene, the goddess of wisdom and enlightened justice, establishes a law court that hears Orestes' case and pardons him of the crime.

Agamemnon's climax builds from the king's victorious entrance. He has defeated the Trojans, destroyed their male population, desecrated their religious altars, and dispersed their women as slaves. His pride blinds him to the meaning of these deeds, and to the import of the carpet spread out before him by Clytemnestra. Agamemnon's and Cassandra's deaths climax the play's events and themes: Barbaric justice will never end unless the system changes. Clytemnestra's rejoicing over the bodies reminds us that her victory will also be brief, for she will die soon at the hands of an avenger like herself—Orestes, her son.

The play's metaphors and color imagery provide a rich complement to Aeschylus' concept. Light and darkness, predatory animals, and blood-red colors serve as metaphors for passions that go wrong and become murderous. Aeschylus' concept is clear: He makes the play's action exemplify *why* enlightened Athenians evolved a judicial system to judge the wrongs and rights of human behavior impersonally.

Othello

The play's action is methodical. Its title, events, metaphors, and themes are clearly stated. Each scene weaves the net of Iago's "motiveless malignity," as Samuel Taylor Coleridge (1772–1834) called it, tighter around Othello, Desdemona, and Cassio. The action shows the process by which Iago—evil disguised as good—transforms Othello from a noble soldier into a murderer. Othello is honestly deceived and chooses evil because he has been so worked upon that he cannot distinguish reality from appearance, truth from falsehood. He learns too late that he has come to see the world through the eyes of Iago and killed the wife who loved him. This concept of human behavior is illustrated in the climactic death of Desdemona, when Othello thinks that he acts as an instrument of God to avenge Desdemona's supposed wrong. Othello's death by his own hand at the play's resolution is a clear statement of the tragic fact that Othello, although misled, was responsible for his own misjudgment and acts.

The Cherry Orchard

Chekhov's play proceeds from the Ranevsky homecoming to the orchard's inevitable sale at auction. The underlying concept is embodied in the orchard. Like the orchard, whose fruit is no longer harvested and used commercially, the Ranevskys are living out the end of a way of life. They are no longer effective members of society, for they cannot deal with life's practicalities: economics, estate management, the future. They live out the routines of rural landowners' lives while failing to come to grips with their finances, loves, careers, and failures. The orchard's sale resolves certain problems for them. They can leave the estate now that Lopahin, who told them in the beginning how to save the orchard, has bought it, and they can return to a drifting existence elsewhere. Chekhov's purpose is to show in the Ranevskys and Lopahin a vanishing way of life and a new breed of entrepreneur. The orchard is Chekhov's metaphor for life's fragile quality; that is, ways of life lose their effectiveness and are replaced by others—sometimes in the name of progress.

A Streetcar Named Desire

Like *The Cherry Orchard,* Williams's play takes its title from an object rather than a person. The "Desire" streetcar literally transports Blanche DuBois to the Kowalski tenement on Elysian Fields Avenue; at the same time her personal desires for refuge, love, and sexual gratification have brought her to an emotional and mental dead end. The fact that the play climaxes with Blanche's rape underscores the purpose of the action: to demonstrate that, without refuge, the emotionally lame cannot survive the brutality of a harsh and insensitive world.

ORGANIZATION

How are the incidents shaped and organized? To visualize a script we must hear what the characters *say* to one another and see what they *do* under the pressure of developing events and relationships. We must also visualize the connections between plot and action, word and gesture. And, what is frequently more difficult while reading, we must see in the mind's eye the changing focus of attention on individuals within a group.

Let us look at an important scene from each of these four plays, considering the organization of that incident and its connection to what has gone before and what is to come after.

Agamemnon's Carpet

The Greek play is formal and stylized, interchanging five episodes with choral odes. Since Aeschylus used only two actors together with the chorus, the focus of attention is controlled by the limited number of actors interacting at any one time and by the differences in costumes. The chorus is simply clothed; the main actors wear colorful robes and masks. Moreover, Agamemnon's entrance is prepared for by the watchman, chorus, messenger, and by Clytemnestra as well. He arrives in a chariot accompanied by Cassandra, the Trojan princess.

This scene is preceded by the episode in which a messenger announces the Greek victory and the desecration of the sacred altars of Troy. It is followed by a choral ode expressing fear of things to come. Both events heighten the emotional tension we feel as we wait to hear what happens in Clytemnestra's death trap. The earlier episode establishes the vindictiveness of the king who destroyed a foreign city "because one woman strayed"—Helen, his brother's wife. It also establishes the pride of the man who will be enticed with flattery to walk to his death on the carpet. In the episode itself, Agamemnon fulfills our expectations. Aeschylus' organization illustrates the working out of Clytemnestra's scheme and the choices made by Agamemnon that fulfill her plans.

Figure 10-6. Agamemnon's pride. The actors' stylized masks and movement visually express the arrogant pride of Aeschylus' doomed characters in the 1977 New York Shakespeare Festival production, Lincoln Center. (Photo by Joseph Abeles.)

Othello's Defense

In reading plays by Shakespeare, or any plays for that matter, the temptation is to concentrate on whoever is speaking and to forget to keep the full stage picture in mind. Although an audience can see everyone on stage and have a sense of simultaneous activity, readers have to keep impressions, characters, sounds, and silences in their heads to visualize the action's physical and psychological impact fully. We have to make mental bridges between one scene and the next. The connections between events give us a sense of progressions as we watch the play.

Othello's defense of his marriage to Desdemona is preceded by the chaotic scene in which her father, Brabantio, discovers her elopement. In the defense scene, Brabantio accuses Othello of practicing magic on his daughter to force her into an "unnatural" marriage. This domestic quarrel is set against the duke's concern for the Turkish fleet's invasion of Cyprus. Sounds of a war council accompany Brabantio's threats to imprison Othello. The scene is a confused one. There are three groups on stage: the duke's, Brabantio's, and Othello's. The focus shifts rapidly from the duke's war council to the father's interrogation of Othello and back again. As the duke's general and Desdemona's husband, Othello links the two groups together. One focuses upon him as a military leader and the other as a devoted husband.

Called to account for his marriage, Othello confesses that he has, indeed, married Desdemona. He describes his courtship in one of the play's famous speeches. Desdemona's entrance is delayed until Othello ends his defense. Then attention naturally turns to her, for she can confirm Othello's story. She argues eloquently that her change of allegiance—from father to husband—was normal and reasonable. Othello wins the day before the duke and leaves Venice to defend Cyprus against the Turks.

This scene establishes Othello's integrity, nobility, and sense of honor. It also shows him as a foreigner—society's attitude is that his marriage is unnatural. The chaos in the street and the events of war that surround the scene mirror the turmoil that is to pervade Othello's life in Cyprus.

Figure 10-7. Othello's speech (I, iii).

Most potent, grave, and reverend signiors,
My very noble, and approv'd good masters,
That I have ta'en away this old man's daughter,
It is most true; true I have married her.
The very head and front of my offending
Hath this extent, no more. Rude am I in my speech,
And little bless'd with the soft phrase of peace;
For since these arms of mine had seven years' pith
Till now some nine moons wasted, they have us'd
Their dearest action in the tented field;
And little of this great world can I speak
More than pertains to feats of broil and battle;

(continued)

Chapter Ten

And therefore little shall I grace my cause
In speaking for myself. Yet, by your gracious
      patience,
I will a round unvarnish'd tale deliver
Of my whole course of love—what drugs, what
      charms,
What conjuration, and what mighty magic
(For such proceeding am I charg'd withal)
I won his daughter.
· · · · · · · · · · · · · · · ·
Her father lov'd me, oft invited me;
Still question'd me the story of my life
From year to year—the battles, sieges, fortunes
That I have pass'd.
I ran it through, even from my boyish days
To th' very moment that he bade me tell it.
Wherein I spake of most disastrous chances,
Of moving accidents by flood and field;
Of hairbreadth scapes i' th' imminent deadly breach;
Of being taken by the insolent foe
And sold to slavery; of my redemption thence
And portance in my travel's history;
Wherein of antres vast and deserts idle,
Rough quarries, rocks, and hills whose heads touch
      heaven,
It was my hint to speak—such was the process;
And of the Cannibals that each other eat,
The Anthropophagi, and men whose heads
Do grow beneath their shoulders. This to hear
Would Desdemona seriously incline;
But still the house affairs would draw her thence;
Which ever as she could with haste dispatch,
She'ld come again, and with a greedy ear
Devour up my discourse. Which I observing,
Took once a pliant hour, and found good means
To draw from her a prayer of earnest heart
That I would all my pilgrimage dilate,
Whereof by parcels she had something heard,
But not intentively. I did consent,
And often did beguile her of her tears
When I did speak of some distressful stroke
That my youth suffer'd. My story being done,
She gave me for my pains a world of sighs.

250

> She swore, in faith, 'twas strange, 'twas passing
>   strange;
> 'Twas pitiful, 'twas wondrous pitiful.
> She wish'd she had not heard it; yet she wish'd
> That heaven had made her such a man. She
>   thank'd me;
> And bade me, if I had a friend that lov'd her,
> I should but teach him how to tell my story,
> And that would woo her. Upon this hint I spake.
> She lov'd me for the dangers I had pass'd,
> And I lov'd her that she did pity them.
> This only is the witchcraft I have us'd.
> Here comes the lady. Let her witness it.
>   *Enter* Desdemona, Iago, Attendants.

The Cherry Orchard's Sale

The climax in Act III of *The Cherry Orchard* is the revelation that Lopahin has bought the estate. Ordinarily, we would expect a triumphant Lopahin to make a grand entrance announcing the purchase of the estate on which his grandfather and father had been serfs. But Chekhov argued that life was "untheatrical" in the sense that real people didn't go about shooting each other and making grand entrances. Chekhov fulfills his concept of life by organizing events in a lower, more realistic key.

> Moscow, April 1, 1890.
> . . . You upbraid me about objectivity, styling it indifference to good and evil, absence of ideals and ideas, etc. You would have me say, in depicting horse thieves, that stealing horses is an evil. But then, that has been known a long while, even without me. Let jurors judge them, for my business is only to show them as they are. . . .
>
> Anton Chekhov, *Letters*

Although the estate is being auctioned in town, Madame Ranevsky is holding a party on the evening of the sale. Couples are dancing to the accompaniment of an orchestra. Varya is weeping as she dances. The outcome of the sale is unknown, for Gaev, Madame Ranevsky's brother, has not returned from town. Unless by some miracle the auction has not taken place, the estate has been sold by now. News comes from the kitchen that a passerby has said that the orchard has been sold but not who bought it.

Lopahin and Gaev, who traveled back from the auction together, come into the drawing room one at a time. As he enters, Lopahin is accidentally hit over the head by Varya, who is chasing a lodger who has annoyed her. Lopahin complains about feeling dizzy, but fails to mention the auction. Gaev enters but is tearful and disinclined to talk about the auction, though Madame Ranevsky begs him to tell her the news quickly. He makes a gesture of resignation, hands over parcels of groceries, and complains that he has not eaten all day. Without delivering the news (although he delivers the groceries), Gaev goes off to change his clothes. We have the climax only when Madame Ranevsky asks Lopahin two direct questions:

> RANEVSKY: Is the cherry orchard sold?
> LOPAKHIN: It is sold.
> RANEVSKY: Who bought it?
> LOPAKHIN: I have bought it.
> *(A pause. Lyubov [Madame Ranevsky] is crushed; she would fall down if she were not standing near a chair and table.)*
> *(Varya takes keys from her waist-band, flings them on the floor in the middle of the drawing-room and goes out.)*

The reader must first observe *what* these characters do, then *why* they do it. For different reasons, Gaev and Lopahin do not want to talk about the auction. Out of the confusion that the characters reveal we see that Gaev was grief-stricken and guilty about his inability to prevent the loss of the estate. Lopahin, according to the stage directions, was *"embarrassed, afraid of betraying his joy."*

Chekhov's change of focus from character to character reveals the emotional confusion over the estate's fate. Madame Ranevsky is at first the center of attention; her tearful waiting indicates that she has abdicated responsibility for the estate's future. As Lopahin comes in, he becomes the center of attention for he has the information they all dread to hear. Although he and Lopahin returned on the train together, Gaev has delayed coming into the room for he prefers that Lopahin deliver the bad news without him. Because Lopahin has not talked about the auction, Gaev becomes the center of attention when he enters and remains so until he escapes. His exit shifts the focus back to Lopahin, who is once again the only character on stage in possession of the information that all want. The tension is go great that Madame Ranevsky must relieve it by asking direct questions, which Lopahin cannot avoid answering. The changing focus of the stage picture is based upon information the characters have but do not share with others. The meaning of the scene is in what the characters try *not* to say, rather than in the information they impart. Varya's throwing of the household keys on the floor signals the end of a regime and the transference of ownership. The *gesture* releases further tension, so that Lopahin can speak uninhibitedly about the details of the auction.

Blanche's Birthday Party

A scene illustrating the beginning of Blanche's retreat from reality begins with Stanley, Blanche, and Stella seated around a table set for four. A birthday cake and flowers are on the table. Stanley is sullen, Stella is embarrassed and sad, and Blanche is putting up a brave front with an artificial smile.

Blanche assesses the situation: Her "beau," Mitch, has stood her up. She tells a lame joke to fill the awkward silence, Stella corrects Stanley's table manners, and he throws his plate on the floor. Blanche wants to know what happened while she was taking a bath, but Stella avoids telling her that Stanley has found out about her past and told Mitch, and that this is the reason Mitch is not coming to the party. Stanley gives Blanche a birthday present: a bus ticket to Laurel. Blanche runs into the bathroom to be sick. Stella and Stanley argue about his treatment of Blanche and he accuses Blanche of changing their lives. The scene ends with Stella quietly asking to be taken to the hospital to have their baby.

Figure 10-8. The birthday party. Marlon Brando as Stanley (left) prepares to throw his cup and plate on the floor during Blanche's birthday party in A Streetcar Named Desire. *Jessica Tandy as Blanche (center) and Kim Hunter as Stella (right) are seated at the table. (Photo Vandamm Collection, New York Public Library, Lincoln Center.)*

Williams shapes scenes vii–ix to illustrate that hostile forces have turned on Blanche. In vii, Stanley tells Stella the facts about Blanche's past and sets the stage for his ultimatum: She must leave. Scene ix is a confrontation between Mitch and Blanche in which she realizes he is not to be that "cleft in the rock of the world" she needs to protect her from the world's harsh realities.

In these three scenes, Blanche is the focus of the conflict between the characters. Williams develops the relationships to the crisis point at which the bus ticket signals to Blanche that she has no place of refuge. What follows is rape—Stanley's final violation of her person—and insanity. Williams's concept is clear: Certain fragile souls must have protection—otherwise they are destroyed by the world's brute forces.

PERFORMANCE STYLE

As readers, how do we think about a play's style of **performance?** *Style* is one of the most difficult words in our language to define. In general, theatrical style is the visual projection of a play's inner nature. In other words, style and the play's *visual reality* are the same. Since the playwright organizes human action into visible action and behavior, the reader must always think visually and three-dimensionally.

There are two principal performance styles in today's theatre: *realism* and *theatricalism*. We need to know what these terms mean, and how to detect these two general styles in the reading of a play.

The most influential book on theatrical style is Michel Saint-Denis's *Theatre: The Rediscovery of Style* (1960). He defines style as "the perceptible form that is taken by reality in revealing to us its true and inner character."[3] What do we look for to visualize this outer reality? What basic questions get at a play's style?

First, we must look for outer or visible characteristics. What are the characters' nationalities and ethnic characteristics? Are they Russian, English, or American? Are they Black, Indian, Italian-American? What dress, manner, and everyday habits do these characters have? What are their ways of speaking, sitting, walking, smiling, eating, and drinking? How are their cultural rhythms expressed?

We must also ask where and when the play takes place. Is it a room, or street, or nonspecific locale? What does the setting look like? Is it a room, or arranged platforms? What is the historical period? And we must ask about the psychological, emotional, and social reality of the characters. How do they speak and behave? Do they speak in verse or ordinary prose? Are their gestures those that we observe around us, or grander? All of these questions about style get at the play's inner nature from the outside—from the setting, costumes, lighting, sounds, speech, and movements.

Realism

Realism is a production style whose intention is to represent life in such a way that the audience accepts what is seen as a picture of *everyday* reality. One major movement of the nineteenth- and twentieth-century European and American theatres has been to recreate everyday life on stage. The American scholar and critic Eric Bentley defines realism as "the candid presentation of the natural world."[4] It is exact, detailed, and recognizable. The actors, dressed as real people, are put in the middle of real furniture, properties, doors, ceilings, and windows. The **box setting**, the basic environment for the realistic play, uses three walls and a ceiling—the illusion is created that the fourth wall, between stage and audience, has been removed.

The Cherry Orchard (1904) In the 1904 production of Chekhov's *The Cherry Orchard* at the Moscow Art Theatre, director Constantin Stanislavsky set a standard for stage realism. He worked to recreate the play's **mise en scène**, or total stage picture. He paid particular attention to stage sounds (birds singing, dogs barking) to create a sense of the play's living reality. Details of costume, setting, locale, furniture, properties, speech, and movement were scrutinized to make certain they were like the life they imitated—rural Russia around 1904. Ordinary details of

Figure 10-9. Stage realism. Stanislavsky's setting for the 1904 Moscow Art Theatre production of The Cherry Orchard *includes* **box set** *(with ceiling), details of a recognizable room (notice the dog), and morning light coming through the windows as essential details of the* **mise en scène.** *(Photo from the New York Public Library, Lincoln Center.)*

everyday existence were brought onstage: samovar, piano, harmonica, stove, lamp, tobacco, singing, drink, twilight, window frost. Stanislavsky's actors turned their backs to the audience, as if it did not exist, and moved with familiarity within their stage environment. There was no star, but a perfect **ensemble**. The foreground and background were one, and properties, costumes, doors, lamps, window curtains, and lights, no less than the actors, performed their parts.

A Streetcar Named Desire (1947)   The 1947 production of Tennessee Williams's *A Streetcar Named Desire*, directed by Elia Kazan and designed by Jo Mielziner, shows us a "selected realism"—a detailed stage environment that also evokes a mood of detachment and fantasy. The blues piano, played in the distance, for instance, is appropriate to the play's setting—New Orleans. "Blues" is an expression of loneliness, rejection, and a longing for love. The piano music is a part of New Orleans's back streets and also a way of calling attention to Blanche's drift into a fantasy world.

The performance style is one of contrasting effects. *Upstage*, there are mood music, soft lighting, and blurred shapes. *Downstage*, there are realistic details: table, chairs, bed, lightbulb, stairwell, flowers, birthday cake, poker game. The style sets forth both the harsh facts of Stanley's world and the dreamlike quality of Blanche's existence. (See Figure 10-3.)

The director's notebook Elia Kazan kept before and during the Broadway rehearsals shows that he concentrated from the beginning on the play's style. For Kazan, *Streetcar* is about a confused bit of light and culture being snuffed out by the violence and vulgarity of Williams's South. Kazan wanted to contrast Stanley's harsh world with Blanche's fragile memories and emotions visually, and the set designer Jo Mielziner selected realistic details to do so. Even though the play's outer world is physically and socially specific, it also calls for moods and sounds that are not objectively present in the environment; for example, polka music plays each time Blanche remembers the past.

Theatricalism

Theatricalism refers to plays performed in a nonrealistic mode. In its broadest sense it represents a revolt against realism by insisting that the stage be used in an openly theatrical way. Under the auspices of such modern directors as Max Reinhardt, Peter Brook, Tom O'Horgan, and Andrei Serban, theatricalism has come to refer to:

large, spectacular productions

a new interpretation of classics or familiar plays

large, spectacular productions

emphasis on pageantry and sensory effect

de-emphasis on the script's verbal qualities

unusual interpretation of the script, rather than a predictable one

the stage emphasized as a stage or medium, rather than de-emphasized and made to look like a living room.[5]

Andrei Serban (b. 1900), Rumanian director, came to the United States in 1970 at the invitation of Ellen Stewart, New York producer-director, to work at La Mama Experimental Theatre on a Ford Foundation grant. After participating in Peter Brook's International Research Institute in Paris and Shiraz (Iran), he returned to New York to direct La Mama productions of *Medea, Electra,* and *The Trojan Women.* During 1975, he directed Brecht's *Good Woman of Setzuan* at the Berlin International Festival; in 1976, he directed Shakespeare's *As You Like It* for summer festivals in France. He recently directed *The Cherry Orchard* and *Agamemnon* at Lincoln Center in New York.

With the success in this country of Tom O'Horgan's *Jesus Christ Superstar* (1971), Peter Brook's *A Midsummer Night's Dream* (1970), and Andrei Serban's *The Cherry Orchard* (1977), we find a growing interest in theatricalism.

Director Andrei Serban has developed a modern theatrical style to project Greek tragedy's inner reality. In 1976, he directed Euripides' *Medea, Electra,* and *The Trojan Women* at the Cafe La Mama Experimental Theatre Club in lower Manhattan. This was followed in 1977 by *Agamemnon* at Lincoln Center in New York City. Using human sounds, stylized costumes and masks, torches, dance, mime, chanting, and new music, Serban tells Aeschylus' story in a blatantly theatrical style. Primitive sounds and physical rhythms project the outer reality of the harsh violence of Agamemnon's world—murder, war, genocide, slavery, and adultery. The staged effects are spectacular. Sound replaces spoken text, dance and pageantry replace normal movement, and the stage becomes an arena for visual and aural effects.

Figure 10-10. Serban's theatrical style. Director Andrei Serban's theatrical style is evident in his treatment of the Greek chorus in Fragments of a Trilogy *(selections from Euripides'* Electra, Medea, *and* The Trojan Women), *produced at La Mama Experimental Theatre Club (New York, 1976). (Photo by Kenn Duncan.)*

Whether we are reading *A Streetcar Named Desire* or *Agamemnon*, a play's performance style is inherent in the script. Reading a play, we must ask if it should be staged with photographic realism or theatrical style. When the experience the play deals with is larger and grander than our living rooms, coffee cups, and card games, its performance style must be theatrical to suggest this larger-than-life quality. Greek and Elizabethan texts lend themselves to the theatrical, while our modern psychological and sociological plays adapt better to realistic staging.

SUMMARY

A play's meaning emerges not just from the words, but from all the relationships that develop between the characters and all other elements of performance. Therefore, it is important to imagine the performance as we read the play. Here is a play-reader's checklist:

1. Imagine the playwright's material three-dimensionally.

2. Visualize the set, atmosphere, costume, decor, and space, and how the actors fill the space individually and in groups.

3. Read all opening speeches and stage directions carefully for details of time, place, weather, and mood.

4. Observe the relationships that develop between the characters. Note what the characters say to one another, as well as what they don't say.

5. Look at the visible relationships and search out the invisible and unspoken. Give attention to pauses, silences, and sounds for related meanings.

6. Observe how the incidents are related to those before and after in the chain of events. Listen in the mind's ear to the story as it unfolds, and visualize in the mind's eye the action's meaningful shape as it develops.

7. Imagine the production style that the script lends itself to, and think in terms of movement, scenery, costumes, and light.

The next and last chapter deals not with the reader, but with critical responses to a play's performance. As audience members, we share opinions and make judgments about what we see. We develop viewpoints for evaluating and sometimes writing about a production's merits. Let us consider, next, essential points in the evaluation of a performance.

Realism *and* Theatricalism are two broad categories of performance styles seen in today's theatre. In realistic style all stage elements, including the actor's performance, simulate details of everyday life appropriate to the play's characters and environment. Realism has predominated in our time, but some theatre artists, feeling constrained by the limitations of stage realism, have sought other modes of expression. They have turned increasingly to purely theatrical devices — open stages, minimal scenic pieces and properties, ritual with highly stylized sounds and movement, and actor-audience participation.

The photographs illustrate these two performance styles, which dominate today's theatre.

Figure 10-11a.   *Chekhov's plays are usually considered major works of modern stage realism. Revolting against contrived artificiality in the nineteenth-century theatre, he asked the audience to believe that they were seeing someone else's everyday life. The play's settings, costumes, dialogue, and general milieu were important to his total purpose. Actor-director Constantin Stanislavsky created a performance style at the Moscow Art Theatre compatible with Chekhov's concepts of stage realism. The actor was placed in the setting, not against a painted drop as background. A "realistic" acting style developed to complement the* **mise en scène,** *and acting became an ensemble art. In the 1978 National Theatre production of the* The Cherry Orchard *in London, Dorothy Tutin (center) as Madame Ranevsky plays in a realistic style. Scrupulous attention has been given to details of* **ensemble** *acting, setting, furniture, and costumes. On stage with her in director Peter Hall's production are Ben Kingsley (Trofimov), Robert Stephens (Gaev), and Susan Fleetwood (Varya). (Photo by Zoe Dominic.)*

Figure 10-11b. Director Andrei Serban collaborated with designer Santo Loquasto to stage in a theatrical style a play long thought to be the hallmark of stage realism. The 1977 production of The Cherry Orchard at the Vivian Beaumont Theatre in New York excited audiences with its boldness and innovation. Dispensing with a traditional room with walls, director and designer opened up the Vivian Beaumont Theatre's stage to suggest a central room flowing into and receding from the orchard. Loquasto designed a vast white carpet, the suggestion of white walls at the side, and a large curtain across the back of the stage. Furniture and actors became sculptured groups in silhouette against the whiteness. Using the metaphor of the death of a house, Serban's production aimed to ritualize Chekhov's play to comment on the death of a civilization. In this photo, actors and furniture half-hidden by dustcovers are sculpted against the vast stage space and the whiteness of the carpet and trees. Irene Worth (center) as Madame Ranevsky is being comforted by Priscilla Smith as Varya upon their return to the old family estate. (Photo by George E. Joseph.)

Figure 10-11c. In a similar way director Peter Brook took Shakespeare's A Midsummer Night's Dream *(1970) out of Elizabethan costumes, painted scenic backdrops, and green forests. Brook's actors performed while balancing on trapezes, juggling plates, hurling streamers, or stumbling about on stilts. The purely theatrical devices of circus clowns and acrobats emphasized the zaniness and physicality of Shakespeare's lovers. (Photo © 1970 by Max Waldman.)*

QUESTIONS FOR STUDY

1. Select a play and discuss the playwright's use of *imaginative material*.

2. How does a playwright indicate the use of *space* in a script?

3. How are *character relationships* illustrated?

4. How does Anton Chekhov use *silences* and *pauses* in *The Cherry Orchard*?

5. How do we discover the *concept* or *purpose* behind a play's action?

6. How are a play's *incidents* or events shaped and organized?

7. Why is *style* a difficult word to define?

8. Does the word *style* mean the same thing when we speak of a person's style of dress as it does when we speak of a play's style?

9. What are some basic questions to ask about a play's style?

10. What is a *box setting*?

11. What is *selected realism*?

12. What is *theatricalism*?

13. How are *pauses* and *silences* used for effect in the theatre?

14. Study the play-reader's checklist on page 260. Select one of the fourteen plays discussed in this book and be prepared to discuss the play using the checklist as a guide.

NOTES

[1]For the discussion of the script-as-model the author is indebted to material from David Cole, "The Visual Script: Theory and Technique," *The Drama Review,* 20, No. 4 (December 1976), 27–50.

[2]Harold Pinter, "Writing for the Theatre," in *Modern British Drama*, edited by Henry Popkin (New York: Grove Press, 1969), pp. 574–580.

[3]Michel Saint-Denis, *Theatre*: *The Rediscovery of Style* (New York: Theatre Arts Books, 1960), p. 62.

[4]Eric Bentley, *The Playwright As Thinker*: *A Study of Drama in Modern Times* (New York: Harcourt, Brace and World, 1946), p. 4.

[5]See John Grassner, *Theatre in Our Times* (New York: Crown Publishers, 1954) and "The Theatricalism Issue," *The Drama Review*, 21, No. 2 (June 1977).

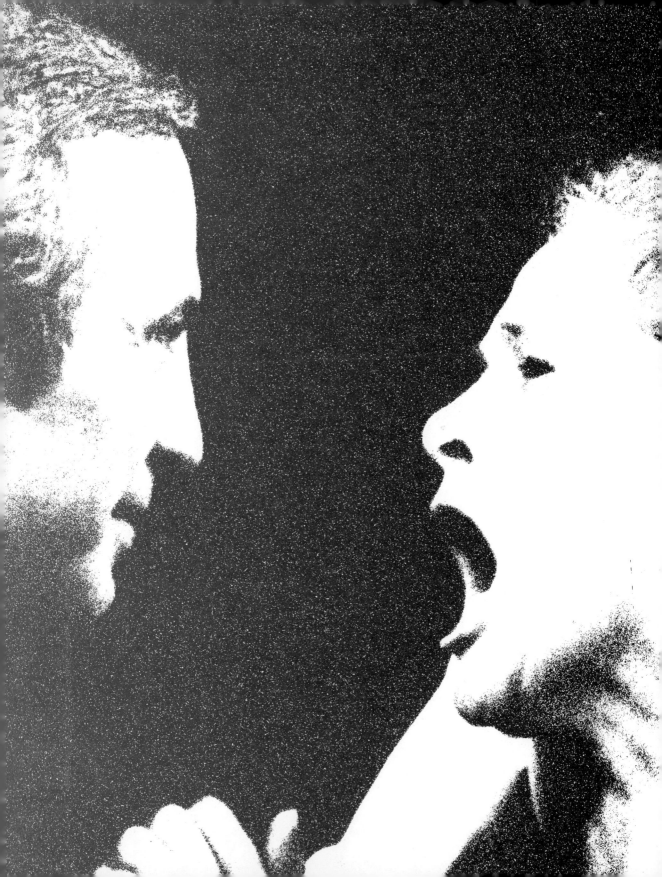

11

Viewpoints

Theatre's artists communicate to us through the performance, and theatre's critics add new dimensions to our awareness of their art.

The critic digests the experience and hands it to the spectator to confirm his own conclusion. The spectator, conditioned to be told what to see, sees what he is told, or corrects the critic, but in any case sees in relation to the response of the critic.

Joseph Chaikin, *The Presence of the Actor*

Theatre criticism gives us a public viewpoint or assessment of what we see in our theatres. Whereas **dramatic criticism** focuses on drama or the written text, **theatrical criticism** is largely concerned with a play's performance.

Present-day theatre criticism reflects the fact that we live in a consumer-oriented society. The business of the journalistic theatre critic is to appraise the theatrical performance, whether it is found on Broadway, in our resident theatres, or on college and university campuses. But, theatre criticism is more than appraisal. It is also an economic force, often determining whether a play will continue to be seen or close after opening night. When the critic for the *New York Times* has the power to close a Broadway play or keep it running for months, it is well to consider how the critic's viewpoint affects the quality of our lives and our theatres.

TYPES OF CRITICISM

Theatre criticism evaluates, describes, or analyzes a performance's merits and a production's effectiveness. It appears in daily newspapers, weekly or monthly magazines, and on television and radio. It is written by men and women with various backgrounds and interests.

The theatre critic traditionally asks three basic questions borrowed from German playwright and critic Johann Wolfgang von Goethe (1749–1832):

What is the playwright trying to do?

How well has he or she done it?

Is it worth doing?

The first question concedes the playwright's creative freedom to express ideas and events within the theatre. The second question assumes that the critic is familiar with the playwright and the forms and techniques of the playwright's time. The third question demands a sense of production values and a general knowledge of theatre. These questions show up in varying degrees of emphasis in two types of theatrical criticism: descriptive and evaluative.

Although descriptive and evaluative materials are

Figure 11-1. Artist Jasper Johns demonstrated his sense of pictorial irony in "The Critic Sees" in 1961 (sculpmetal on plaster with glass). (Photo reprinted by permission of the artist and Leo Castelli Gallery.)

found in all theatre criticism, *descriptive criticism* describes the production: who is in it, what takes place during the performance, and what theatre artists are "behind the scene." The descriptive article on *Candide* (see Figure 11-2) appeared in 1974 in *The Drama Review.* For the most part, descriptive criticism offers no judgment, but simply a record of the theatre event.

Evaluative criticism (the kind found most often in newspaper and magazine reviews) deals directly with our three basic questions and passes some types of value judgment on the production (see Figure 11-4). Whether we like it or not, this type of criticism most directly affects the theatre's welfare and the audience's response.

Most evaluative critics consider the performance from these three viewpoints. First, they consider what the playwright was trying to do—the imaginative material, the concept, and the themes. Second, they judge how well the performance accomplishes what the playwright has set about to do. Plot, character, setting, lighting, costume, acting, or directing may be considered, depending upon their relative contribution to the effectiveness of the production. Third, they answer the question, Was it worth doing? This answer is the most sensitive and influential aspect of the review, for critical standards are on the line as well as the fate of the production.

Candide at the Broadway Theatre

The United States Institute of Theatre Technology recently honored *Candide's* director Harold Prince for his "special combination of courage and experience" in bringing "the first successful large-scale environmental production to Broadway." Eugene and Franne Lee, who designed the set for the Chelsea Theater Center production at the Brooklyn Academy of Music, recreated the set in The Broadway Theatre, removing all 1,800 seats. The new space seats 840 on fixed stools, benches, and benches with backs.

Prince presents Voltaire's 1759 satire as a burlesque in support of the bourgeoisie: "For man, it is only work that makes life endurable." Leonard Bernstein's operetta score satirizes the Grand Opera. In most of the songs, the lyrics advance the plot. The orchestra is divided into four sections coordinated by closed-circuit television. The playing areas are electronically amplified. Louis Stadlen, who plays Voltaire, wears a Vega microphone strapped to his leg for three quarters of the performance. The acting style is presentational.

To stage Voltaire's odyssey of an indefatigable optimist who endures the most grotesque buffetings of nature, the plot has been streamlined and fit into many short scenes, set, introduced, or connected by a speech from the character

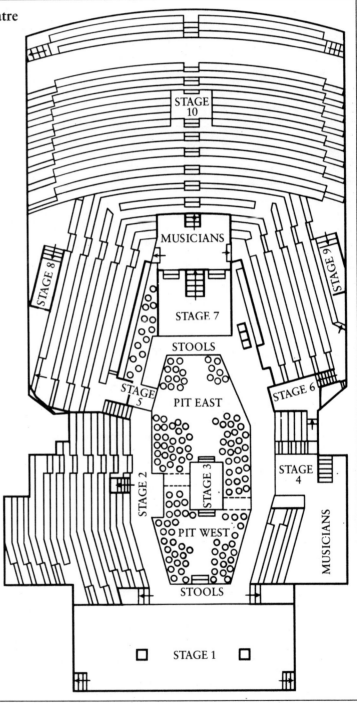

Figure 11-2. A descriptive review of the Broadway musical Candide *(1973).*

of Voltaire. This device permits the description of shipwrecks, wars, volcanoes, and other unstaged material to be included in the development of the plot. The chief omissions are the characters and events of Candide's companions, Cacambo and Martin. Ten different stages permit simultaneous action and rapid scene changes. There is an over-all sense of variety and speed. In "Auto Da Fé," a cast song number, the effect is similar to the circus with more actions happening than can be entirely taken in. Most of the scenes are played on the oval ramp and the stages adjacent to it. Frequently, action begins on the stairways and moves down to a stage. Entrances and exits are made through the stairways and areas off-stage of the ramp. The proscenium stage (1) and the platform stage (4) are used more often than the others to suggest different places.

The audience gathers at the box-office and waits there until 7:30 when the doors to the foyer are opened. Inside, hot-dogs, peanuts, soda, beer, T-shirts, buttons, and cast record albums are hawked by vendors at a central booth. At either side of this stand are stairways leading to the bleachers and covered wooden corridors leading to the pit. The spectators wait in their seats until 8 p.m. when a costumed actor enters (by stage 4) to announce the location of the ten stages and two drawbridges and to caution against leaving programs, peanut shells, and feet on the ramps and stairs where the actors may trip over them. Before he leaves, he announces that the performance lasts an hour and forty-five minutes and is performed without intermission. He invites the audience to "stretch" during the following four-minute overture. No one has left his seat as the overture concludes.

Wearing a white nightshirt and wig, Stadlen introduces Candide, who is singled out by spotlights above stage 5 singing his verse of "Life Is Happiness Indeed." As the lights fade on Candide, he remains in place and the procedure is repeated for Cunegonde, Paquette, and Maximillian. Lastly, Stadlen, as Voltaire, introduces Pangloss and changes into that character by altering his voice and putting on a black periwig and frock-coat. A final chorus is sung by these five and the lights dim. During the blackout, the actors take their places on the proscenium stage (1) for the next scene. The curtains are separated disclosing a painted backdrop of a blackboard on the rear wall of a one-room schoolhouse. Four real chairs and a small wooden desk are set facing the audience to suggest the classroom. In other scenes, this stage is set with backdrops of "a fishing village near the equator," the city and harbor of Montevideo, a landscape of an American colony (for the final tableau), life-sized corpse dummies, a grass hut, and a rowboat wagon.

To turn the entire pit into "the jungle of El Dorado," about two dozen crepe paper streamers drop and hang from the light-pipes above while the cast make jungle noises. An actor in a grass skirt with a bone in his topnotch slides across on a wire from stage 6 to stage 2 over the heads of the audience in the pit. Two actresses in pink fleece accompanied by an actor in a lion suit sing "Sheep's Song." The entire theatre is made to suggest a frigate at sea by the extension of ropes from a mast inserted in stage 3 to the corners of the theatre. A recording of surf is played over the loudspeakers. The stage 3 platform rocks from side to side.

Actual audience participation is limited to a few well-rehearsed instances. During his song "It Must Be So," Candide walks through the pit where the people on the fixed stools edge around to make way for him. He stops on his line "but men are kindly," continuing when the person in front edges over for him. At another moment he hands his shirt and Cunegonde's blouse to the people near stage 2.

Candide has won five Tony Awards this year and has performed to full houses. At a total budget of $475,000, Prince says that one week of capacity audiences brings in $8,000 above running cost.

B.E.

George Jean Nathan (1882–1958) was for many years a leading American theatre critic. Writing largely for New York City newspapers, he fought for a drama of ideas in America, and introduced plays by Henrik Ibsen, George Bernard Shaw, and August Strindberg. He discovered the great American playwright Eugene O'Neill, and published his early work in *The Smart Set,* a magazine he edited with H. L. Mencken. Nathan's more than thirty books on theatre include the volumes on the New York season that he produced annually for many years.

It takes years of seeing theatre to develop critical standards. It is like the appreciation of a sports event. The more we know about the game of football, for example, the better we are able to judge the coach's strategy, the execution of plays, the players' individual and collective skills—those factors contributing to success or failure.

In the theatre critical standards can begin with concern for the old and the new. We might ask the following: Does the performance retread old ground and deal in clichés, or does it add a new dimension to our lives, telling us something new? Perhaps it tells us something old, but in a new and fresh way. The musical *Candide* is an adaptation of a satirical novel written in 1759 by the French philosopher Voltaire. Produced originally on Broadway in 1956, this first musical version of Voltaire's novel didn't succeed; but in 1973, the new environmental staging and the new lyrics, script, and music, permitted audiences to experience this story about an irrepressible optimist in "the best of all possible worlds" in a fresh way.

George Jean Nathan, an American critic writing in the 1920s and 30s, said: " . . . Criticism, at its best, is the adventure of an intelligence among emotions."[1] After all is said and done, theatre criticism is the encounter of one person's sensibility with the theatrical event. Thus it is important that the critic tell us about the theatre, humankind, society, and perhaps even the universe in the course of evaluating the theatre event. American director-critic Harold Clurman once said that whether the critic is good or bad doesn't depend on his opinions, but on the reasons he can offer for those opinions.[2]

Too often theatrical criticism runs to critics' personal likes and dislikes—opinion without critical judgment. In an effort to avoid the "I liked it or didn't like it" approach, critics have been urged in recent years to define as exactly as possible the nature of the performance.

SEEING THEATRE

Although there is no general agreement on criteria for judging a performance, the first step in writing theatrical criticism is the ability to see. If we can describe what we see

Harold Clurman (b. 1901) is an American director, author, and critic. Founding member and managing director of The Group Theatre (1931–41), he directed the early plays of American playwright Clifford Odets. Director of many original Broadway plays, Clurman has also been the theatre critic for newspapers and magazines. He told the story of The Group Theatre in his book *The Fervent Years* (1945) and has published collections of his theatre essays and reviews.

in the theatre, then we can begin to arrive at critical judgments. The play and/or the production determine the type of review the critic writes. If the staging justifies a description of what we observe, then the review will be largely descriptive, dealing with observed details. In Bill Eddy's review of *Candide* (see Figure 11-2), he describes the theatrical space's configuration, particular events, costumes, movement, lighting, scenic and sound effects. He forms a general impression of the performance in the reader's mind. Moreover, he achieves in the review a sense of the creative process at work during the performance. For example, he writes:

Wearing a white nightshirt and wig, Stadlen introduces Candide, who is singled out by spotlights above stage 5 singing his verse of "Life Is Happiness Indeed." As the lights fade on Candide, he remains in place and the procedure is repeated for Cunegonde, Paquette, and Maximillian. Lastly, Stadlen, as Voltaire, introduces Pangloss and changes into that character by altering his voice and putting on a black periwig and frock-coat. A final chorus is sung by these five and the lights dim.

These descriptive lines give us a sense of the 1973 production of *Candide,* including the event's structure, the staging, the actors' choices, and the integration of music with story line.

However, what we see in the theatre must connect with the play's meaning. For this reason, all theatre criticism involves both description and evaluation. The critic's priorities are determined by the play and by the production. For instance, Edward Albee's *Who's Afraid of Virginia Woolf?* challenges the mind more than the eye and is usually staged in a traditional box setting. Critic Howard Taubman's review of Albee's play for the *New York Times* sets forth his general impression of the production, as well as the play's meaning and merits (see Figure 11-4).

WRITING THE THEATRE REVIEW

What J. L. Styan calls "percepts"[3] are those simultaneous sensory impressions and details that are seen and heard in the theatre and in life. Since theatre is something perceived by the audience, our first efforts to criticize

273

The New York Times *logo for Albee's play published in the October 15, 1962 edition of the newspaper.*

The Cast

Who's Afraid of Virginia Woolf?, a play by Edward Albee. Directed by Alan Schneider, presented by Richard Barr and Clinton Wilder; production designed by William Ritman; stage manager, Mark Wright. At the Billy Rose Theater, 208 West 41st St.

Martha ..... Uta Hagen
George ..... Arthur Hill
Honey ..... Melinda Dillon
Nick ..... George Grizzard

---

theatre should be based on sensory stimuli or impressions received during the performance. As audiences, we are exposed to many significant details, impressions, and images, and only on the basis of them do we construct concepts or abstract meanings. Thus the critical process begins, not with the concept, but with what we perceive. We build critical concepts on the foundation of our perceptions, and we can begin the process of seeing theatre critically by learning to describe our perceptions in the theatre. What we say about the performance's meaning and value is based on a prioritizing of our experience. A model for a review written according to this method might take the following form:

Heading or logo

Substance or meaning of play

Setting or environment ⎫

Costumes

Lighting and sound effects

Acting (actor and character) ⎬ Select and prioritize these elements

Stage business

Directing

Other significant human details ⎭

In writing any commentary it is necessary first to identify the performance to be discussed. Eddy chose to identify *Candide* as an environmental production in his opening sentence: "The United States Institute of Theatre Technology recently honored *Candide's* director Harold Prince for his 'special combination of courage and experience' in bringing 'the first successful large-scale environmental production to Broadway.'" Second, commentary upon the play's substance or meaning informs the reader about the playwright's special concern with human affairs. Third, the performance exposes the audience to what Styan calls "an environment of significant stimuli":[4] sights, sounds, color, light, movement, space. These stimuli can be described by answering questions related to setting, costumes, lighting, acting, and stage business. For instance, what details of color, mass, line, space, texture, and movement affect our senses? Is the stage environment open or closed—symbolic or realistic? What are the effects of the stage shape on the actor's speech, gesture, and movement? Is the lighting symbolic or suggestive of realistic light sources? What details of color, line, texture, period, taste, and socioeconomic status are established by the costumes? What emphasis does the performance place on setting, costume, color, light? Are these representational or nonrepresentational? What use is made of music and sound or light effects? What details separate the actor-at-work from his or her character-in-situation? (Eddy tells us that actor Stadlen, as Voltaire, introduces Pangloss and changes into that character by altering his voice and putting on a black periwig and frockcoat. The first is the actor-at-work; the second is the actor becoming the character.) What does the character do in the play's action? What stage properties does the actor use and how do they make meaningful dramatic statements? Are the properties realistic or symbolic? Finally, what visual and aural *images* of human experience and society develop before us during the performance? And how effectively do the play and the actors create these images on stage? All of these elements of light, sound, space, movement, color, properties, and setting guide the eye and ear to meaning and value.

As we gain experience "seeing" theatre and describing our perceptions, we learn that in some performances elements such as costumes or lighting may be more important than in others. We become able to select priorities, describe those human details that enhance the performance, and omit those that contribute little to it. In other words, we become selective, developing criteria based on sensory stimuli for judging the performance's effectiveness.

A performance's meaning or social content is the sum total of the audience's perceptions. Meaning does not precede the performance. It is our experience of the relationship of visual and aural stimuli that leads us to conclusions about the meaning of *Othello* or *Candide*. To become skilled theatre critics is to hone our perceptions of the when, where, and how of the event taking place before us.

Who's Afraid of Virginia Woolf? is Edward Albee's realistic drama in three acts—"Fun and Games," "Walpurgisnacht," and "Exorcism"—about the marital war between George, a college history professor, and his wife Martha, the daughter of the college president. Martha has invited Nick, a new faculty member, and his wife Honey for a late-night drink. George and Martha engage in verbal sparring while the young couple remain, at first, as bewildered onlookers. As the evening wears on and liquor is consumed, the fun and games involve the guests as well. Despite George's warnings, Martha reveals their secret: They have a son. They exchange insults in a "Walpurgisnacht" of mutual loathing. Martha taunts George about his unpublished novel; George goads her to an act of adultery with Nick. Nothing happens, but nevertheless George retaliates by inventing a telegram with news of their son's death. Martha collapses, and Nick realizes that the "child" is an illusion sustained by the childless couple. Nick and Honey leave; George and Martha are left emotionally spent by the child's exorcism from their lives.

Let us test our critical perceptions by studying photographs of two New York productions of Who's Afraid of Virginia Woolf? In Figure 11-3a we see actors Arthur Hill as George, Uta Hagen as Martha, and George Grizzard as Nick in the original 1962 New York production directed by Alan Schneider. Martha dances with Nick, and their flirtation excludes her husband, who contemplates the couple. Consider the details of environment, lighting, decor, and costumes worn by the actors, and the physical relationship of the actor/characters. What are the most important details? (Photo by Joseph Abeles.)

Figure 11-3b is from the 1976 New York revival of the play directed by playwright Edward Albee, Ben Gazzara as George taunts Colleen Dewhurst as Martha, telling her of their "child's" death while Richard Kelton as Nick restrains her. This photo emphasizes the physical and emotional relationships among the actor/characters. (Photo by Joseph Abeles.)

Figure 11-4. Drama critic Howard Taubman reviewed the opening performance of Edward Albee's Who's Afraid of Virginia Woolf? *for the* New York Times *(October 15, 1962).*

The Theater: Albee's "Who's Afraid"

Dramatist's First Play
On Broadway Opens

By Howard Taubman

Thanks to Edward Albee's furious skill as a writer, Alan Schneider's charged staging and a brilliant performance by a cast of four, "Who's Afraid of Virginia Woolf?" is a wry and electric evening in the theater.

You may not be able to swallow Mr. Albee's characters whole, as I cannot. You may feel, as I do, that a pillar of the plot is too flimsy to support the climax. Nevertheless, you are urged to hasten to the Billy Rose Theater, where Mr. Albee's first full-length play opened Saturday night.

For "Who's Afraid of Virginia Woolf?" is possessed by raging demons. It is punctuated by comedy, and its laughter is shot through with savage irony. At its core is a bitter, keening lament over man's incapacity to arrange his environment or private life so as to inhibit his self-destructive compulsions.

Moving onto from off Broadway, Mr. Albee carries along the burning intensity and icy wrath that informed "The Zoo Story" and "The American Dream." He has written a full-length play that runs almost three and a half hours and that brims over with howling furies that do not drown out a fierce compassion. After the fumes stirred by his witches' caldron are spent, he lets in, not sunlight and fresh air, but an agonized prayer.

Although Mr. Albee's vision is grim and sardonic, he is never solemn. With the instincts of a born dramatist and the shrewdness of one whose gifts have been tempered in the theater, he knows how to fill the stage with vitality and excitement.

Sympathize with them or not, you will find the characters in this new play vibrant with dramatic urgency. In their anger and terror they are pitiful as well as corrosive, but they are also wildly and humanly hilarious. Mr. Albee's dialogue is dipped in acid, yet ripples with a relish of the ludicrous. His controlled, allusive style grows in mastery.

In "Who's Afraid of Virginia Woolf?" he is concerned with Martha and George, a couple living in mordant, uproarious antagonism. The daughter of the president of the college where he teaches, she cannot forgive his failure to be a success like her father. He cannot abide her brutal bluntness and drive. Married for more than 20 years, they claw each other like jungle beasts.

In the dark hours after a Saturday midnight they entertain a young married pair new to the campus, introducing them to a funny and cruel brand of fun and games. Before the liquor-sodden night is over, there are lacerating self-revelations for all.

On the surface the action seems to be mostly biting talk.

Underneath is a witches' revel, and Mr. Albee is justified in calling his second act "Walpurgisnacht." But the means employed to lead to the denouement of the third act, called "The Exorcism," seems spurious.

Mr. Albee would have us believe that for 21 years his older couple have nurtured a fiction that they have a son, that his imaginary existence is a secret that violently binds and sunders them and that George's pronouncing him dead may be a turning point. This part of the story does not ring true, and its falsity impairs the credibility of his central characters.

If the drama falters, the acting of Uta Hagen and Arthur Hill does not. As the vulgar, scornful, desperate Martha, Miss Hagen makes a tormented harridan horrifyingly believable. As the quieter, tortured and diabolical George, Mr. Hill gives a superbly modulated performance built on restraint as a foil to Miss Hagen's explosiveness.

George Grizzard as a young biologist on the make shades from geniality to intensity with shattering rightness. And Melinda Dillon as his mousy, troubled bride is amusing and touching in her vulnerable wistfulness.

Directing like a man accustomed to fusing sardonic humor and seething tension, Mr. Schneider has found a meaningful pace for long— some too long—passages of seemingly idle talk, and has staged vividly the crises of action.

"Who's Afraid of Virginia Woolf?" (the phrase is sung at odd moments as a bitter joke to the tune of the children's play song, "Mulberry Bush") is a modern variant on the theme of the war between the sexes. Like Strindberg, Mr. Albee treats his women remorselessly, but he is not much gentler with his men. If he grieves for the human predicament, he does not spare those lost in its psychological and emotional mazes.

His new work, flawed though it is, towers over the common run of contemporary plays. It marks a further gain for a young writer becoming a major figure of our stage.

SUMMARY

Theatre artists communicate their experience of life through the use of its raw materials and the theatre's specific means. The critic confronts this creative process and, at best, enhances our understanding of it by enabling us to perceive the theatrical experience from a perspective other than our own or that of our friends.

Theatre criticism—carefully weighed by the reader—adds a new dimension to our discovery of theatre.

QUESTIONS FOR STUDY

1. What is criticism?

2. What is the difference between *theatrical* criticism and *dramatic* criticism?

3. What is the difference between *descriptive* and *evaluative* criticism?

4. In what ways is the review of *Candide* an example of descriptive criticism?

5. Examine the photograph of a play production from elsewhere in this book and write a paragraph describing the sensory stimuli that appear to be at work in the scene.

6. Attend one or more plays on your campus or in your community; write a *review* of each performance, keeping in mind the model on page 274.

NOTES

[1]George Jean Nathan, *The Critic and the Drama* (New York: Alfred A. Knopf, 1922), p. 133.
[2]Eric Bentley and Julius Novick, "On Criticism," *Yale/Theatre*, 4, No. 2 (Spring 1973), 23–36.
[3]J. L. Styan, *Drama, Stage and Audience* (London: Cambridge University Press, 1975), pp. 1–67.
[4]Ibid., p. 33.

Glossary

Angelika Hurwicz as Grusha in
the 1954 Berliner Ensemble
production of The Caucasian
Chalk Circle, directed by Bertolt
Brecht. (Photo courtesy of The
Berliner Ensemble.)

GLOSSARY OF THEATRE TERMS
Arena stage   See **Stages.**

Box set   An interior setting, such as a living room, using flats to form the back and side walls and often the ceiling of the room. The Moscow Art Theatre setting for Chekhov's *The Cherry Orchard* has a box set (see Figure 10-9).

Convention   An understanding established through custom or usage in the theatre that certain devices will be accepted or assigned specific meaning or significance on an arbitrary basis, that is, without requiring that they be natural or real. In a soliloquy the actor stands alone on stage speaking to himself so that the audience can "overhear" his thoughts. Since this behavior is accepted as a convention we do not think it odd or unnatural when it occurs. An example of a Shakespearean soliloquy is found on pages 205–06.

Criticism   In drama and theatre, criticism is the understanding and assessing of the play either as a text or as a performance. Two types of theatrical criticism *(descriptive* and *evaluative)* are discussed in Chapter 11. There is a third type, usually called *dramatic criticism.* Dramatic (or interpretive) criticism is usually associated with scholarly articles, books on theatre, and classroom teaching. The critic is concerned with the what and how of the play—with historical background, themes, genre, character, plot, and action. Martin Esslin's book, *The Theatre of the Absurd* (1961), is an explanation of the term *absurd,* and a testing of the concept against the works of such modern playwrights as Eugene Ionesco, Samuel Beckett, and Harold Pinter. *The Drama Review, Theater* (formerly *Yale/Theater*), *Theatre Journal,* and *The Performing Arts Journal* publish articles on contemporary theatre and avant-garde movements.

Dramaturg   The dramaturg's profession, which was created in eighteenth-century Germany, has only recently been instituted in United States resident theatres. Sometimes called a literary manager or advisor, the dramaturg is a critic-in-residence who performs a variety of tasks before a play opens. He or she selects and prepares playtexts for performance; advises directors and actors on questions of the play's history and interpretation; and educates the audience by preparing lectures, program notes, and essays. To accomplish all of this, the dramaturg serves as script reader, theatre historian, translator, play adaptor, editor, director's assistant, and critic of work-in-progress. The commitment to producing new plays has given rise to the dramaturg's employment by a number of resident theatres in America, including The Guthrie Theater in Minneapolis, the Mark Taper Forum in Los Angeles, the O'Neill Theater Center in Connecticut, and the Manhattan Theatre Club in New York.

Ensemble playing or **performance**   Acting that stresses the total artistic unity of the performance rather than the individual performance of a specific (or "star") actor. The photo of Stanislavsky's production of *The Cherry Orchard* at the Moscow Art Theatre shows the unity of acting style as the visitors are welcomed to the estate (see Figure 10-11a).

Mise en scène   The arrangement of all the elements in the stage picture either at a given moment or dynamically throughout the performance. Modern directors give careful attention to the *mise en scène* or total stage picture, integrating all elements of design, lighting, acting, etc. The *mise en scène* established by director Andrei Serban and designer Santo Loquasto for the 1977 New York production of *The Cherry Orchard* reflects the director's emphasis on the cherry trees and the dying civilization (see Figure 10-11b).

Open stage   See **Stages**.

Performance   A word used, especially in modern theatre criticism, to describe the whole theatrical event. In environmental theatre the performance begins as the *first* spectator enters the performing space and ends when the *last* spectator leaves. (See Figure 3-6 for an example of environmental performance.)

Proscenium stage   See **Stages**.

Properties   These fall into two categories: *set* and *hand* properties.

Set properties are those items of furniture or set pieces that the actor uses; they are placed on stage for design reasons, to accommodate the actor's movement, and to place the actors in the right degree of emphasis with relationship to them. The size and structure of properties, especially furniture, determine the sort of movement the actor can make around them and the use of costume.

Hand properties, such as fans, pistols, or telephones, are required for personal use by the actor. Sometimes the distinction between the set and hand prop is unclear, but design is the main function of the set prop; the hand prop first satisfies the needs of the actor using it even though its "look" is important to the designer. The table lamp that Mrs. Alving turns out in the final act of *Ghosts* is a hand prop, one with symbolic significance. As a set prop, the tree in *Waiting for Godot* is part of the scenic design (see Figure 8-5). Properties are the initial responsibility of the designer. There is a property crew responsible for acquiring or making props, supplying rehearsal props, handing out and storing props during the production, and repairing and returning props to storage at the production's close.

Scenographer   A designer with artistic control over all design elements, including set, lighting, and costume. The recent development of theatre technology, particularly the use of film projections and moving scenery, has called for unified production with one person integrating the various design elements. Although the scenographer works closely with the director, he or she is responsible for the totality of theatrical expression in time and space. Artistic unity is the goal. The idea that one person must have total control over design is derived from the theatrical concepts of the early twentieth-century theorists Adolphe Appia and Edward Gordon Craig (see pages 123–25).

One of the world's most famous scenographers today is Josef Svoboda (b. 1920), the leading designer of the Prague National Theatre in Czechoslovakia. He became known in America through the Czech Pavilion at the 1967 Montreal Exposition, where he orchestrated films and stills, cascading images over surfaces and spectators. The result was a visually kinetic assault on the spectators. Svoboda's stage designs feature moving blocks, projections, and mirrors. The basis of his theory is that all scenic elements must appear and disappear, shift and flow, to complement the play's development.

Soliloquy   A speech delivered by an actor alone on stage, which, by stage convention, is understood by the audience to be the character's internal thoughts, not part of an exchange with another character or even with the audience. Hamlet's speech on page 205 is a soliloquy.

Spine   In the Stanislavsky method, a character's dominant desire or motivation, which underlies his or her action in the play. Director Elia Kazan conceived of the spine of Tennessee Williams's character Blanche DuBois in *A Streetcar Named*

Figure G-1. Three types of stages

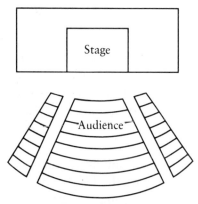

Proscenium Stage

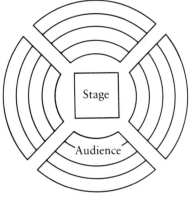

Arena Stage

Desire as the search for refuge from a brutal and hostile world.

Stages—proscenium, arena, thrust or open   Throughout theatre history there have been four types of theatre buildings and basic arrangements of audience seating: (1) the proscenium or picture-frame stage, (2) the arena stage, or theatre-in-the-round, (3) the thrust or open stage, and (4) created or found stage space of the kind discussed as environmental theatre in Chapter 3.

The proscenium or picture-frame stage is most familiar to us. Almost all college and university campuses have proscenium theatres, and our Broadway theatres have proscenium stages. The word *proscenium* comes from the wall with a large center opening that separates the audience from the raised stage. In the past the opening was called an "arch" (the proscenium arch), but it is actually a rectangle. The audience faces in one direction before this opening, appearing to look through a picture frame into the locale on the other side. The auditorium floor slants downward from the back of the building to provide greater visibility for the audience; usually there is a balcony above the auditorium floor protruding about halfway over the main floor. Frequently there is a curtain just behind the proscenium opening that discloses or hides the event on the other side. The idea that a stage is a room with its fourth wall removed comes from this type of stage; the proscenium opening is thought of as an "invisible wall."

The arena stage (also called a theatre-in-the-round) breaks away from the formality of the proscenium theatre. It places the stage at the center of a square or circle with seats for the spectators around the circle or on the four sides. This stage offers more intimacy between actor and audience since the playing space usually has no barriers separating them. In addition, arena

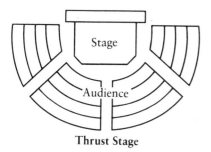

Thrust Stage

productions can usually be produced on low budgets since they require only minimal set pieces and furniture to indicate scene and place. Margo Jones (1913–1955) pioneered arena theatre design and performance in America, establishing Theatre 47 in Dallas, Texas, in 1947. Today, the Arena Stage in Washington, D.C., founded by Zelda Finchandler and Edward Mangum, is one of the most famous (see Figures 1-7c and 1-7d).

The thrust or open stage, which combines features of the proscenium theatre and the arena stage, usually has three-quarter seating for the audience. The basic arrangement has the audience sitting on three sides or in a semicircle around a low platform stage. At the back of the stage is some form of proscenium opening providing for entrances and exits as well as scene changes. The thrust stage combines the best features of the other two stages discussed here: the sense of intimacy for the audience, and a stage setting against a single background that allows for scenic design and visual elements. After World War II a number of important thrust stages were built in the United States and Canada, including The Guthrie Theater in Minneapolis (see Figure 1-8), and the Shakespeare Festival Theatre at Stratford, Ontario (see Figure 2-7).

Thrust stage   See **Stages.**

Well-made play *(pièce bien faite)*   A commercially successful pattern of play construction. Its techniques were perfected by the nineteenth-century French playwright Eugene Scribe (1791–1861) and his followers.

The well-made play uses eight technical playwriting elements: (1) a plot based on a secret known to the audience but withheld from certain characters until it is revealed at the climax to unmask a fraudulent character and restore the suffering hero, with whom the audience sympathizes, to good fortune; (2) a pattern of increasingly intense action and suspense prepared by exposition, contrived entrances and exits, and devices like unexpected letters; (3) a series of gains and losses in the hero's fortunes, caused by a conflict with a hostile opponent or force; (4) a major crisis in the hero's bad fortune; (5) a revelation scene brought about by the disclosure of a secret that brings a turnabout in the hero's bad fortune and defeats the opponent; (6) a central misunderstanding made obvious to the audience but withheld from the characters; (7) a logical, credible resolution or tying-up of events with appropriate dispensations to good and bad characters; and (8) an overall pattern of action repeated in each act, and act-climaxes that increase tension over the play's three or four acts.

The features were not new in Scribe's day, but represented the technical methods of most great writers of comedy and even serious drama. Scribe and his followers turned the techniques into a formula for commercially-entertaining plays as well as serious plays dealing with social and psychological subjects. In plays by Henrik Ibsen, George Bernard Shaw, and Oscar Wilde we can see the well-made play machinery underpinning the action.

Suggested Readings

From Samuel Beckett's Waiting for Godot *produced 1961 at the Odéon, Théâtre de France, directed by Jean-Marie Serreau. (Photo courtesy of Cultural Services, French Embassy, New York.)*

SUGGESTED READINGS

Chapter 1

Brockett, Oscar G. "The Humanities: Theatre History," *Southern Speech Communication Journal,* 41 (Winter 1976), pp. 142–150.

Brook, Peter. *The Empty Space.* New York: Avon Publishers, 1969.

Cole, David. *The Theatrical Event: A Mythos, A Vocabulary, A Perspective.* Middletown, Conn.: Wesleyan University Press, 1975.

Chapter 2

Bowers, Faubion. *Japanese Theatre.* New York: Hill and Wang, 1952.

Brockett, Oscar G. *History of the Theatre.* Third Edition. Boston: Allyn and Bacon, 1977.

Hodges, C. Walter. *The Globe Restored.* Second Edition. London: Oxford University Press, 1968.

Kirby, E. T. *Ur-Drama: The Origins of Theatre.* New York: New York University Press, 1975.

Lommel, Andreas. *Shamanism: The Beginnings of Art.* New York: McGraw-Hill Book Company, 1967.

Mullin, Donald C. *The Development of the Playhouse: A Survey of Theatre Architecture from the Renaissance to the Present.* Berkeley: University of California Press, 1970.

Southern, Richard. *The Seven Ages of the Theatre.* New York: Hill and Wang, 1961.

Chapter 3

Grotowski, Jerzy. *Towards a Poor Theatre.* New York: Clarion Books, 1968.

McNamara, Brooks, Jerry Rojo, and Richard Schechner. *Theatres, Spaces, Environments: Eighteen Projects.* New York: Drama Book Specialists, 1975.

Schechner, Richard. *Environmental Theatre.* New York: Hawthorn Books, 1973.

Chapter 4

Canfield, Curtis. *The Craft of Play Directing.* New York: Holt, Rinehart and Winston, 1963.

Clurman, Harold. *On Directing.* New York: Macmillan Company, 1972.

Cohen, Robert, and John Harrop. *Creative Play Direction.* New Jersey: Prentice-Hall, 1974.

Cole, Toby, and Helen K. Chinoy. *Directing The Play: A Source Book of Stagecraft.* New York: Bobbs-Merrill Company, 1953.

Dean, Alexander. *Fundamentals of Play Directing.* Revised by Lawrence Carra. Third Edition. New York: Holt, Rinehart and Winston, 1974.

Hodge, Francis. *Play Directing: Analysis, Communication and Style.* New Jersey: Prentice-Hall, 1971.

Macgowan, Kenneth. *Primer of Playwriting.* New York: Random House, 1951.

Playwrights on Playwriting. Edited by Toby Cole. New York: Hill and Wang, 1960.

"Playwrights and Playwriting Issue." *The Drama Review,* 21, No. 4 (December 1977).

Chapter 5

Benedetti, Robert L. *The Actor at Work.* Revised Edition. New Jersey: Prentice-Hall, 1976.

_____. *Seeming, Being and Becoming: Acting in Our Century.* New York: Drama Book Specialists, 1976.

Boleslavsky, Richard. *Acting: The First Six Lessons.*

New York: Theatre Arts Books, 1933.

Chaikin, Joseph. *The Presence of the Actor: Notes on The Open Theatre, Disguises, Acting and Repression.* New York: Atheneum, 1972.

Cohen, Robert. *Acting Power: An Introduction to Acting.* Palo Alto: Mayfield Publishing Company, 1978.

_____. *Acting Professionally.* Palo Alto: Mayfield Publishing Company, 1975.

Cole, Toby, and Helen K. Chinoy, eds. *Actors on Acting: The Theories, Techniques and Practices of the Great Actors of All Times as Told in Their Own Words.* Revised Edition. New York: Crown Publishers, 1970.

Goldman, Michael. *The Actor's Freedom: Toward a Theory of Drama.* New York: Viking Press, 1975.

Hagen, Uta, with Haskel Frankel. *Respect for Acting.* New York: Macmillan Company, 1973.

Harris, Julie. *Julie Harris Talks to Young Actors.* New York: Lothrop Lee and Shephard Company, 1971.

Stanislavsky, Constantin. *An Actor Prepares.* Translated by Elizabeth Reynolds Hapgood. New York: Theatre Arts Books, 1936.

_____. *Building a Character.* Translated by Elizabeth Reynolds Hapgood. New York: Theatre Arts Books, 1949.

_____. *Creating a Role.* Translated by Elizabeth Reynolds Hapgood. New York: Theatre Arts Books, 1961.

_____. *My Life in Art.* Translated by J. J. Robbins. New York: Meridian Books, 1956.

Chapter 6

Bay, Howard. *Stage Design.* New York: Drama Book Specialists, 1974.

Bellman, Willard F. *Lighting the Stage: Art and Practice.* Second Edition. San Francisco: Chandler Publishing Company, 1974.

_____. *Scenography and Stage Technology: An Introduction*. New York: Thomas Y. Crowell, 1977.

Benda, Wladyslaw T. *Masks*. New York: Watson-Guptill Publishers, 1944.

Burdick, Elizabeth B., and others, eds. *Contemporary Stage Design U.S.A.* Middletown, Conn.: Wesleyan University Press, 1974.

Burris-Meyer, Harold, and Edward C. Cole. *Scenery for the Theatre*. Revised Edition. Boston: Little, Brown and Company, 1971.

Corey, Irene. *The Mask of Reality: An Approach to Design for Theatre*. New Orleans: Anchorage Press, 1968.

Corson, Richard. *Stage Makeup*. Fifth Edition. New York: Appleton-Century-Crofts, 1975.

Izenour, George C. *Theatre Design*. New York: McGraw-Hill Publishing Company, 1977.

Parker, Oren, and Harvey K. Smith. *Scene Design and Stage Lighting*. Third Edition. New York: Holt, Rinehart and Winston, 1974.

Rosenthal, Jean, and Lael Wertenbaker. *The Magic of Light*. New York: Theatre Arts Books, 1972.

Russell, Douglas A. *Stage Costume Design: Theory, Technique and Style*. New York: Appleton-Century-Crofts, 1973.

Simonson, Lee. *The Stage Is Set*. New York: Theatre Arts Books, 1962.

Chapters 7 and 8

Beckerman, Bernard. *Dynamics of Drama: Theory and Method of Analysis*. New York: Alfred A. Knopf, 1970.

Bentley, Eric. *The Life of the Drama*. New York: Atheneum, 1964.

Corrigan, Robert W., ed. *Comedy: Meaning and Form*. Revised Edition. New York: Harper & Row, 1980.

_____, ed. *Tragedy: Vision and Form*. Revised Edition. New York: Harper & Row, 1980.

Esslin, Martin. *An Anatomy of Drama*. New York: Hill and Wang, 1977.

Fergusson, Francis. *The Idea of a Theater*. Princeton: University Press, 1968.

Heilman, Robert B. *Tragedy and Melodrama: Versions of Experience*. Seattle: University of Washington Press, 1968.

Langer, Susanne K. *Feeling and Form: A Theory of Art*. New York: Charles Scribner's Sons, 1953.

Marranca, Bonnie. *Theatre of Images*. New York: Drama Book Specialists, 1977.

Nichol, Allardyce. *The Theory of Drama*. New York: Thomas Y. Crowell, 1931.

Schechner, Richard. *Public Domain: Essays on the Theatre*. Chicago: Bobbs-Merrill Company, 1969.

Smith, James L. *Melodrama*. London: Methuen, 1973.

Chapter 9

Boulding, Kenneth. *The Image*. Ann Arbor: University of Michigan Press, 1956.

Cole, David. *The Theatrical Event: A Mythos, A Vocabulary, A Perspective*. Middletown, Conn.: Wesleyan University Press, 1975.

McLuhan, Marshall. *Understanding Media: The Extensions of Man*. New York: McGraw-Hill, 1964.

Styan, J. L. *Drama, Stage and Audience*. London: Cambridge University Press, 1975.

Chapter 10

Bentley, Eric. *The Playwright As Thinker: A Study of Drama in Modern Times*. New York: Harcourt, Brace and World, 1946.

Hayman, Ronald. *How to Read a Play*. New York: Grove Press, 1977.

Saint-Denis, Michel. *Theatre: The Rediscovery of Style*. New York: Theatre Arts Books, 1960.

Styan, J. L. *The Dramatic Experience: A Guide to the Reading of Plays.* London: Cambridge University Press, 1965.

"Theatricalism Issue." *The Drama Review,* 21, No. 2 (June 1977).

Chapter 11

"Criticism Issue." *The Drama Review,* 18, No. 3 (September 1974).

Clurman, Harold. *Lies Like Truth: Theatre Reviews and Essays.* New York: Macmillan Company, 1958.

_____. *The Naked Image: Observations on the Modern Theatre.* New York: Macmillan Company, 1966.

Nathan, George Jean. *The Critic and the Drama.* New York: Alfred A. Knopf, 1922.

Sontag, Susan. *Against Interpretation and Other Essays.* New York: Doubleday and Company, 1966.

Acknowledgments

Selections used with permission of the following sources appear on the pages shown in parentheses.

Atheneum Publishers: Selections from Peter Brook, *The Empty Space,* 1968 (3, 149). Selection from the text of *Who's Afraid of Virginia Woolf?* by Edward Albee; copyright © 1962 by Edward Albee (93). Selection from Peter Weiss, *The Persecution and Assassination of Jean Paul Marat as Performed by the Inmates of the Asylum of Charenton under the Direction of the Marquis de Sade;* English translation copyright © 1965 by John Calder Ltd.; originally published in German under the title *Die Verfolgung und Ermordung Jean Paul Marats Dargestellt Durch die Schauspielgruppe des Hospizes zu Charenton unter Anleitung des Herrn de Sade;* copyright © 1964 by Suhrkamp Verlag, Frankfurt Am Main (216–217). Selection from Joseph Chaikin, *The Presence of the Actor,* 1974 (267).

The Bobbs-Merrill Company, Inc.: Selection from *A Book on the Open Theatre* by Robert Pasolli. Copyright © 1970 by The Bobbs-Merrill Company, Inc. (219).

Cambridge University Press: Selection from J. L. Styan, *The Dramatic Experience,* 1965 (229).

Coward, McCann & Geoghegan, Inc.: Selection from *America Hurrah!* by Jean-Claude van Itallie. Copyright © 1966 by Jean-Claude van Itallie as unpublished plays. Copyright © 1966, 1967 by Jean-Claude van Itallie (220–221).

Crown Publishers, Inc.: Selection from *Actors on Acting* by Toby Cole and Helen Krich Chinoy. Copyright 1949, 1977 by Toby Cole and Helen Krich Chinoy (101–102).

The Drama Review: Selection from Jean-Claude van Itallie, "A Reinvention of Form," first published in *The Drama Review,* T76, December 1977 (218).

Bill Eddy: Review by Bill Eddy, "*Candide* at the Broadway Theatre: A Theatre Review," *The Drama Review,* September 1974 (270–271).

Farrar, Straus & Giroux, Inc.: Selections from *Brecht on Theatre* translated by John Willett. Copyright © 1957, 1963, and 1964 by Suhrkamp Verlag, Frankfurt Am Main. This translation and notes © 1964 by John Willett. Reprinted with permission of Hill and Wang, a division of Farrar, Straus & Giroux, Inc. (187, 189, 211–212).

Granada Publishing Ltd.: Selections from Peter Brook, *The Empty Space,* 1968 (3, 149).

Grove Press, Inc.: Selection from Samuel Beckett, *Waiting for Godot,* 1954 (15). Selections from Eugene Ionesco, *Notes and Counternotes,* Donald Watson, translator, © 1964 by Grove Press, Inc. (191, 199). Selection from Eugene Ionesco, *The Bald Soprano,* Donald Watson, translator, © 1958 by Grove Press, Inc. (192–194). Selection

from Harold Pinter, "Writing for the Theatre" in *Modern British Drama,* Henry Popkin, editor, 1969 (241).

Harcourt Brace Jovanovich, Inc.: Selection from Mircea Eliade, *The Sacred and the Profane,* Willard R. Trask, translator, 1959 (25).

Harper & Row, Publishers, Inc.: Selection from Mircea Eliade, *Birth and Rebirth,* Willard R. Trask, translator, 1958 (28–29).

Hawthorn Books, Inc.: Selection from Richard Schechner, *Environmental Theatre.* Copyright © 1973 by Richard Schechner. All rights reserved (65).

International Publishers: Selection from *Brecht: As They Knew Him,* Hubert Witt, editor, 1974 (85).

International Theatre Institute of the United States, Inc.: Patricia Zipprodt, "Designing Costumes," in *Contemporary Stage Design U.S.A.,* Elizabeth B. Burdick *et al.,* editors, 1974 (131).

Alfred A. Knopf, Inc.: Selection from Albert Camus, *The Myth of Sisyphus and Other Essays,* Justin O'Brien, translator, 1955 (191).

Richmond Lattimore: Selection from Aeschylus, *Agamemnon,* translated by Richmond Lattimore in *Oresteia I,* 1953 (238).

Little, Brown and Company: Selections from Harold Burris-Meyer and Edward C. Cole, *Scenery for the Theatre,* copyright 1938, renewed © 1966, 1971 by Harold Burris-Meyer and Edward C. Cole (126, 127). Selection from Jean Rosenthal and Lael Wertenbaker, *The Magic of Light,* copyright © 1972 by the Estate of Jean Rosenthal and by Lael Wertenbaker (142).

Lothrop, Lee & Shepard Company: Julie Harris with Barry Tarshis, *Julie Harris Talks to Young Actors,* 1971 (110).

Macmillan Publishing Co., Inc.: Selection from Uta Hagen with Haskel Frankel, *Respect for Acting,* 1973 (111–112).

The New American Library, Inc.: Selection from *Ghosts* from *Henrik Ibsen: The Complete Major Prose Plays,* translated by Rolf Fjelde. Copyright © 1965, 1970, 1978 by Rolf Fjelde (208–209).

New Directions: Selections from Tennessee Williams, *A Streetcar Named Desire.* Copyright 1947 by Tennessee Williams (235, 236).

The New York Times Company: Selection from an interview with Irene Worth, © 1976 by The New York Times Company (114). Review by Howard Taubman, "The Theater: Albee's 'Who's Afraid,' " © 1962 by The New York Times Company (278).

Odin Teatret: Selections from Jerzy Grotowski, *Towards a Poor Theatre,* 1968. Reprinted by permission of H. M. Berg, Odin Teatret, Denmark (59, 60, 64).

Oxford University Press: Selections from *Chekhov Plays*, translated by Ronald Hingley. © Ronald Hingley 1965 (210, 234–235, 242, 252).

Random House, Inc.: Selection from *Actors Talk about Acting*, Lewis Funke and John E. Booth, editors, 1973 (102–103). Selection from Bertolt Brecht, *The Caucasian Chalk Circle*, translated by Ralph Manheim, in *Collected Plays*, Volume 7, edited by Ralph Manheim and John Willett (213).

Theatre Arts Books: Selections from Robert Edmond Jones, *The Dramatic Imagination*. Copyright 1941 by Robert Edmond Jones. Reprinted with permission from the publisher, Theatre Arts Books, New York (75, 121).

The University of Chicago Press: Selection from Aeschylus, *Agamemnon*, translated by Richmond Lattimore in *Oresteia I*, 1953 (238).

The Viking Press: Selections from *Letters of Anton Chekov*, edited by Avrahm Yarmolinski, 1973 (230, 251).

Wesleyan University Press: Selection from David Cole, *The Theatrical Event*, 1975 (222–223).

Index

Index